THE BECOMING OF THE CHURCH

THE BECOMING OF THE CHURCH

A Process Theology of the Structures of Christian Experience

by
Bernard Lee, S. M.

Carmelite Monastery
1381 University Ave.
Bronx, New York

PAULIST PRESS
New York / Paramus / Toronto

Library of Congress
Catalog Card Number: 73-90718

ISBN: 0-8091-1816-5

Published by Paulist Press
Editorial Office: 1865 Broadway, N.Y., N.Y. 10023
Business Office: 400 Sette Drive, Paramus, N.J. 07652

Printed and bound in the
United States of America

ACKNOWLEDGMENTS

The author wishes to express his gratitude to the publishers designated
for their permission to quote from the following works:

Man and Sin by Piet Schoonenberg. Copyright © 1968. Reprinted by
permission of Henry Regnery Co.

Reconstruction in Philosophy by John Dewey. Copyright © 1957. Reprinted by permission of Beacon Press.

The Future of Belief by Leslie Dewart. Copyright © 1966 by Herder
and Herder, Inc. Reprinted by permission of the publisher, The Sea-
bury Press, New York.

The Function of Reason by Alfred North Whitehead. Copyright 1929,
© 1957. Reprinted by permission of Princeton University Press.

Quest for Certainty by John Dewey. Copyright © 1960. Reprinted by
permission of G. P. Putnam's Sons.

Philosophical Writings of Peirce, edited by Justus Buchler. Copyright
© 1955. Reprinted by permission of Dover Publications, Inc. and Rout-
ledge & Kegan Paul Ltd.

CONTENTS

INTRODUCTION

If the twentieth century has given us reason to be proud (and it has), with just as much earnestness it gives us reason for a more serious humility than we've ever known. Knowledge is not unlike a circle of light in a dark field of unknowing. The circumference of the circle of light is the size of our exposure to the dark. Each time the circumference of knowledge becomes larger, the length of our exposure to the unknown advances geometrically. Proud, because of so much new light! Humble, at the expansiveness of dark's parameter!

We know about our very act of knowing that at the height of its yield about reality, it is a highly conditioned act of knowing: conditioned by our times, by our language and symbols, by both the opportunities and restrictions of whatever world view we claim. We know about each statement that we articulate that it gives us a perspective—hopefully a valid one—on reality, but only a perspective. Part of our new humility is a hesitancy to claim anything like exhaustiveness for anything we know or say. Our perspective might be really fine, but it is only *a* perspective. And a highly conditioned perspective at that.

1

It is not enough even to say that our various perspectives are historically conditioned. Our perspectives mediate our experiences themselves. We experience through our perspectives and out of them. We use their symbols, and the meanings of words (especially the nuances) which derive from the perspectives. The presuppositions, seldom part of our conscious equipment, which underlie our world view necessarily shape our experiences and communicate value judgments to our pursuits and upon our actions.

There are several implications to draw from these considerations for theology. Theology is a systematic, organized attempt to articulate, elaborate and interpret faith experience. It is primarily a living-act directed upon living-experience, and for those who *do* the act, it is directed to the betterment of the quality of life (of faith). There may be others with serious interests in theology for different reasons, but their studies at that point are historical, anthropological, etc. But for those for whom theology is their own action (and that includes many who study it and pursue it, many who read it and digest it—without creating it or writing it), I think it stands to reason that theological formulation needs to stay very close to the experiences it elaborates and interprets. The more the historical conditioning of the theological articulation resembles that of the recent faith experience which it elaborates, the more "living" is the theology (or to use that hackneyed word, the more "relevant" is the theology). Each Gospel is such an example, for each is conditioned by both a world view and by highly particular concerns and problems of either the redactor or the earlier oral and written traditions. The "livingness" of each Gospel is most available to us when we gain access (always limited, of course) to the world view and the particularity of concerns which animated it. But present "livingness" demands a constant recasting and reappropriation of the initial hold of the Jesus-event on human lives.

In recent generations our awareness of the extent of such

historical conditioning on both human experience and human articulations of that experience calls for many theologies, side by side, for there are many experiences side by side. That awareness—which we could not have had until the modern period—makes us wary of "an" official theology. There has, of course, always been a certain amount of theological plural- ism. Yet in popular consciousness there has been, for the most part, a strong conviction in favor of *an* official theology. Of course, that conviction is really deeper too than popular consciousness. There has been (and is, though much less) an official "orthodoxy," with an official Office of the Church as overseer. But in recent times even that office is straining into a new self-definition, something more modestly in the direc- tion of a facilitator. By that, I mean not a conscious, verbal redefinition, but nonetheless a functional one. For the "doc- trine" and "dogma" of any era stand in need of exegesis, historical criticism, redaction criticism, etc., as much as the Scriptures themselves.

Process theology is one of the living ways in which theology is moving today. (There are, of course, many ways in which theology is moving today.) It is an attempt to bring con- temporary consciousness to bear upon the life of faith. There are several elements in contemporary consciousness with which process theology tries especially to reckon. The most obvious is the stress upon "process" or "becoming." There is the conviction that reality is really on the move; or more dramatically perhaps, that being-on-the-move is the heart of reality.

The accent upon process has come from many quarters: from physics, biology, paleontology—from the sciences in general. It is an insight that is equally at work in psychology, sociology, etc. A second accent in process thought is upon the universe as a community of events, interlocked and inter- related. This sense of "organicness," whether about the com- munity of man or the universe of events, is a very real preoccupation for modern man. The categories of process thought try to help us interpret our individual experiences against or within an organic whole of reality. A third point of emphasis in process thought is upon radical openness to the future. It is a belief that all that is real feels, or should feel, a summons to be more, to move beyond a present into futures that offer something really new. Process perspectives, and this is important for theology, tend to see God at work in the world basically through a persuasiveness (never a coerciveness) which exerts a gentle pressure on the inside of every reality's summons to be "more."

Philosophies and theologies have a technical aspect about them that normally distances them from the proverbial man in the street. In some ways that is regrettable, especially if it should mean that the philosophies and theologies are out of touch with the questions which contemporary living has raised. But from another point of view, some distancing between the technical and the popular is unavoidable. The existentialists are in touch with contemporary sensitivities at very many points, but neither Sartre's *Being and Nothingness* nor Heidegger's *Being and Time* stands a chance for the best-seller list. And if their chances are slim, Whitehead's chances for *Process and Reality,* the classic expression of process metaphysics, are infinitesimal to the point of practical nonexistence.

Yet philosophies and theologies spawn a mood, an atmosphere, a mystique. Sartre's plays and novels catch and communicate the mood of anyone who has felt the alienation of the modern world. Through Bultmann and Bultmannians Heidegger has helped Christians make new sense out of their own Christianity. Someone who has read only Paul Tillich's *Systematic Theology* may well have caught less of the man than one who has read only his sermons, for there the mood of the man catches us up. One who knows Tillich's systematic work as well as his sermons knows that the vision at work in his system is a necessary precondition for the poignancy of his sermon. One major gauge of a system-of-thought's vitality is the extent to which the understandings which emerge out of it can, to use a fine expression of Whitehead, command immediacy of assent.

My concern in this work is with philosophy and theology which are cast in process modes of thought. Philosophically I draw principally upon the work of Alfred North Whitehead. Theologically I am principally concerned with Church and Sacrament, especially (not exclusively) with Roman Catholic experience as a frame of reference. Pierre Teilhard de Chardin has seemed important to me, not so much because of a systematic process approach in his work—he is a process thinker, but not in a systematic or even in an entirely cohesive way—but because he has done more than anyone to spawn a process mood in the Church, especially through the kind of spirituality that his work engenders.

When it comes to precise statements made about the Church and the Sacraments in process modes of thought, at many points they will sound surprisingly similar to traditional formulations, e.g., to speak in terms of a society and its defining characteristics; or to speak of symbols (sacramental signs) as both eliciting a past event and effecting a new event in continuity with it. But that similarity is deceptive because it may so easily overlook the fundamentally different meanings and attitudes with which the similar expressions are invested. And that is why Whitehead has, in fact, introduced new philosophical language at many points, and why it behooves us to learn his language. I have gone into some detail in the chapter on Whitehead to introduce his thought in his own language. We learn a foreign people best by learning their language. And even if someday we forget that language quite completely, there's a fair chance that we will retain a feel for that people's feel for reality. That is my justification for the long chapter on Whitehead: to see what his thought feels like, through the admittedly tedious task of learning some of his language.

Trying to catch the meaning of a mood for Church and Sacrament in process modes of thought is part of the reason for this work. The other part is to use many of the White-headian categories to see how he understands a society to put itself together, to maintain itself in existence (survival), and to occasion for its members a rich and meaningful life (intensity). I want to look at the implications of that analysis for the Church, and to show the intimate relation of Sacramental Life to the Church's "becoming," that is to say, to the Church's reality. My focal interest is in the "how" or the "dynamics" of the Church's reality. It is difficult, of course, to avoid "what" questions: what exactly is the Church's defining characteristic; what is the content of the Jesus-event. I want to avoid, somewhat at least, those "what" questions, not because they are not important—they obviously are—but because they would enlarge the scope of this work beyond manageability. I also believe that enough work has been done on process natural theology and process Christology to be able to "get on with the show." Any talk of Church cannot but elicit some sense of the Jesus-event. I am, therefore, briefly citing two process Christologies as possible "whats" to keep in mind during the discussion of Church and Sacrament, namely those of John B. Cobb, Jr., and Pierre Teilhard de Chardin. But my purpose here is not a theological construct of "whats"; I am interested rather in the "hows" of the Church's reality, especially those "hows" which are the Sacraments.

Of course I work at this as one who confesses to being held by the claim of Jesus—which implies a "what." I also work as one whose experience of Christianity is primarily within Catholic Christianity. Both that faith claim and that affiliation contribute to the "whats" with which I work. But my aim here remains the limited one of trying to say something (not everything) about the dynamics of the Church's actuality, and about Sacramental Life which is the communal mainstay of those dynamics which continually "become" the Church into existence through their on-going appropriation of the Jesus-event into present history and for future history.

Process theology is a relatively new enterprise in the Catholic Church. It is only of late that it begins to feel its way into theological consciousness. This work is hopefully a participation in that new enterprise. And if I need a tag for this work it is this: a probe, and only a probe, in the genre of philosophical theology.

In the first chapter I will pay some attention to the context in which the theological act is pitched today. The two chapters which follow are about Alfred North Whitehead and Pierre Teilhard de Chardin. Each of those two chapters treats a Christology. The next two chapters deal respectively with Church and Sacrament. The final section of the book discusses certain implications of these understandings for pastoral concerns.

1

THEOLOGIZING TODAY

Webster says that a melodrama is "a drama with sensational action, extravagant emotions, and, generally, a happy ending." [1] Life in the postconciliar Catholic Church seems to qualify, though there may be those who doubt the happy ending, or at least its proximate appearance. It is commonplace now to allude to the end of the Modern World, or to Man's Coming of Age, or to say in the words of Vatican II that "the living conditions of modern man have so profoundly changed in their social and cultural dimensions, that we can speak of a new age in human history." [2] Alternately the masterpieces and the faux pas, the glorious celebrations and the glorious flops in recent Sacramental Life in the Church, above all in the celebration of the Eucharist, attest to the new freedoms (official or not) and the new faces of things in the Church. Sometimes these new experiences are satisfying or not, depending upon the aesthetic sensitivities (official or not) of their authors. But equally often, the satisfaction or the lack of it derives from the soundness and the true contemporaneity of the theological bases (also, official or not) underpinning the creative efforts.

It is the purpose of this present work to suggest a theological basis, hopefully sound and faithful to our times, for understanding the Sacramental Life of the Church. The work is honestly a thesis, i.e., *a* position, proffered with the tentativeness that any such historically conditioned proposal makes exigent. It is only recently that process thought is commending itself to the attention of Catholic theology; this I hope is a further "commendment." For reasons that I shall explore shortly, it is my belief that process thought has great potential for the act of theologizing within the Catholic Church. I would like for this project to be an act of such theological dialogue.

Of the many handles that might be used to try to get a hold on the contemporary situation in theology, I am choosing the secularization phenomenon as the point of view from which to work. I want to refer also to some earlier historical situations in which some of the current issues showed themselves quite a while ago. For, though many of the current issues are really quite new, there are past "intuitions," if I might call them that, that were bones of contention because we lacked certain intellectual equipment, either for posing the question correctly, or for fielding an adequate reply. And now there are good reasons for re-viewing and re-assessing many of those situations.

I suggest Harvey Cox's short description of secularization as a good working definition:

It represents "defatalization of history," the discovery by man that he has been left with the world on his hands, that he can no longer blame fortune or the furies for what he does with it. Secularization occurs when man turns his attention away from worlds beyond toward this world and this time . . .[3]

Secularization is predominantly a western phenomenon, to a great extent because technology is also a predominantly western phenomenon. Technology is born of science and is the most effective medium of the message of science: that the world indeed is plastic and sooner or later yields to being molded by the touch (or grasp) of man; that it may be difficult, but it is largely a matter of time—the moon, the planets, the stars are all touchable, by our instruments if not by our hands.

Although secularization is mostly a western phenomenon, not much of the world is untouched by it because technology, secularization's ordained preacher, touches the world at nearly every juncture of life. I think that Van Leeuwen may be right, that while Christianity failed to move much beyond western modes of thought, it may finally make substantial sorties into the non-west by riding on the coat tails of technology.[4] Of course this presumes, along with Van Leeuwen, Cox, Gogarten and other secularizationists, that the secularization movement is not only *not* the demise of Christianity, but its natural development and expression, and that in many real ways (though not conscious or deliberate) the Church has fostered the development. Whitehead, for example, has pointed out how the scholastic theology of the high middle ages gave the western mind the kind of faith in reality's fundamental orderliness that it had to have for science to emerge and develop.

It would be a mistake to expect every man one meets to exemplify secularized man. It may even be few who, in the daily run of things, appear as typically secularized. There are many church going Christians who would be horrified at the propositions of secularization. Yet many of these same Christians have had to compartmentalize their secular and religious experience, albeit unconsciously, to go on believing. And there are few who would not be touched in some way by the values of secularization.

The sources of secularization are manifold and interrelated. I will treat individually the three sources which I think are the critical ones: science, historical and Biblical criticism, and existential thought. I will also state here my conviction that the problems and obstacles which secularization presents to religious belief are fundamentally theoretical, and that the linguistic problems, for example, are at base theoretical problems even though the problem of speaking about God is indeed very real.

It would be nearly impossible to overestimate the impact of science upon the modern mind. I will indicate three of the aspects of the impact that have contributed greatly to the development of secularization.

The first of these impacts is epistemological. One locus of the epistemological problem is in British empirical thought, and the derivative tendency to eliminate from consideration anything that is not verifiable through sense experience. The linguistic analysis school of philosophy reflects empirical thought at this point—the analysts hold Berkeley in high esteem as a precursor. The American "death of God" movement, especially in William Hamilton and Thomas Altizer, manifests that aspect of secularization which finds it difficult to speak about God because such speech is not verifiable and therefore lacks meaning.

Another locus of the epistemological problem is American pragmatic thought. The manner of scientific inquiry generates an epistemology applicable to all inquiry, not just to scientific knowing. Scientific inquiry becomes the model of human experience (especially for John Dewey). In this regard, individual experiences tend to generate habitual ways of understanding them and coping with them. Those habitual ways become the theses. Some thesis or another articulates the understanding, but it remains subject to modification and improvement, and it can be discarded if it cannot effectively provide guidance for anticipating and coping with the experience which it purports to understand. The Modernist, George Tyrrell, who was familiar with American pragmatic thought, especially with William James, introduces this epistemological material into his understanding of dogma, credal statements, and into the relation between theology (statements of theses) and devotion (ground of verification). I will deal with Tyrrell again later when I consider Modernism.

There is an ethical analogue to the epistemological issue. Natural law is replaced by the law built on the model of the scientific thesis. The "law" helps us to understand, anticipate, and cope with our experiences. Formerly, in presecular experience, man was responsible *to* the law in order to cope with reality. But today man tends to see his ethical formulations as thetic; they are positions which enable him to carry out his responsibility not *to* but *for* the world. Friedrich Gogarten calls the responsibility *for* the world the law which must direct man, and he inserts this secularized understanding of law into the Pauline theology of law and grace.[5]

The second aspect of the impact of science on the modern mind which I wish to indicate is metaphysical in import. A clear example of this is Dewey's thought:

Instead of a closed universe, science now presents us with one infinite in space and time, having no limits here or there, at this end, so to speak, or at that, and as infinitely complex in internal structure as it is infinite in extent. Hence it is an open world, an infinitely variegated one . . . so multiplex and far reaching that it cannot be summed up and grasped in any one formula. And change rather than fixity is now a measure of "reality" or energy of being; change is omnipresent . . . He [modern man] does not try to define and delimit something remaining constant *in* change. He tries to describe a constant order *of* change. And while the word "constant" appears in both statements, the meaning of the word is not the same. In one case, we are dealing with something constant in *existence,* physical or metaphysical; in the other case with something constant in *function* and operation.

The world of modern science is an open world, a world
varying indefinitely without the possibility of assignable
limit in its internal makeup, a world stretching beyond
any assignable bounds externally.[6]

Another way of contrasting the classical world view with
that of science is to say the "becoming" rather than "being" is
normative of the real way that things are. This has many
implications that are reflected in the theological problems of
secularization thought, since most of the traditional religious
formulations in the western world reflect a "being" rather than
a "becoming" understanding of the world.

Institutional religion has found it increasingly difficult to
register change. Some of the difficulty comes from the sheer
weight of institutionality; but a larger factor is that the Church
has not self-understood itself with "becoming" as its normal
mode of existence. Cf. Whitehead, in *Science and the Modern
World:*

> . . . for over two centuries religion has been on the defen-
> sive, and on a weak defensive. . . . Consider this con-
> trast: when Darwin or Einstein proclaim theories
> which modify our ideas, it is a triumph for science. We
> do not go about saying that there is another defeat for
> science, because its old ideas have been abandoned. We
> know that another step of scientific insight has been
> gained.
>
> Religion will not gain its old power until it can face
> change in the same spirit as does science.[7]

The presupposition that becoming is normative presents
further problems for the understanding of revelation and of
dogma. Does revelation have a once-and-for-all character,
the full content of which was developed by the close of the

apostolic age? Is dogma, then, the unfolding of the content of revelation—the *depositum fidei*—which awaits the deeper understandings of later generations to be unfolded, though there would be no change or increase of size in the folded fabric? Newman grappled with the notion of development in his *Essay on the Development of Christian Doctrine*. Although the Modernists used Newman, perhaps because his ecclesiastical prestige made him a respectable source, they found him not to go far enough, in that he still held to the notion of a *depositum*. Modernist understandings needed a revelation and a dogma which themselves evolved. Nothing short of that could respect the "becoming" nature of the world, nor the necessarily tentative nature of formulations about it.

In this regard, the theologies of Karl Barth and Rudolf Bultmann are probably quite limited in their contributions to solving the religious problems of secularization. In Barth, revelation and subsequent Christian history receive God's unfolding of himself—but development only regards the unfolding, and not the essential givenness of God. For Bultmann, Jesus is a definitive revelation of man's original potential for authentic human existence. And it seems to me that there is also an essential givenness to human nature, and that what unfolds is a clearer revelation of human potential, which was there all along, and not human nature itself. I think it may be that Tillich's "New Being" in Jesus falls under the same critique.

God too must really change if his reality is to respect the nature of all reality as modern man tends to understand it. God too would become. (To say that "God becomes" is *not* to say that "something or someone becomes God"—rather, that "God as God, in some real ways, is engaged in becoming." A possible interpretation of this will emerge later in the discussion of Whitehead.) The First Vatican Council in its *Dogmatic Constitution on the Catholic Faith* had little choice but to affirm that God is "entirely simple and unchangeable,"

since in asserting that "he is one unique spiritual substance,"
it set itself within the framework of a metaphysics of substance. The *Syllabus of Errors* of Pius IX, only a few years
before Vatican I, considered the proposition that "God is
actually in the process of becoming" as one of the modern
errors, and as untenable. Teilhard de Chardin seems to have
attributed something of a "becoming" nature to Christ in
speaking (de Lubac considers it an unfortunate phrase) of
the cosmic nature of Christ. That was one of the Teilhardian
items which came under fire in the *monitum* on his works.
For that matter, already in the fourth century, the Council of
Nicea condemned anyone "alleging that the Son of God is
mutable or subject to change." I mention these instances to
indicate the theological problems that traditional Christian thought has with the contemporary evolutionary world
view as all-embracing.

Less specifically, the general attitudes that science has
tended to propagate are characteristic of the secular man. The
following remarks of Gogarten, in which he cites Jaspers,
illustrate the serious problem a scientifically minded man
would have as his religious attitudes push against centuries of
orthodox theology:

> There, however, are the attributes of modern science.
> Its questioning is unlimited. It is directed to everything
> man encounters. In its research it is never finished with
> even a single phenomenon. It is dominated by a con-
> sciousness of the presuppositions from which one pro-
> ceeds continually. Everything is there to be overcome
> (for the presuppositions are grounded and are relativized
> by more comprehensive presuppositions). Or, if there are
> facts, they are there to be developed in the continuity of
> increasing and more penetrating knowledge. (Karl Jas-
> pers, *Vom Ursprung und Ziel der Geschichte,* Munchen,
> 1940, p. 112) [8]

The third area of impact of science on modern consciousness that I wish to indicate is the attitude of independence that has been generated. I think it is clear from the previous sections that modern man tends to feel no absolute commitment to verbal formulations about reality. He senses his independence in this regard because he feels the tentative nature of theoretical statements, and knows that he uses his theories to bring "nature" under the control of his understanding and experience. Dewey has emphasized the contrast of this mentality with the earlier world view:

> Greek and medieval science formed an art of accepting things as they are enjoyed and suffered. Modern experimental science is an art of control.[9]

If science has encouraged man to look upon the world as plastic and under his control, it is technology that has assured him that he is indeed in control, or that if he is not yet in control, it is only a matter of time. One can't imagine a meteorologist consulting the parish priest about having a votive Mass offered for rain. But he might, if the situation were bad enough, make a series of long distance phone calls to inquire about having the clouds seeded with silver iodide particles. We no longer feel so threatened by the powers and the whimsy of nature. We seek to be autonomous of them by learning to predict and control their energies. We become responsible *for* these forces and not *to* them. As Gogarten has observed:

> Compared with New Testament times, our time is different in respect that it is no longer the worship of the cosmic powers which threatens its freedom. Something like a religious worship absolutely cannot be given to a world toward which man has realized his autonomy in the degree and in the kind that modern man has in rela-

tion to his world. The decisive thing is that man is no longer responsible to the world and to its power as the classical man was and, in a modified way, even the medieval man was. Instead, he has become the one who is responsible *for* his world. This is so exactly to the extent and in the way in which he has become independent toward it.

Man owes this independence to science.[10]

When man feels that he is responsible for the world and that he cannot any longer blame fortune or the furies for how *he* handles it, he begins to sense, out of his new found and larger independence, a correspondingly new found and larger responsibility. Vatican II even accepted such as a definition of man:

> Thus we are witnesses of the birth of a new humanism, one in which man is defined first of all by his responsibility toward his brothers and toward history.[11]

As he senses more that *he* carries such a responsibility, man is less likely to turn to any God for help or to any Providence for assistance, for that no longer seems to be how God relates to the world. Religious feeling, therefore, cannot be rooted in the old understanding of Providence. Whitehead remarked in *Process and Reality*:

> The secularization of the concept of God's function in the world is at least as urgent a requisite of thought as is the secularization of other elements in experience. The concept of God is certainly one essential element in religious feeling. But the converse is not true; the concept of religious feeling is not an essential element in the concept of God's function in the universe.[12]

When man can no longer fall back upon a Providence that will intervene, is there any kind of ultimate assurance that things will work out? Here secularizationists differ. For Dewey,

> Denial to nature of all inherent longings and aspiring tendencies toward ideal ends removed nature from contact with poetry, religion and divine things.[13]

For Leslie Dewart, too, there is no assurance about history, even given the fact of the Christian dispensation. History may ultimately fail:

> All history is free and possible, in the first place, against God, given man's real freedom. His real self-creative possibilities and his true ability to create in time any possible world mean he can actually create a history without, or against, God. The creation of such a history is what Christianity calls *sin,* and its outcome *hell,* (and evidently it is we, not God, who create it and establish its gates at the very center of the earth). This means that history can actually fail . . . For there is no decree to insure the inevitability (any more than there is one to forbid the actuality) of unending progress or the ultimate success of man. Even the definitive and utter failure of history as a whole is a real possibility.[14]

On the other hand, Whitehead is committed to a belief in an evolutionary *upward* trend, or a creative *advance,* with human reason in a directive function:

> Reason finds its scope here in its function of the direction of the upward trend.[15]

Teilhard de Chardin also presupposes a world which has within it the dynamics to insure its upward trend, even though he admits that biologists who allow a teleological interpretation of evolution are in the minority.

For better or for worse, then, the secularizationists leave the world on its own to work out its history. All the dynamics of the working-out are within the universe. If there is a way in which God functions relative to historic process, it can only be from within history, never from without.

In ways that touch most modern men in the western world, whether they are conscious of it or not, science has presented us with a world that is plastic, whose history is truly open, and for which we are responsible. It has encouraged us to act upon our understandings, but to be tentative for not only do our understandings develop and become clarified through experience, but the very objects of our understanding develop and change. Science has given us a new autonomy by urging that history submit to us, rather than that we capitulate to history. We are instructed to look *within* history for reasons for things, and only there, and to be offended by two-world explanations. The phenomena that were once attributed to the supernatural must submit to one of two destinies: either be discredited and discarded (or, as is often the case, be shown to have resulted from mythological worlds); or find new explanations that account for them within a single metaphysic, as in Whitehead, where God too never fails against metaphysical first principles. Rather, he is their chief exemplification, and they never in their sway, therefore, take a holiday.

After this brief look at the impact of science on the contemporary mind, I would like to turn attention to a second originating factor, historical and biblical criticism. It is not surprising that for most of its existence Christianity felt confident in leaning upon the accounts of Scripture, for there were not the tools of historical criticism which we have today. And there was such confidence too in the logical procedures used to develop the "givens" of revelation, that the Church could speak unabashedly of truths that are derived from Scripture with theological certainty. Crisis after crisis after crisis was met through the formulation of credal summaries and doctrinal propositions that removed or at least attenuated the "apparent" ambiguities of faith. No wonder that under the promptings of historical and biblical criticism, the Churches felt—and reacted accordingly—that the ground upon which they had stood full of confidence was disintegrating; they felt the footing disappear.

Serious application of historical criticism to the Bible begins early in the eighteenth century. Albert Schweitzer, in his classic *The Quest of the Historical Jesus,* says that the work of Hermann Samuel Reimarus "was the first time that a really historical mind, thoroughly conversant with the sources, had undertaken the criticism of the tradition"; and of Reimarus' fragment, "The Aims of Jesus and His Disciples," Schweitzer says that "this essay is one of the greatest events in the history of criticism." [16]

Protestant Christianity fared better than did the Catholic Church in accepting the historical criticism of Biblical texts. It was the French priest and scholar, Alfred Loisy, who, at the turn of the present century, tried to introduce Biblical criticism into Roman thought and theology. His books were placed on the Index and he later came under an edict of excommunication. In many ways, Biblical criticism was the principal instigator of the Modernist movement, toward which Catholic officialdom felt something less than affection. Among other reasons, the relativizing tendencies of historical criticism came at a time when the temporal power and political suasion of the papacy were crumbling, and the papacy (my guess) reacted by asserting ever more strongly its absolute authority in matters of faith and morals. Papal infallibility was defined, and Rome was in no mood to have her corpus of dogma tampered with and subjected to historical criticism. In the Catholic Church, it has only been in the years following Vatican II that form criticism has become in fact an acceptable scientific method in Biblical research.

A sense of relativity regarding all matters of historic process is one of historical criticism's contributions to the mentality of secularization; for that means a relativity that is equally operative in the New Testament and the Church as well. Gogarten says that,

> . . . the research of history acknowledged the almost un-limited metamorphosis of the historical orders of human life in state and society. Scarcely any of the forms that once existed and that will yet develop can claim for themselves an absolute validity.[17]

It would be a serious mistake to understand secularization as something happening over and against religion, and therefore as something with which religion must contend. For in a number of very real ways, religion has itself been a source of secularization. And the influence of Biblical scholarship has been one way in which secularization pressures have arisen from within religion. In what is probably the best known of the presentations of secularization, *The Secular City,* Harvey Cox has insisted that secularization is the rightful effect of authentic directions of Judaeo-Christian faith. Cox, Gogarten, the "death-of-God" theologians, and so many others who have urged religious acceptance and affirmation of secularization are themselves Churchmen. In the Catholic Church some of the strongest secularization pressures have come in the wake of Vatican II and especially the document *Gaudium et Spes* which reminded us that "according to the almost unanimous opinion of believers and unbelievers alike, all things on earth should be related to man as their center and crown" (n. 12). Religion, it seems, will play an increasingly large role in the secularization processes in which it participates.

The third locus for looking into the development of secularization thought is existentialism. I want to call attention to two of the concerns of existentialism that reflect the mind of secularization: the radical freedom of man; the presence and problem of evil, with the questions that evil raises about God's relation to the world, or even about his existence at all.

To have spoken as we did about man's sense of autonomy, independence and responsibility is to have considered, in other terms, his recent sense of his radical freedom. He is not held to the "givens" of some essence of human nature, for nature, like all things historical, is open-ended and is itself subject to further development. A sense of alienation from religion accompanies a realization of the ways in which institutionalized religion has infringed upon freedom of thought and conscience. "The Legend of the Grand Inquisitor" in Dostoevsky's *The Brothers Karamazov* is a classic statement of that alienation. Ivan relates the parable to his saintly brother, Alyosha, who is a young monk. Jesus turns up in the streets of Seville during the days of the Inquisition. The Grand Inquisitor has him arrested. As he visits Jesus at night in prison, he rebukes him with stinging irony for continuing to assert man's freedom:

> "For fifteen centuries we have been wrestling with Thy freedom, but now it is ended and over for good. Dost Thou not believe that it's over for good? Thou lookest meekly at me and deignest not even to be wroth with me. But let me tell Thee that now, today, people are more persuaded than ever that they have perfect freedom, yet they have brought their freedom to us and laid it humbly at our feet. But that has been our doing. Was this what Thou didst? Was this Thy freedom?"

> "I don't understand again," Alyosha broke in. "Is he ironical, is he jesting?"

> "Not a bit of it! He claims it as a merit for himself and his

Church that at last they have vanquished freedom and have done so to make men happy." [18]

One of the recurrent themes in Jean-Paul Sartre's work reflects the Grand Inquisitor's realization that freedom frightens men, and that they easily surrender it to be happy. For Sartre, that is bad faith on man's part, for he is condemned to absolute freedom. Reflecting upon his own existentialist philosophy, Sartre queries:

Can it be that what really scares them in the doctrine that I shall try to present here is that it leaves to man a possibility of choice? [19]

If we grant the existentialist positions about man's radical freedom (responsibility), even the freedom to create his own essence (which is therefore subsequent to his existence), then the classical doctrine of God and creation is unmanageable. (The -theism of Sartre's atheism certainly seems to me to be not God necessarily, but classical theism.)

When we conceive God as the creator, He is generally thought of as a superior type of artisan. Whatever doctrine we may be considering, whether one like that of Descartes or Leibniz, we always grant that will more or less follows understanding or, at the very least, accompanies it, and that when God creates He knows exactly what he is creating. Thus, the concept of man in the mind of God is comparable to the concept of the paper-cutter in the mind of the manufacturer, and, following certain techniques and a conception, God produces man, just as the artisan, following a definition and a technique, makes a paper cutter. Thus, the individual man is the realization of a certain concept in the divine intelligence. . . .

Atheistic existentialism, which I represent, is more coherent. It states that if God does not exist, there is at least
one being in whom existence precedes essence, a being
who exists before he can be defined by a concept, and
that being a man, or, as Heidegger says, human reality.
What is meant here by saying that existence precedes
essence? It means that, first of all, man exists, turns up,
appears on the scene, and only afterwards, defines himself. If man, as the existentialist conceives him, is de-
finable, it is because he is at first nothing. Only afterward
will he be something, and he himself will have made what
he will be. Thus, there is no human nature, since there
is no God to conceive it. Not only is man what he
conceives himself to be, but he is what he wills himself
to be after his thrust toward existence.[20]

A major challenge of secularization to Christianity is for
its philosophers and theologians, respecting the intuitions of
modern experience, to understand God as one who confers
on man the freedom and responsibility for fashioning history,
without *outside* assistance or interference—and still be a God
who is comfortable to the innermost convictions of the Old
and New Testament faith. This requires the careful use of
research and historical criticism to sort out the cultural husks
(using Harnack's imagery) and retain the grain-beliefs about
God and Jesus (though some critics have felt that Harnack
ended up with neither husk nor grain).

Although the roots of secularization theology go considerably back into history, it was in the 1960's that these intuitions reached into a broader popular consciousness. But the
1970's have begun to identify a sort of haughtiness in some
of those formulations, although most of the basic secularization intuitions are intact. We know that while history is
plastic, any conviction about its easy (or even difficult) manageability is misplaced. That's why the increased popular

humility before history seems quite in order. In a sense, history seems to have a movement of its own. Process philosophers name it "creative advance." Theologians call it "salvation history." Marxists identify it as the inevitable sweep of Communism over historical configurations.

There is a useful analogue in personal experience. Carl Jung has called our attention to the collective unconscious, which is a way of affirming that we are ourselves and yet more than ourselves. The elements of consciousness which we are apt to identify exhaustively with our ego-content are indeed but a small part of what accounts for our selfhood. Each of us has a personal unconscious and a collective unconscious also which keeps us in touch with the whole history of man, where we have been and where we are going. The symbols and fantasies of both our daydreams and our night dreams puzzle us often by their content, by the pressures they exert, and sometimes even by the movement they instigate. And that sometimes happens, as it were, in spite of ourselves. Sometimes to our delight, other times to our chagrin:

> Whether primitive or not, mankind always stands on the brink of actions it performs itself but does not control. The whole world wants peace and the whole world prepare for war, to take but one example.[21]

We must likewise not identify history exhaustively with those movements of which we are conscious, as if those were the sum total of history's ego content. The return, these recent years, to a concern with transcendence and to reinterpretations of it, are a kind of corrective to the radical secularization theologies. That portion of history that we deal with consciously is but a small part of what accounts for historyhood. What we know about personhood should keep us alerted to that.

A second frequent concern in existential thought is that of evil. Modern man has been confronted with evil in overwhelming dimensions not previously part of human consciousness: the atomic attacks on Hiroshima and Nagasaki; the extermination of millions of Jews under National Socialism in Germany; the new consciousness of intense suffering throughout the world—starvation because of a tragically inequitable distribution of the world's goods, persecution because of the color of one's skin or the place of one's birth, savage killing in the name of peace. Rabbi Richard Rubenstein's book *After Auschwitz* is a clear presentation of the question: how can these monstrous evils be squared away with a God whom we call the Lord of History:

> After the experiences of our time, we can neither affirm the myth of the omnipotent God of History nor can we maintain its corrolary, the election of Israel. . . . Jews do not need these doctrines to remain a religious community. . . .

> If there is a God of History, he is the ultimate author of Auschwitz. I am willing to believe in God, the holy nothingness who is our source and final destiny, but never again in a God of History. . . . What the death of God theologians depict is an undoubted *cultural* fact in our time: God is totally unavailable as a source of meaning or value. There is no vertical transcendence.[22]

If there is an answer to this within the Judaeo-Christian framework, in some way or another it will have to be by way of a God who left it fully up to man to fashion him as a Lord of History by fashioning history after what man understands to be the configuration of God's extraordinary love. If history fails, it is through the irresponsible use of human freedom; and God must not be dragged in vertically to make history safe. Man may have been irresponsible for history at times because his expectation of vertical assistance to horizontal problems was misplaced and misconstrued.

Some of the matters of secularization are twentieth century matters. But some of them are matters that have been with us a long while and have kept asserting themselves at different points of history because no sufficient answers were offered when the questions were posed. And, to be sure, many of these same matters will continue past our present century in pursuit of answers. But it does seem helpful to our present understanding of secularization thought to probe the childhood and adolescence of some of the members of its family. I will deal briefly with the Pelagian and semi-Pelagian heresies of the fifth century; the thirteenth century joust that St. Thomas Aquinas had with one of the same issues; and then the Modernist movement within the Roman Catholic Church in the late nineteenth and early twentieth centuries.

Pelagius was born probably in Britain around the middle of the fourth century and moved to Rome around 380. Here, though not ordained, he became the spiritual director for many laity and clergy alike. He left for Africa shortly before the capture of Rome by Alaric in 410, and soon after went to Palestine, and no more is heard of him after 418. It was his friend Coelestius who propagated his views, for Pelagius confided his beliefs to a select few only. Coelestius was summoned before the African Bishops in 411 in Carthage, and refused to recant from the Pelagian things he was teaching. St. Augustine dispatched a Spanish priest, Orosius, to Palestine to alert the Church there, especially St. Jerome, to the presence and the teaching of Pelagius. Augustine and Jerome both wrote tractates against the Pelagian teaching (Jerome's with such invective as to be almost ineffective). The teaching was condemned by Innocent I in 417, who also excommunicated both Pelagius and Coelestius. Innocent's successor, Pope Zosimus uncondemned and unexcommunicated the teaching and the men, only to renew both at a later time, by way of ratifying the Acts of the Sixteenth Council of Carthage.

The essential part of the teaching of Pelagianism is that the human will is completely free and is equally ready to do good or evil. Pelagius felt that if Adam's sin tilted the will toward evil, or if there was a necessity of grace to do any good act at all, then the perfect freedom of the will would be removed.

I believe this teaching is in touch with secularization matters at two points. The first is the issue dealt with in Sartre, that man is radically free, and that his freedom is a neutral state: he may choose good, he may select evil. The second issue is analagous to the first, the feeling that history too is neutral, that it is truly open-ended, not precommitted to any particular outcome but waiting, for better or for worse, the decisions of man out of which history is processed.

Semi-Pelagianism is a variation on the Pelagian teaching, the leading exponent being John Cassian, against whom Augustine also wrote. Semi-Pelagianism teaches that while grace is necessary for the Christian life, it is without grace and solely by a human decision that a man opens himself to the life of grace; the initial act of faith he is able to make on his own. If a true act of faith is possible without grace, then the supernatural character of Christianity is jeopardized.

Christian theology had already been cast in the modes of thought taken from the Greek world view, though certainly with no consciousness of the presuppositional elements of Hellenistic categories of thought. I will return to this shortly when I consider St. Thomas' treatment of the same problem. But the issue that puts semi-Pelagianism in touch with the problem areas of secularization thought is its attempt to

break down the division between nature and supernature—
or, in other terms, between nature and grace, or between
reason and faith. For secularization thought will have nothing
to do with a two-realmed reality, having such a chasm between that the members of the lower realm can in no way
cross unless the upper realm somehow elevates the power of
the lower so that it can make the crossing.

With the greater and more sophisticated elaboration of
theology in Aristotelian categories by the Scholastics, it became possible to state the problem of semi-Pelagianism more
succinctly. There is a life which is *natural* to God and a life
which is *natural* to man. *Nature* details what something is.
Nature defines both the character of something's actuality and
also the scope of its potentialities. The summarizing phrase is:
agere sequitur esse, what something can *do* is *consequent*
upon what something *is*. Human (or divine) *agere* is defined
by human (or divine) *esse*. What one is capable of doing is a
real expression of one's nature. Theology has described the
Christian vocation as a call to participate in God's own life.
If a man were capable on the basis of his own nature (his
esse) of participating in the life (the *agere*) of God, then his
own nature would in some way be "naturally" divine, since
agere sequitur esse; and that is what was implied by the semi-
Pelagian belief in even an initial but real faith act, without
grace first elevating the human *esse* beyond its natural capacity. The tightly knit category of nature in scholastic philosophy
and theology requires the position that God must *first* elevate
human nature before it is capable of true faith acts, which
are participations in the life of God.

That still leaves us with a dilemma. If a man's nature is
graced to do something which otherwise *in no way* would it
be capable of doing, then whether we use the name "supernatural" or the phrase "life of Grace," we are still describing
something not-natural to man, something unnatural. Yet if

it does lie *in some way* within man's power that he can participate in divine life, how can we avoid attributing divine *esse* to him? And how could the gratuity of grace be maintained?

The solution presented by Thomas was the concept of "obediential potency." As we think of the real potentials that we have for doing things, we know that these potentials differ greatly; some are very easy to invoke, but other potentials would need such a specialized set of circumstances to be actualized that they will almost surely never be tapped. Nevertheless, such highly specialized potentials are still real potentials, even though barely so. We might think of the easier-to-realize potentials as being near to realization, and the latter as being so barely potential, so far removed from the likelihood of realization, as to be almost pure potential and nothing more. Thomas posits for human nature a real potential for participating in divine life, but so much at the remote end of potentiality that *absolutely the only* circumstance that can evoke it is a summons from God. That summons is grace and is the only way in which the potential can be touched off. It can obey the summons if it comes. That is the concept of obediential potency. In this way, the potential for participating in divine life is posited in man so that supernatural life is not unnatural. The potential, however, cannot be actualized by any human initiative; it can be actualized only by a summons from grace. Thus the gratuity of grace is preserved, and the supernatural character of the Christian vocation sustained.

I am inclined to think that the Thomistic solution is at least semi-semi-Pelagian, for the potential *is* in man, and that substance categories leave no fully legitimate way out. Secularization is putting extraordinary pressure upon the theological enterprise to find a way out. Within the framework of philosophical theology, removal of the barriers between the natural and the supernatural of traditional theology must, I think, involve a single metaphysic within which all the phenomena fit. This leaves two options: one is to reject the entire supernatural package and thereby avoid a dualistic package, e.g., John Dewey and Jean-Paul Sartre; the other option is to account for the contents of the supernatural package within the single metaphysic, e.g., Whitehead, and certain of the process theologians such as John Cobb, Jr.

And now it remains to say something about the Modernist controversy in the Catholic Church. After a gestation period that began about the middle of the nineteenth century, and which was already fraught with prenatal complications, the Modernist movement was born to light in 1903 with the publication of Alfred Loisy's *L'Evangile et L'Eglise*. And it died an early and somewhat violent death in Rome, on September 8, 1907, with the encyclical *Pascendi Gregis* of Pius X. There is the sneaking suspicion that it has resurrected, its Easter date being October 11, 1963, the opening of the Second Vatican Council.

George Tyrrell, the Irish-English Modernist, defined a Modernist as "a Churchman, of any sort, who believes in the possibility of a synthesis between the essential truth of his religion and the essential truth of Modernity." [23] The tension of that struggle is caught anew by a contemporary poet, cited in a recent book by Norman Pittenger:

I come to you in anxiety, and you give me uncertainties.
I come without meaning, and you preach nonsense.
I come in confusion, and you cry "Miracle."
If my only choice is to be a Christian or a modern man,
I have no choice. Modernity is my name—I am its
    child.[24]

The Modernist movement represents the struggle of exegetes and theologians to take historical criticism and evolutionary and developmental thought seriously enough that one could be a thoroughly Christian man.

From some points of view, it is not accurate to refer to a Modernist *movement*. Those usually considered to be Modernists do not form a single school of thought. They have no common point of origin. They work with no deliberate collusion. There is none of the internal cohesion among the members and their positions that normally marks a movement.

But there are at least two reasons that justify speaking of Modernism as a movement. First of all, Baron Friedrich von Hügel served as something of an architect for the movement. He got in contact with those whom he was able to identify with the cause. With England as his home base, but being at ease in several languages and having contacts and prestige in many places upon the continent, he kept interested parties mutually informed of each other's efforts, and served as a sort of "nervous system" among the various members.

And secondly, there is the fact that *Pascendi Gregis* spoke of Modernism as a movement, attributing to it a developed system of presuppositions, though (the encyclical held) the Modernists were clever enough to keep the systematic nature of their presuppositions out of purview. I think there might well be, on the part of Rome, a projection of a system into the Modernist movement, because she felt—and rightly so—that the entire fabric of her system was under fire at almost every point, and this suggested an opposing system spread out against her with contact at almost every point.

I want to quote at length from *Pascendi Gregis,* both to show the scope of the threat which Rome felt, and because of how strangely that which was condemned sounds like a description of the Aggiornamento in the Roman Church following Vatican II:

It remains for us now to say something about the Modernist as a reformer. . . . They wish philosophy to be reformed, especially in the ecclesiastical seminaries. They wish the scholastic philosophy to be relegated to the history of philosophy and to be classed among obsolete systems, and the young men to be taught modern philosophy which alone is true and suited to the time in which we live. They desire the reform of theology: rational theology is to have modern philosophy for its foundation, and positive theology is to be founded on the history of dogma. As for history, it must be written and taught only according to their methods and modern principles. Dogmas and their evolution, they affirm, are to be harmonised with science and history. In the catechism no dogmas are to be inserted except those that have been reformed and are within the capacity of the people. Regarding worship, they say, the number of external devotions is to be reduced, and steps must be taken to prevent their further increase, though, indeed, some of the admirers of symbolism are disposed to be more indulgent on this head. They cry out that ecclesiastical government needs to be reformed in all its branches, but especially in its disciplinary and dogmatic departments. They insist that both outwardly and inwardly it must be brought into harmony with the modern conscience, which now wholly tends towards democracy; a share in the ecclesiastical government should therefore be given to the lower ranks of the clergy, and even to the laity, and authority which is too much concentrated, should be decentralised. The Roman Congregations, and especially the *Index* and the *Holy Office,* must likewise be modified. The ecclesiastical authority must alter its line of conduct in the social and political world; while keeping outside political organisations, it must adapt itself to them, in order to penetrate them with its spirit. With regard to morals, they adopt the principle of the Americanists, that the active virtues are more important than the passive, and are to be more encouraged in practice. They ask that the clergy should return to their primitive humility and poverty, and that in their ideas and action they should admit the principles of Modernism; and there are some who, gladly listening to the teaching of their Protestant masters, would desire the suppression of the celibacy of the clergy. What is there left which is not to be reformed by them and according to their principles? [25]

As evidence, compelling though not conclusive, of Modernism's empty tomb, I would like to cite from Vatican II:

May the faithful, therefore, live in very close union with the men of their time. Let them strive to understand perfectly their way of thinking and feeling, as expressed in their culture. Let them blend modern science and its theories and the understanding of the most recent discoveries with Christian morality and Christian doctrine. Thus their religious practice and morality can keep pace with their scientific knowledge and with an ever increasing technology. Theological inquiry should seek a profound understanding of revealed truth without neglecting close contact with its own times.[26]

In his 1934 book, *The Modernist Movement in the Catholic Church*, and his 1970 book, *A Variety of Catholic Modernists,* Alec Vidler insists upon the centrality of Biblical criticism to the Roman Modernist crisis. The Catholic world had kept apart from the mainstream of Biblical criticism, and thus was deprived of a somewhat slow and organic period of adjustment to it, though it would not have been easy in any event. Friedrich Strauss' *Life of Jesus* was translated into French in 1840. However, it was only with Ernest Renan's *La Vie de Jesus* in 1863 that the fruit of German criticism, along with Renan's own critical work, came to the attention of the Catholic world. He was, says Schweitzer, "a writer with the characteristic French accent, who gave to the Latin world in a single book the result of the whole process of German criticism." [27] However, the crisis emerged full blown with Alfred Loisy's *L'Evangile et L'Eglise* in 1903, which had the subtle added attraction of being a formidable Catholic response to and criticism of Adolf Harnack's liberal Protestantism in his *What Is Christianity?* Loisy's historical critique was tucked into the folds of the apologetique. Baron von Hügel put George Tyrrell in touch with Loisy, and with wider literature in the field. From Loisy on, the action of the Roman Church was swift and severe as the works of the Modernists fell to the Index, and the authors came under excommunication.

Historically, it was certainly Biblical criticism which precipitated the Modernist crisis. In that sense, I agree with Vidler on the centrality of Biblical criticism to the crisis. But in my opinion, the critical work raised issues which in their turn caused the crisis mentality. As I see it, the issues raised were almost immediately philosophical and theological because of the Church's strong commitments to the structures and articulations of her belief. In a letter to the Baron, Loisy reflected upon an early apologetic work he had planned and partly written, though it had not been published:

> The first sketch shows that the fundamental and dominating idea of the whole work was the reform of the intellectual system of the Catholic Church; neither more nor less; and all the rest, criticism, history, philosophy, were to be ordered to this end.[28]

In the *Syllabus of Errors* there is already a strong resistance to notions of evolutionary development, especially as these apply to dogma and revelation. I agree with Leslie Dewart's assessment of the problem:

> The fundamental mistake of the Modernists consisted

in attempting to reinterpret the traditional doctrines of the development of dogma and the nature of revelation in line with the contemporary awareness of human evolution and historicity, but on the continued assumption of the traditional theory of knowledge, in which a subject enters into union with an object to overcome an original isolation between the two.[29]

Because the scope of this presentation is necessarily limited, I would like to concentrate briefly upon George Tyrrell since I feel that he, more than the other Modernists, directly attempted to meet the epistemological issue.

George Tyrrell was born in Ireland, and raised in the Low Church. He later moved to London where he became a Catholic, and a year later entered the Jesuit order. In his early training he was an ardent disciple of Thomas and went through a period of militant orthodoxy. After ordination he had some parish experience, and then began teaching and writing, when his "troubles" began. An 1897 work, *Nova et Vetera*, got him the attention of Von Hügel through whom he became acquainted with the work of Blondel, Laberthonnière and Bergson. He became increasingly disenchanted with classical philosophy and theology. He became a sore presence to the Jesuit order, from which he was dismissed in 1906; shortly after he was excommunicated. And even so, he continued his deep interest in the reform of the Church. Before he died in 1909, he received the sacraments from another priest closely associated with the movement, Abbé Henri Bremond.

Tyrrell felt that his essay, "The Relation of Theology to Devotion," was fundamental to his thinking. Years after he wrote it, he said that it marked "a turning point in my own theological experience." He added that,

. . . on rereading it carefully I am amazed to see how little

I have really advanced since I wrote it; how I have simply eddied round and round the same point. It is all here— all that follows—not in germ but in explicit statement —as it were a brief compendium or analytical index.[30]

In addition to this early essay, I shall be referring principally to *Christianity at the Crossroads,* the final work of his life.

Tyrrell insists on keeping clear the distinction between our immediate, crass, unsophisticated experience, and the neater, sophisticated theories and principles by which we generalize and interpret it. Regarding that unsophisticated immediate experience, "the world at large refuses to be harnessed to our categories, and goes its own rude, unscientific way." [31] And while he refuses to allow the vulgar experience of the generalizing formulations to become absolutized, he knows that theorizing is necessary to help us handle the accumulation of immediate experience. Our theories engender for man

> . . . a new source of vision, a power of observing and recognising and remembering order where before he had only seen chaos. And in this lies the great advantage of abstract and scientific consideration; of precisions that are unreal; of suppositions that are impossible. Only by these devices can we digest our experience piecemeal, which else would remain in confused and unsorted masses.[32]

These remarks are equally true for the generalizations of both philosophy and theology.

Revelation did not arrive in propositional form, but via everyday, ordinary means, i.e., the crass, daily experiences. It is up to theology in succeeding ages (at its own risk, he insists) to translate and systematize, but not to finalize any of the articulations. For the articulations are always highly shaped by the historical conditions and the mind-sets at work where they are uttered, and are always relativized, therefore. For example,

> If she [Church] says the soul is the "form" of the body, it is not because she has a revelation of philosophy to communicate, but because the question is asked by a hylo-morphist; and it is the nearest way the truth can be put to him.[33]

Tyrrell sees that the Gospels themselves are already attempts to formulate the Idea of Jesus, and are therefore a combination of experience and of theorizing upon it—of theology and devotion, the interplay of *lex orandi* and *lex credendi* (though more of the former).[34] The Church, through its devotion (*lex orandi*) and its theology (*lex credendi*) continues to work out its understanding of the Idea of Jesus.

The influence of William James upon Tyrrell is quite marked. It is undoubtedly through James that he acquired his sense of scientific method and his insistence upon experience as the test of truth, whether of the hypotheses of science and theology, or of religious symbols. Tyrrell considers the ideas of rational theology and of creeds to be symbolic:

> Hence all our theology of the Incarnation deals, not with transcendent realities, but with the visions or revelations in which they are symbolised. Its purpose is to preserve the original force and usefulness of that symbolism; to secure its correct rendering for other ages and people; to make it coherent within itself and with the equally symbolic ideas of rational theology.[35]

What is important about the experience that authenticates propositions and symbols is not so much reference to the past, at least not principally so, but to the future and to control:

The value of all these symbols and hypotheses is in the extent to which they anticipate and control that order of experience upon which they are founded; and every new success deepens that foundation and strengthens our faith.[36]

Tyrrell clearly means that not only the value of symbols but their truth is involved in this verification. Scientific inquiry is his model:

So with the hypotheses of physical science, which are fictions founded in fact. Not one of them is absolutely true as resting upon a complete comprehension of the whole universe. But one is truer than another as yielding a wider anticipation and control of experience; and that it does so means that it is, in some degree, *like* nature —not merely analogous, since the fiction and the fact are in the same order. Aided by art and reflection, they are suggested, criticised and improved by experience. They are self-revelations of physical nature; to which science is related as is theology to Divine revelation.[37]

And as an example:

The Father of Jesus is a far richer and truer symbol than the War-God of early Israel. . . . As the spirit grows in man his symbolism grows truer and more spiritual. "Truer," because it gives a fuller anticipation and control of spiritual experience.[38]

From a pastoral point of view, Tyrrell is quite aware of the personal difficulties that are involved for those who attempt to move from the older systems of truths, when symbols and propositions tended to be treated with high literalness, to an understanding such as he has elaborated. I would judge that a fair amount of contemporary disillusionment about religion in our secularized world stems from just that:

> This transitional state between consistent literalism and consistent symbolism is distressing and dangerous. What retards the liberation is the fear of losing the experience and guidance so long associated with simple literalism. But only when the liberation is completed will it be possible to go back with safety and profit to the integrity of the Christian revelation, and realise its truth as a guide to spiritual experience and a vehicle of transcendent meanings.[39]

The reluctance of the Church to change her understandings of the nature of her symbols and propositions, in so many ways an epistemological issue, accounts for much of her difficulty in the modern world:

> Nay, her [Church's] fidelity to the letter; her unwillingness to tamper with what has been the vehicle of much spiritual life and experience; her refusal to admit the symbolic character of the apocalyptic vision; her determination to treat it as revealed truth of the phenomenal order and make it a criterion of history and science—all this has gradually weakened her influence and brought her into conflict with the modern mind.[40]

For me, this points again to the theoretical nature of the Modernist crisis and also of secularization today. The reason why the Church was unwilling to tamper with her symbols and formulas was obvious to most of the Modernists, and especially to Tyrrell: if any one of the major premises of the Modernists were granted, the whole system of thought upon which orthodoxy was constructed would be up for grabs, so tightly knit is the system:

> In the Roman Church . . . scholastic logic has bound
> these positions into a system so compact as to obliterate
> any distinction between fundamental and contingent ele-
> ments. They all stand or fall together, for they are all at-
> tached to the one root of ecclesiastical inerrancy. Other
> systems, more loosely organized, could survive the am-
> putation of this member or that; Rome would bleed to
> death if she sacrificed her little finger.[41]

It is on grounds like this that I feel, with Dewart, that the
Modernist crisis was first of all a theoretical crisis. There was
no epistemology in the tradition that could handle the notion
of real development. Nor was there a metaphysics that could
handle "becoming" and change as not merely what happened
to being, but as the nature and condition of the real.

I believe that Tyrrell is a better key to the Modernist
crisis than Loisy, though Loisy is of course better known.
Tyrrell was conditioned by the *two* streams from which the
Modernists crisis emerged, historical criticism and the method
of scientific inquiry. Admittedly, these influences were second
hand, for Tyrrell was neither critic nor scientist; but he was
a good pupil of the pragmatic thought of James and Schiller
and of the critical work of Loisy. Tyrrell considered himself
more radical than Loisy, and I tend to agree. His relativiza-
tion was more thoroughgoing. I doubt whether Loisy would
seriously have entertained the possibility of Christianity or
Catholicism ultimately disappearing, as did Tyrrell:

> We may be sure that religion, the deepest and most uni-
> versal exigency of man's nature, will survive. We cannot
> be so sure that any particular expression of the religious
> idea will survive . . . Should Christianity be unable, or
> unwilling, to conform to these laws, it must perish, like
> every other abortive attempt to discover a universal
> religion as catholic as science.[42]

Yet, notwithstanding the pain that he experienced as Christian and Catholic, especially his excommunication, he continued his interest and writing till the end of his life.

In trying to sketch out the situation in which theologizing is being carried out in the Catholic Church today, I am aware of a selectivity that is operative. A caricature lacks the full detail of a photograph, but hopefully selects enough significant and tell-tale items to be a faithful communication of a familiar face. Two of the principles of selectivity are an awareness of the close liaison that Roman theology and philosophy have long maintained (and a continuing conviction about the high value of that liaison); and secondly, that there is no single other factor that is even close to science in its importance as a force that shapes contemporary consciousness.

Theology today must present a world, a reality, with a credible unity. There cannot be two sets of rubrics, one for this world, one for the "other" world. Charles Hartshorne has presented this case very forcefully in his book, *The Divine Relativity*.[43] A knower is shaped in a real way by what he knows. Should a man in fact know *this* rather than *that,* he would be different as a knower. Our knowledge depends for its content upon the objects of knowledge (as well as upon the interpretative equipment the knower brings to bear, but certainly and really too upon the objects of knowledge). Hartshorne points to the logical contradictions involved in having a God who does not in any real way depend. God may in his abstract characteristics be all-knowing; but when he actually knows, he knows *this* as actual rather than *that;* thus his knowledge depends upon what is actual. Knowing-all is a matter of relating perfectly (cognitively) to what is real. No aspect of what is real lies outside the cognitive relation. Cognitive error reflects a breakdown in the cognitive relationship. In this way, a perfect knowledge requires an unflawed cognitive relationship, a super-relativeness, or in Hartshorne's words, sur-relativity. To allow for such a relativity in God, a dependence upon what is real, means that as what is real changes and becomes, so God's knowing changes and becomes. And that means, therefore, that God as well as all else that is real is subject to becoming. In classical theology, the epistemology of our knowing follows one set of rubrics, and God's epistemology follows another since it was not possible to attribute any kind of real change to God. In order to protect God from change, which in Aristotelian thought is always an indication of imperfection, it has to be held that God knows all-at-once all that will ever be, thus no new knowledge comes to him. That may save him from the classical imperfection of being engaged in change. But it is difficult then to salvage what we experience as history from mere appearance. For even though we *seem* to experience a free unfolding of event in temporal sequence, there is "someplace" a once-and-for-all grasp of the total configuration. Not only is the nature of God's knowing at stake, but the genuine open-endedness of historical event and real human freedom. So much of the classical problem derived from a strong philosophical presupposition that change is always a matter of imperfection. Scientific experience communicates to our consciousness today in a myriad of ways that "becoming" is normative of all that is, even constitutive of all that is. What I am suggesting strongly throughout this present work is the importance of a process world view and of process categories of thought for elaborating our contemporary experience in many fields: psychology, sociology, philosophy, theology.

Theology today must further be able to maintain man's responsibility for how history turns out, and yet understand God's commitment to history. If there is a way that God touches history, yet never interventively, then perhaps it is simultaneously true that man is fully responsible, yet that God makes a difference and that religion may matter substantially to the world's becoming. Here again, I feel that the world view of many of the process thinkers has an understanding of reality that is consonant with the scientific mind and also offers to religion the possibility of addressing secular man.

One way of understanding the theological task today is to realize that the symbol making factory has changed its address. And if there is still some stock on hand from the old factory, it is largely unmarketable.

Symbols emerge out of a culture. They reflect how a culture understands itself. They express those understandings and even reinforce them. New eras usher in new sets of symbols. I use "symbol" here in a very broad sense. Language is a symbolic code, for example. The Hebrew language expresses a people's self-understanding and an interpretation of experience that differs greatly from that of the Greek world or the modern English speaking world. Music is another example of symbol. Spanish music is almost immediately identifiable in comparison with German music, whether folk or popular or classical. There's just a different feel for life in each. Romantic music symbolizes one era; baroque quite another. In recent American history, very different moods and approaches to life are evident in the various musical styles, from the dance-bound sounds of the forties, to the rock music that emerged in the fifties, and later branched into folk rock and hard rock, while folk music had a large hold for a while also; protest music both had a life of its own, and also influenced other trends in music. As McLuhan has observed, the medium of one age becomes the art material of the next: so we have rock operas in the early Seventies. Catch phrases become symbols. For many years "renouncement" was a symbol around which spiritualities formed themselves, partly because of the extent to which monasticism shaped the liturgical experience and passed its symbols on to the laity. Today "insertedness" is symbol of the spiritual life.

Symbols in this sense cannot be created or manipulated at will. They just happen-out. If we want to point a finger more precisely at the agencies that are most responsible for what symbols emerge, it would be toward those factors in a culture which contribute most to a culture's self-understanding. They are the symbol making factories. Although the impact of education varies in historical periods, the educational institution (in a large sense) has often been a symbol factory. Today business and advertising are also symbol factories. As Roszak has recently pointed out, the counter-culture in the United States has been responsible for the emergence of new symbols which have worked their way into a broader consciousness: long hair (music from the musical "Hair"), flower power, colors and styles of clothing that are much more informal and often more flamboyant in celebration of life. "Celebration" itself has become a symbol.

It is critical for theology that it realize that the major symbol making factory changed its address in the late sixteenth and early seventeenth centuries. For obvious and understandable reasons, the Church was the major symbol making factory from the early centuries of Christianity (from Constantine onward, if we need a date for a symbol) until, roughly, the dawn of science. Monasteries were frequently *the* centers of learning. In their libraries the major texts of western culture were kept and copied and passed on. Clerics were the best educated people in most communities. The contact which most people had with learning was their contact with the Church. There were sometimes schools attached to monasteries. The early thirteenth century saw the rise of the medieval universities, and here again the Church was the major controlling influence. Most of the great thinkers in the western world during this long period were Churchmen: Augustine, Scotus, Bonaventure, Anselm, Thomas Aquinas, Bernard, etc. The few non-Churchmen are scattered. Most of the men who were responsible for the rise of science are not

Churchmen. Most of the great philosophical explorations after the sixteenth and seventeenth centuries are not by Churchmen. Nor is that any kind of indictment. There is just the fact that centers of learning have passed from ecclesiastical locations to secular locations. The symbol making factory changed its address. Today it is largely out of secular experience that the world's self-understanding emerges, and out of which many of our symbols take shape. Freud, Jung, Adler, Rogers, Maslow, Perls, etc., have supplied us with much of our picture of man. College students, and sometimes even high school students, are able to use their symbols: id, superego and ego; archetype; self-actualization; gestalt.

Some part—and I am inclined to think some large part—of why the Church felt herself losing touch with modern man is because she continued to work with symbols and symbol systems from an earlier age. Liturgical symbolism continued to reflect medieval court practice in many aspects of its solemnity, monastic life-style in other aspects, such as music. The scholastic theology of the thirteenth century continued to be the official theology. There is no question here of good and bad, or right and wrong. But if the symbols used are not the vital ones of an age, then they cannot command immediacy of assent.

The symbol making factory has changed its address! Theology today has got to do business with the new address. That challenge, not just to theology but to the Church, holds out rich possibility for a still deeper incarnational life. We used to use the expression: We will go to Church Sunday. Man went to Church. Now the Church must go to the world, for less and less does the world go to Church. The Word was made flesh, and *pitched his tent* in our midst. During much of their history the Jewish people were nomads and wanderers. They literally lived a tent life. We do little justice to St. John's word ἐσκήνωσεν when we translate it: dwelt among us. It means *pitched his tent*. That means living just like us. It means being truly at home. It means in today's symbols that the Word is as intimate as the friend who can take off his shoes and put his feet on the coffee table, or who will help himself to a beer from the refrigerator, or who'll take a mug instead of a cup and saucer for coffee. The Word was made flesh, not the other way around. And that's the incarnational way that salvation came to us and continues to come to us. Because the symbol making factory has indeed changed its address, the Church has no choice but to become world, and to bring salvation by becoming world. Jesus was man in every way save sin. The Church has no choice but to become world in all ways save sin. But let us remember how instinctively we still are tempted to think of our task as making the world into the Church. We who are Church bring salvation by pitching our tent in the midst of man.

This present work attempts to be such an incarnational venture, that is, to take a system of thought which seems to reflect a lot of contemporary understanding, and to let theological elaborations of our faith experiences express themselves through those symbols. There is more involved, of course, than just a new set of symbols. The symbols of process modes of thought have arisen out of new apprehensions of the world, of our own existence. Those new understandings of what reality is are the basis for many rather fundamental re-interpretations of the Christian experience.

It is my intention to attempt an elaboration of Church and Sacrament using process modes of thought. I am indebted to many resources and many influences. The two men, however, who are clearly the dominant influences throughout this work are Alfred North Whitehead and Pierre Teilhard de Chardin.

Whitehead's period of philosophical construction followed a long and distinguished career in mathematics and physics, and for the most part occurred in the years he spent at Harvard following his "retirement" from the Imperial College of Science and Technology of the University of London at the age of sixty-three. His *opus magnum* in philosophy is *Process and Reality;* this work is the Gifford lectures which he delivered in 1927-28, and which were published in 1929. I shall be making extensive use of the philosophical categories in *Process and Reality*. In one place, Whitehead summarized the work of *Process and Reality* as an attempt to show how actual entities are truly *present* in other actual entities. That is perhaps not the best summary statement of his work in terms of showing the full sweep of his creative philosophical construction. But it is a good insight into what he is about and is an indication of why I find his work helpful in a discussion of Church and Sacrament. Loosely put, the Christian Church has understood itself as that society where Jesus Christ is "present" and "at work" in us, personally and corporately. We shall explore how the presence of Jesus, the Christ, is a constitutive element of that society which we call the Christian Church; or, in Whitehead's terminology, we will examine the "defining characteristic" of that society. And we shall try to show how the Sacraments have been the principal means, in the life of the Church, for re-creating, maintaining, and passing on the Church's defining characteristic, i.e., Sacramental Life as that which *makes* the Church, Sacramental Life as the "becoming" experiences constitutive of Church. My aim is to engage in the theological task of using process modes of contemporary thought to elaborate an understanding of Christian life that is faithful to its inner-self, and that relates it to contemporary man in ways that he can "buy," and in ways that demonstrate values that make him eager to "buy" for the good of man.

While in the main I shall be availing myself mostly of the Whiteheadian synthesis for technical categories, I feel that it is very worthwhile to introduce Teilhard de Chardin into the work I have set out. First of all, there is an amazing similarity in the world views of the two men. And at many points, even the language used and the names of their respective categories have an uncanny resemblance. However, Teilhard was not a philosopher—this he knew well enough about himself. I am convinced that some of the inconsistencies and incompletions in Teilhard are the result of not having a process philosophical system to help him along the way. In a later chapter I will develop this more fully. But Teilhard is extremely important as a Catholic, as a distinguished scientist, working out a magnificent synthesis of new thought. Teilhard is a "place" where many of the issues raised by the Modernist crisis continued to be agitated, though the Modernist movement was reputedly dead. Apparently the Modernist "insiders" were aware that Teilhard quietly carried on many of the Modernist programs. Vidler reports a conversation with Maude Petre (a close friend of George Tyrrell and very active in the Modernist movement) in 1941, in which she said that "modernism was still at work in the Church, though not under that name, and she now instanced the writings of Père Teilhard de Chardin." [44] Teilhard's close personal relationship with Edouard Le Roy, a French Modernist, certainly kept him appraised of the Modernist movement. Their own mutual influences on each other were marked. Le Roy (as well as the Russian geologist Verdatsky) took from Teilhard and used his word "noosphere" to describe a kind of cosmic envelope created by the presence of reflective mind.[45] And Teilhard considered the regular Wednesday evenings that he spent with Le Roy in Paris "among the best spiritual exercises of the week. I always come away from them," he wrote, "better and refreshed." [46]

Teilhard's life and thought have a history of almost unremitting problems in his order and in the Church. Those of his writings which touched upon theology and spirituality were not allowed to be published. When they were published after his death (still without approval), a *monitum* from Rome was placed upon them. But by that time, the Catholic world was readier and more in need of his offering. Not too

many years previously he surely would have rated the Index
and not merely a *monitum*. He immediately became very
popular in the Catholic Church, especially through the kind
of spirituality which he generates. At the somewhat "popular"
level, I believe his spirituality was assimilated somewhat before the theoretical implications of that spirituality were
realized. But fortunately by that time, much of the needed
theoretical equipment to take care of those evolutionary
modes of thought was becoming more readily available. This
seems to bear out the insights of Tyrrell's development of the
relation of theology to devotion. And for these reasons Teilhard has been an important figure in recent years in helping
Roman thought and Roman theology meet problems and challenges emerging out of the secularization phenomenon.

In developing a process explanation of Church and Sacrament, I am going to focus principally upon the *dynamics*
that constitute a society, and those that enable the members
of a society to be members through an organic assimilation
of the society's defining characteristic. In the first place, we
are concerned with that society of men who, in a central way,
find meaning and ways of interpreting existence in the Jesus-
event; and in the second place, we are concerned with the
important function of symbol in human consciousness, and
in particular those symbols through which ages of Christians
have over and over again re-appropriated the Jesus-event,
namely, the Sacraments.

My concern, then, is with a "how": how the active presence of the Jesus-event is maintained and propagated. My
focus is not upon the "what" of the Jesus-event. But that is
obviously of extraordinary concern. I would like, therefore,
to present very briefly two process Christologies to keep in
mind as possible understandings of the "what" of Jesus. In
connection with a chapter on Whitehead, I will summarize
some of the Christological formulations of an excellent Whiteheadian theologian, John Cobb, Jr. And then as part of the

chapter on Teilhard, I will single out some of the aspects of his Christology that point up his own process underpinnings.

The five chapters that follow, therefore, are: a summary of the Whiteheadian synthesis, along with a Whiteheadian Christology. Then a chapter on Teilhard de Chardin and his Christology. The final three chapters will take up respectively Church, and Sacrament, and certain pastoral implications of these process interpretations.

While I approach the work with great conviction about the importance and availability of process thought to the theological act today within the Catholic Church, I cannot insist enough on the tentativeness of these forays. It is a rather new undertaking in Catholic thought. Beginnings must be made, then discussed and revised.

2

WHITEHEAD AND
A WHITEHEADIAN
CHRISTOLOGY

It is very difficult to speak in English about process modes of thought in such a way as never to manifest an inconsistency. The structure of thought reflected in the Indo-European languages is based upon unconscious presuppositions that vary greatly with the presuppositions of process thought. The very use of the English language for process thought, always reflecting "other" presuppositions, cannot but present problems. But what other options are there? The subject/predicate structure of grammar unfolds a world of things or substances about which predications are made reflecting what the subject is or does or sustains. In each case there is first the subject, then the experience of the subject. This principle is generalized into a metaphysical position by Aristotle: "For everything that changes is [first] something, and is changed by something into something." [1] This is the philosophical world of subject and accident. For Whitehead there is not first a subject and then its experiences; rather, "each actual entity is a throb of experience." [2] "The notion of 'substance' is transformed into that of actual entity." [3] "Experiencing" is the fundamental unit of reality, not

some*thing* which experiences. The very *act-of-becoming is*
what is real. The identity or sameness that we experience in
reality is a predication that is made about the "becoming" or
about successive acts of becoming that belong together historically. For all practical purposes, this represents a reversal
of the grammatical structure, for the event is the subject. The
subject is a verb. And the identities that we have called subjects before are the predicates, the functions of event or
process.

There is an American Indian language in which all indications of time are made by way of inflections of nouns, not of
verbs. Nouns are past, present and future; not verbs. While
this might sound clumsy and primitive to us, we would also
have to admit that such a grammatical structure would reflect
better than ours the radical historicity of things. Time is a
dimension of things. Time belongs in things. Our instinct has
been to make time a sort of continuum in which things are at
one point or another. Our instinct is that time is adverbial,
i.e., a dimension of the predication. In the Indian dialect referred to, time belongs *in* the subject, not in the predicate.
How difficult it would be to translate one of our history books
into this dialect, for the greatly differing linguistic structure
reflects a greatly different structure of psychic experience out
of which the language arose.

More accessible to us, yet still at times appallingly elusive,
is the Hebrew language and the Biblical mind. The grammatical structure contrasts greatly with ours. In the Indo-
European language system, of which English is a derivative,
there were eight cases for nouns, three genders, and not just
singular and plural, but special forms for dual. In contrast,
the Hebrew noun is very simple. Nouns are derived from
word roots which are the verbs. But the verb system is highly
inflected, manifesting nine different moods. Yet there are no
tenses, properly speaking, in classical Hebrew. No past, present and future; the only distinctions are between completed

events and non-completed events, i.e., perfect and imperfect. Were I to speak of a meal that was *going on* yesterday, I would use the same form as that which indicates a meal that will be going on tomorrow. Such a structure reveals a very event-ful oriented system of perception. The event-centered perception, rather than a thing-and-place-centered perception, must surely explain in part the Jewish phenomenon of maintaining Judaism wherever Jews are found. Their identity is not absorbed when they are placed outside their geographical boundaries; and for a long time they had no geographical location. But their self-understanding as a people is in terms of events primarily, not in terms of national boundaries. They *are* where Covenant *is,* and Covenant is the major *event* of self-constitution and self-understanding. Even though Hebrew has the grammatical structure of subject/predicate, its strong event-orientation gives it a closer kinship with process thought than the Indo-European languages could have.

This discussion of language is simply to admit, at the outset, that there are linguistic problems in trying to elaborate process thought in a language which itself is closer to a substance mind-set. And this is the reason, too, why Whiteheadian language is a strange, new world. The new language is often a help for staying reminded that the very solid looking world of things is not really so solid after all. There are several factors that have unsolidified the world for our understanding, factors that conditioned Whitehead very much. In a highly descriptive expression, Marshall McLuhan has called many of technology's instruments "extensions of the senses." [4] The part of the world which is "our" world is that which presents itself to our perception. And McLuhan rightly understands "our" world to have been extended through ears like radar, eyes like microscopes and telescopes, fingers like laser beams. We understand today that the "insides" of apparently solid substances are the scenes of prodigious electron activity—that is the microscopic world. The heavenly bodies we no longer hold, as did Aristotle, to be eternal (in contrast to earth), but rather quite like the earth in following the behavior of matter and in being engaged forever in their respective rhythms of movement. The evolution of the earth instructs us to be tentative in our descriptions of the "natures" of things. Man has come from someplace in history, he is on the move now, we tend to believe that he continues to go someplace in the future. What we describe as human nature is a description of a temporal cross section out of man's history. If the cross section described is from recent history it has one appearance; a cross section from 20,000 years ago would hardly be recognizable against today's description. The speculative philosophers of science fiction offer projections and alternatives for a future cross section. And those become increasingly important with man's realization of his own power to shape himself and his future. In sum, the spectacle of reality which we encounter is one of unremitting process. It is only by abstraction that we can stop the process. And though those abstractions are often necessary, we need to be reminded that the still shots are abstractions from the *concrete* fact of process. The word *concrete* has suffered a betrayal in linguistic history. *Concrescere's* root sense is "to grow together," i.e., for some kind of a multiplicity to become a unity. The word concrete has in recent times certainly lost its dynamic sense, at least in general common usage. Frequently in Whitehead the word concrescence is used instead of the broader term "process" to call attention to a particular act of becoming, a particular instance of a many becoming a one by growing together. Concrescence is present reality—what is becoming. Concrete reality is finished fact.

The philosophy of Whitehead is a thoroughgoing metaphysical assertion that "the event is the real unit of things." [5] He remarked while teaching at Harvard: "Reality is becoming; it is passing before you—a remark too obvious to make

. . . You can't catch a moment by the scruff of the neck—it's gone, you know." [6] In his earlier writings, Whitehead used the word event for the basic unit of reality. In *Process and Reality* he rather consistently speaks of "actual entities," also termed "actual occasions." It is important never to associate any kind of "thing" notion with an actual entity (although the language makes it difficult to avoid that totally), at least in any sense suggestive of the Aristotelian position that there is first something, and afterward the thing undergoes its various adventures. For Whitehead, "an actual entity is a process, and is not describable in terms of the morphology of a 'stuff.' " [7] "The process itself is the constitution of the actual entity; in Locke's phrase, it is the 'real internal constitution' of the actual entity." [8] "Its 'being' is constituted by its 'becoming'. This is 'the principle of process.' " [9]

Whitehead preferred William James' picture of process to that of Bergson's steady flux. The Jamesian version is not one of uninterrupted flux, but one of "drops of experience" which follow upon each other. For the most part, one drop of experience conforms to its immediate predecessor, which is our experience of identity or sameness; there are, however, interstices between the drops of experience. As each new occasion gets under way, it is possible to diverge from the past and to incorporate some element of newness. The point I want to underline here is Whitehead's use of the word "experience" for the content of process. It calls attention to an element of interiority, to some principle which "gets it all together." This is not an attribution of experience in the sense of human conscious awareness to every concrescence. It is another way of affirming that "what's going on" is what is real. "Each actual entity is a throb of experience." [10] "Its experience is its complete formal constitution." [11] "Process is the becoming of experience." [12]

Whitehead's own name for his philosophical system is "the

philosophy of organism." Before looking at some of the details of his system I would like to stress his organic understanding of the world. The law of universal gravitation posits an attraction or force that is operative between all bits of matter anywhere. The formula for that force of attraction is $F = \dfrac{m_1 m_2}{d^2}$, where m_1 and m_2 are the masses of the two particles, and d is the distance between them. While it is obvious that the gravitational world of measureable influences requires a certain closeness and size, it would be possible to fill in the formula with the mass of a piece of dust on the earth and the mass of a piece of dust at a distance of thousands of light years, though in fact the gravitational force between them is indeed negligible. But there. As Whitehead says, "any local agitation shakes the whole universe. The distant effects are minute, but they are there." [13] "Accordingly the full universe, disclosed for every variety of experience, is a universe in which every detail enters into its proper relationship with the immediate occasion." [14] Such is the organic unity of the universe. Analogous to the position that every item in the universe bears a gravitational relationship with every other item and is thus present through its gravitational pull, so, says Whitehead, "we must say that every actual entity is present in every other actual entity. The philosophy of organism is mainly devoted to the task of making clear the notion of 'being present' in another." [15] "In the philosophy of organism, an actual occasion—as has been stated above—is the whole universe in process of attainment . . ." [16] Thus, in a real sense, "the whole world conspires to produce a new creation." [17] The entire universe is inter-related. And differences between actual entities are differences, therefore, in their patterns of relatedness. Similarities too are due to similar patterns of relatedness. In the Aristotelian framework, a discussion of differences would be in terms of qualities. However, in the Whiteheadian framework, " 'relatedness' is dominant over 'quality.' " [18] "The organic starting point is from the analysis of process as the realization of events disposed in an interlocked community." [19]

Before beginning a presentation of some of the specifics from the Whiteheadian system that will pertain to the discussion of Church and Sacrament in the latter chapters, I want to call attention to an important aspect of his systematic work. That aspect is to some extent a mood, and to some extent a pervasive, if sometimes lurking, model. I mean the aesthetic mood, with beauty as a model of the goal of all process. In as lovely a tribute as I think any man might make to his wife, Whitehead wrote:

> The effect of my wife upon my outlook on the world has been so fundamental that it must be mentioned as an essential factor in my philosophic output . . . Her vivid life has taught me that beauty, moral and aesthetic, is the aim of existence; and that kindness, and love, and artistic satisfaction are among its modes of attainment.[20]

The structure of beauty, as outlined most clearly in *Adventures of Ideas,*[21] is all put paradigmatic for the synthesis of *Process and Reality,* the major work of Whitehead. Beauty is a larger category even than truth or goodness or value, each of which can be considered an aspect of beauty.

In view of the organic nature of the universe, relating is a picture of what is and relatedness is a picture of what has already come to be. For Whitehead, the aim of the process of relating is beauty, as he said in the citation just above: beauty is the aim of existence. Higher forms of beauty require a much more intricate pattern of inter-relations. The degree of beauty achieved in a particular act of becoming depends upon how the parts that can possibly go into some unity are selected, and how effectively they meet the demands of mutual inter-relatedness. A minor form of beauty, i.e., low intensity, derives

from the simple fact that the mutual inhibition has been eliminated from the multiple parts that have entered into a harmony. There is simply a lack of discord. However, when there
are strong contrasts among the many items that might possibly
be unified, the various relations between those items must be
much more intricate and delicate and nuanced, if the final
result is to be one of harmony. But when such an arrangement
is brought off satisfactorily, the beauty achieved is more intense and more interesting.

Take, for example, possible room decor and arrangements.
If the possible furnishings for a drawing room include both
French provincial and colonial American, and several colors,
a usual procedure would be to sort out the two styles, and
keep all the pieces that are green or go easily with green (or
some other color unity). Someone with a keener sense of color
might keep not only what blends with green, but what contrasts sharply with it. Perhaps a still keener eye would hold
on to pieces of furniture from both styles, since finding a way
to put them together successfully would heighten attention to
the particularities of each style. But it would take much more
arranging and rearranging to achieve such an aim. When it's
all French provincial and green it is relatively easy for any one
item to be placed almost anywhere in the room and still relate
well to the whole. But as styles and colors are mixed, each
item must relate not just vaguely to the whole, but specifically
to each constituent part, and especially to the nearer parts.
Altering the position of any one piece of furniture might call
for re-arranging the entire room. And two colors which would
be incompatible next to each other, will often, through the
intervention of colors placed between them, contribute more
to the intensity of the overall effect than either color alone.
But in that case, a *very* special arrangement is needed so that
those colors can be entertained as effective contrasts rather
than as incompatibles. Called for are a delicate balance and
a keen sense of pattern, if "variety with effective contrast" [22]
is to be achieved as a more intense mode of the beautiful.

Beauty is the internal conformation of the various items of experience with each other, for the production of maximum effectiveness. Beauty thus concerns the inter-relations of the various components of Reality . . . Thus any part of experience can be beautiful. The teleology of the Universe is directed to the production of Beauty.[23]

Whitehead accepts the notion that the trend of evolution is upward or forward; it is a creative *advance*. It is clear from the text just cited that he has chosen an aesthetic model to describe the teleology which accounts for the creative advance:

The metaphysical doctrine, here expounded, finds the foundation of the world in aesthetic experience . . . All order is therefore aesthetic order . . . The actual world is the outcome of the aesthetic order.[24]

While the influence of his wife and his natural temperament are important factors in accounting for Whitehead's aesthetic sensitivity and orientation, his world over many years was the world of mathematics. When Whitehead turned to philosophy as a main preoccupation and occupation, he by no means took leave of his mathematical abode to do so. Ralph Norman has pointed out that there are two approaches to mathematics, the skeptical and the aesthetic.[25] The skeptical version of mathematics is built around a concern for the deduction of strict consequences from sure premises, this being the most certain knowledge possible. The aesthetic role of mathematics concerns the discovery and unfolding of pattern:

Whitehead remained fascinated by the mathematical method, not in its function of building upon certainties but in its characteristically modern function of exhibiting types and modes of coherence. This is mathematics in its *aesthetic* philosophical use—i.e., in its use as the search for infinitely rich and diverse patterns of order, in its confidence that the conception and enjoyment of such coherence is an open-ended enterprise . . .[26]

Whitehead's essay on "Mathematics and the Good"[27] is a clear example of the influence of mathematics upon his philosophical aesthetique. If the many are to become one, the action which makes them one must have a "pattern of assemblage"[28] according to which the multiple can be coordinated. Mathematics is the study of pattern; and philosophically, for Whitehead, beauty is the structure of the pattern as it relates to the creative advance of the universe. In yet another of his works, Whitehead characterizes the essence of the underlying power of the creative advance as the "drive towards aesthetic unity."[29]

Such is the world, as Whitehead understands it and describes it systematically. Events, not things, are the basic units of reality. It is process (or becoming, or experiencing) that constitutes events. The most common name for these basic units of reality is "actual entities." The entire universe of actual entities is inter-related. It is an inter-locked community of events. As such, the universe is an organic whole. It is a reasonable universe. Things are reasonably together. That is, there are patterns of assemblage. The Whiteheadian way of understanding the patterns is after the aesthetic model. The creative advance of the universe demands pattern or order in each actual entity and in the infinitely varying groupings of actual entities. "The heightening of intensity arises from order such that the multiplicity of components in the nexus can enter explicit feeling as *contrasts,* and are not dismissed as *incompatibles*."[30] "The whole universe is the advancing assemblage of the processes."[31]

In presenting now some of the Whiteheadian categories

that explicate the dynamics of process in this organic universe I want to stay somewhat close to Whitehead's language. Even when there are familiar expressions or words that are extremely close to some notion or other, often that tiny nuanced difference is of such importance that the special language of Whitehead is critical in maintaining the specifically and radically processive thrust of his modes of thought. We will first look at the "private life" of an actual entity, i.e., how it puts itself together. Then we will look at the "public career" of an actual entity, i.e., how it, in its turn, goes "out" into the public world and becomes present in the private life of other actual entities. I will also consider Whitehead's natural theology, and understandings of society and of symbols. I will not relate Whitehead's categories to the question of Church and Sacrament in this chapter. I simply present some of the main lines of his schema. However it is certainly the case that my selection of material is guided by my concern for developing a process understanding of Church and Sacrament.

The universe is a "universe of many things." [32] Or, to put it another way, "the ultimate metaphysical truth is atomism." [33] But that world of many things is not a radically disjunct world, for there are patterns of assemblage among the many that create unities out of the multiplicity. That is the irreducible picture of the real, or, in Whitehead's words, the category of the ultimate. That category embraces three notions: creativity, the many, the one. The super-notion of the three is creativity, "the universal of universals characterizing ultimate matter of fact," for it names the process through which the many become one; the many is the universe taken *disjunctively;* and the one is a real, actual occasion wherein the universe is taken *conjunctively*. And that is the story line of reality. The plot is fundamentally simple: "it lies in the nature of things that the many enter into complex unity." [34]

The unities which creativity forges out of multiplicity are the actual entities or actual occasions. Each actual entity has its own particularity and individuality which is not shared with any other entity; there might be many similarities, but no total identity. Each actual entity, therefore, represents the appearance of something really new. That "really new" might mean the addition of some new element to the process of becoming, a new form, for example, in the pattern of assemblage. Or, more simply, the "novel" may be a matter of a *new* instance of becoming that conforms to the preceding instance of becoming. The meaning of that becomes clearer when we see that "atomism" in Whitehead's framework has a time meaning as well as a sort of thing meaning.

Whitehead followed the lead of William James in understanding the movement of process to be not a steady flow but successive drops of experience. There is a "thing" kind of atomism in the molecules that constitute a drop. But there is also a temporal kind of atomism in that each drop is a unit of experience, a unit of becoming. When each drop of experience conforms to the defining characteristics of the previous drop, there is what we experience as identity. Yet each drop of experience in that closely knit series is a new moment of the same identity. There is novelty, therefore, even in identity. Thus it is that creativity, i.e., the process of becoming, "is the principle of novelty." [35]

The strong empirical bent of Whitehead is manifest in his "ontological principle," which is his way of insisting upon sticking to "irreducible and stubborn facts" (and here he again borrows words from William James).[36]

The final facts are, all alike, actual entities; and these actual entities are drops of experience, complex and interdependent.

"Actual entities"—also termed "actual occasions"—are the final real things of which the world is made up. There is no going behind actual entities to find anything more

real. They differ among themselves: God is an actual
entity, and so is the most trivial puff of existence in far-
off empty space.

The ontological principle can be summed up as follows:
no actual entity, then no reason.[37]

According to the ontological principle, there is nothing
which floats into the world from nowhere. Everything in
the actual world is referable to some actual entity.[38]

The ontological principle means that actual entities are
the only *reasons*; so that to search for a *reason* is to
search for one or more actual entities.[39]

The ontological principle is an essential factor in the development of Whitehead's natural theology, which will be treated
later in this chapter.

Not unlike Plato (to whom Whitehead claims a closer relationship) and Aristotle, Whitehead gives "form" a large
place in his philosophy, i.e., the doctrine of eternal objects.
Eternal objects are forms of definiteness which *can* contribute
specification to actual entities. I stress that they *can* give such
specification; but as such eternal objects are pure potentials,
and they bear no "necessary reference to any definite actual
entity of the temporal world." [40] That is their "eternal" aspect: no necessary tie-in with any actual entity existing in
time. Yet every actual entity is what it is because it is defi-
nitely one thing rather than another. All actual entities have
forms of definiteness. Every "drop of experience," therefore,
involves eternal objects. The eternal objects are objects, therefore, of experience. To speak of these eternal objects right
after considering the ontological principle raises a question.
Evidently, eternal objects help account for reality in Whitehead's system. Yet eternal objects are not actual—they are

purely potential. How then can they explain reality, since to search for a reason is to search for one or more actual entities? Yet without eternal objects, there is no room for the appearance of the really "New" in concrete actuality—there would be only the already actual to draw upon and to arrange and rearrange. Since all explanations (reasons) for reality must have to do with actual entities, then "the general potentiality [eternal objects] must be somewhere";[41] since the possibilities are relevant to process and available, what actual entities may be invoked to account for that availability? Where is the "actual somewhere" that harbors all the eternal objects (although the form of the question might be poor in suggesting too visual a storehouse)? That is the question that leads into Whitehead's natural theology, for God—who is an actual entity—has a primordial characteristic in that he envisions all possibility, i.e., all eternal objects. The point, for the moment, is that eternal objects are part of the explanation of reality. They help make understandable the appearance of true novelty, as well as being explanatory of the definiteness that all actuality manifests. True novelty is possible because there are possible forms of definiteness which need not yet be anywhere manifest as a form of some actuality. Eternal objects may be awaiting ingression into some actuality. It is one of the functions of God that he, an actual entity, *conceptually* envisions all potential forms of definiteness, knowing them as purely potential. He, in his primordial nature, maintains the availability of the world's potentiality. Thus there can be new actualities under the sun. And the eternal objects do not fail against the ontological principle, for they too are actual-entity-based.

Concrescence is frequently Whitehead's word for a particular act of becoming. It suggests the "getting it together" notion, for *concrescere*'s root meaning is to grow together. The "-scence" part of the word also suggests, in its root meaning, the actual *becoming*. The relationship between concrete and concrescence might be seen by analogy with the words obsolete and obsolescence, the latter being the fact of becoming obsolete, whereas obsolete means that obsolescence is over and done with. Concrescence is the "on-going" or becoming stage of "a growing together," a creation of a unity out of a many. The period of becoming or concrescing is what we are calling the private life of an actual entity. When it is no longer in the process of concrescing, when that is finished, then we have concrete reality with a public life. A concrete actual entity may participate in the reality of other actual entities. A concrescence cannot. Our focus now is on concrescence. How does the "growing together" take place? The key notion for this discussion is that of "prehension," a characteristically Whiteheadian word.

Taking up the notion of "prehension" means taking up a whole cluster of notions. That is one of the interesting and disconcerting things about Whitehead's thought. He is describing an organic universe where all items form an interlocked community, where everything needs everything else, where there is nothing that needs only itself to exist. A philosophy which hopes to describe such a universe will manifest the same features. Every category in Whitehead needs all the others, for no one can exist as understandable alone. Each successive chapter in *Process and Reality* sheds light upon the whole system of categories.

It helps an understanding of Whitehead's notion of prehension to see that he is using a psychic model for the development of most of his categories. It is axiomatic for Whitehead, as for most contemporary philosophers, that there is but one world, one reality. That is, of course, not a brand new problem. But it has a brand new urgency. Philosophy has grappled with so many dichotomies, trying to overcome them: animal, mineral, vegetable; life and non-life; matter and spirit; natural and supernatural; subject and object; etc. If one set of categories is going to be generalized for all experience, then categories from non-psychic phenomena will have to be up-graded for descriptions of the psychic; or else categories de-rived from psychic experience will have to be downgraded to describe sub-psychic phenomena. Whitehead (like Teilhard de Chardin) opts for the second. There is more at stake than choosing what fits the philosophical strategy best. Whitehead holds that the full potentiality of reality is always there seeth-ing below the surface of the real, and all the dynamics needed to actualize any of it are already operative. For example, the fact of definiteness or particularity is an indication that the many that grow together in one actual entity grow together in the pattern or form that finally characterizes them. That kind of ordering, however primitive, is an indication of men-tality (though in no sense does that mean conscious, human mentality). A sunflower "knows" to follow the sun. A plant "knows" what it needs from the soil and tries to take it. There is something internal that directs the concrescence so that, in fact, it becomes in *this* way rather than in *that* way. Each concrescence has at its disposal a whole universe as its data; but it trims that vast amount of data down for its own be-coming. Whitehead, therefore, attributes subjectivity to his and James' "drops of experience." Again, he does not neces-sarily imply conscious subjectivity. But he does want to indi-cate that there is a process of gathering together what is rele-vant to a particular concrescence. There must be some kind of control factor, too, that enables a concrescence to "know" what it should accept into its act of becoming, and also how to make such an acceptation. Every actual entity is experienc-ing a universe of other entities that might be "matter" for its own act of becoming. In terms of that toward which its be-coming is directed, it accepts some of the world at its disposal and dismisses the rest. That is the sense in which every actual entity experiences. Thus, too, Whitehead can speak of the subjectivity of every actual entity, meaning that each one is experiencing. "The actualities of the Universe are processes of experience, each process is an individual fact." [42] "Process is the becoming of experience." [43] Whitehead calls this the "reformed subjectivist principle," that "apart from the experiences of subjects, there is nothing, nothing, nothing, bare nothingness." [44]

Actual entities experience with their prehensions. "Actual entities involve other actual entities by reason of their prehensions of each other." [45] It is prehensions that mediate an actual entity's relationship with the rest of the universe while it is in the process of becoming. Prehensions are how an actual entity responds to all the items of the universe that might become part of its own constitution. Sometimes the response is a Yes—a positive prehension; sometimes it is a No—a negative prehension. A concrescing entity is faced with an entire universe that offers itself as objects of experience. But practically, that is too large a universe. A concrescing entity has to make a selection of those items that will contribute to its own internal constitution. Negative prehensions trim a whole universe of data down to manageable size.

Positive prehensions are also called feelings. [46] Here the psychic model is clearly operative. We use feelings in both a sense meaning and an emotional meaning. But senses and emotions are both ways of reckoning with items of experience. Even if a feeling is a matter of repulsion, we still experience being touched and conditioned by that feeling. That kind of repulsion is not analogous to a negative prehension. Negative prehensions simply eliminate from experience items that are so totally irrelevant that they receive no positive notice. " 'Negative prehensions' . . . are said to 'eliminate from feeling.' "[47]

An actual entity is a drop of experience, and "its experience is its complete formal constitution." [48] Feelings effect that formal constitution. "A feeling is the appropriation of some elements in the universe to be components in the real internal constitution of its subject. The elements are the initial data; they are what the feeling feels." [49] "Feelings are 'vectors'; they feel what is there and transform it into what is *here*." [50] It is not stretching things too far to say that "the first analysis of an actual entity, into its most concrete elements, discloses it to be a concrescence of prehensions, which have originated in its process of becoming." [51]

One way of characterizing prehensions is, as we have indicated, in terms of being positive or negative—that is, either feeling some piece of data positively, in which case it enters into the experience of an actual entity; or else eliminating a piece of data from feeling, in which case the datum plays no part in the real internal constitution of an actual entity. Another way of characterizing a prehension is in terms of the kind of object which is a datum of experience. If the object of a prehension is an actual entity, Whitehead calls this a physical prehension. If the object of a prehension is an eternal object, it is a conceptual prehension.

The first phase of a concrescence is a response to the actual world that is given, and physical prehensions feel those occasions that are there to be felt. Sometimes these are called conformal feelings or responsive feelings. They feel what is *there* and transform it into what is *here*. These feelings will involve the conceptual pole also. Another actual entity is the initial datum for the physical prehension of a concrescing entity. But there will be some aspect of that other actual entity through which it is objectified for the concrescing entity. That aspect, or form of definiteness, through which an initial piece of data becomes objectified is the object of a conceptual prehension. At this juncture novelty becomes a possibility. The form of definiteness through which an entity becomes objectified participates in a structure—what Whitehead has called graded relevance among eternal objects. It is the structure of possibility. What that corresponds to in concrete experience is the realization, for example, that at a certain juncture of a man's life, some possibilities are open to him; but as a result of decisions that he has already made in the past, some potentialities which are "out there" in the world of possibility are not real possibilities. A person who has become a parent can never be a non-parent. A woman ninety-five who has never been a parent cannot become a parent. In other words, the forms of definiteness which are data are able, in a sense, to suggest other forms which, with graded degrees of possibility, are new possibilities. Those new possibilities which may become actualized allow the possibility of novelty. Conceptual prehensions, therefore, open the road to novelty. Not every conceptual prehension results in novelty. But every time there is novelty, it is the result of a conceptual prehension which proposed a new possibility, one not contained in the givens of its actual data. Physical prehensions tie the experiencing of an occasion to the already actualized givens. It is the conceptual prehension which is able to break the tyranny of the given world and allow for a departure from what has been the story up to this point. An entity need not always conform to its past. It may always instigate a new version of itself. Whitehead calls that new version a reversion—a "conceptual reversion." "Conceptual" here does not, of course, necessarily mean conscious human awareness, although human consciousness is a more developed form of the conceptual pole's operation. Whitehead also calls this the mental pole. The root sense of mentality is its concern with forms of definiteness and it is the power for newness. "Reason," says Whitehead, "is the organ of emphasis upon novelty. . . . The essence of Reason in its lowliest forms is its judgment upon flashes of novelty." [52] Whitehead holds that process is a history of creative advance. He does not mean that naively; there are repeated set-backs, errors, failures. Yet there is forward movement. There is a three-fold urge on the inside of reality:

first, to be; second, to do it well; third, to do it better and better, that is, to acquire an increase in satisfaction. The urge toward something better requires going beyond the present. It means transcending. It means finding newness. It means a constant quest for novelty, and it requires that an entity be able to conceptualize a new way of being, a new form of definiteness that is not yet actual. That is the contribution of the mental pole. "Reason finds its scope here in its direction of the upward trend." [53]

Another kind of prehension is that which Whitehead calls a "hybrid prehension," a combination of physical and conceptual. A hybrid prehension is a physical feeling which objectifies an actual entity through one of that actual entity's own conceptual feelings. A hybrid physical feeling gives rise to a conceptual feeling, since it will have for a datum the eternal object which the other entity's conceptual feeling also had for a datum. Somewhat crassly put, it's like stealing an idea from someone else, an idea which another person had, perhaps not even an actualized idea. To summarize for a moment: the universe is radically organic. All actual entities exist in an interlocked community. Prehensions attend to the organization of that community. Prehensions are the relatings. The life history of an actual entity is the history of all its prehensions. Each new concrescence is faced with the entire universe of all actual entities that ever came to be. Some very few of those actual entities will contribute to the makeup of the newly concrescing occasion. Prehension explains the transfer of energy from a past occasion into a present occasion. Physical prehensions give rise to conceptual prehensions, for a past occasion is experienced through some aspect or another of its constitution, that is, some form of definiteness. That form of definiteness is an eternal object and is the datum of a conceptual prehension. Since the data of the past actual world are so manifold, they must be trimmed down to size. What is of no possible interest or use, given the subjective aim of an occasion, is eliminated from feeling. Those prehensions which eliminate from feeling are called negative prehensions. Positive prehensions relate data to a concrescing occasion in ways that make that data enter into the real internal constitution of the new entity. A conceptual prehension may also arise if a concrescing entity prehends the conceptuality of another actual entity. A hybrid prehension is a prehension of an eternal object which a conceptual feeling of another actual entity felt, and the eternal object is accessible through another entity's prehension of it. An eternal object is part of a structure of possibility. Within that structure the forms of possibility are inter-related; they have a graded relevance to each other. On the basis of that structure of possibility, a form of definiteness which has been prehended can elicit other forms of definiteness as new possibilities. In that case a conceptual prehension entertains for a concrescing occasion a new possibility which would mark a departure from the shape of its past. This mental or conceptual pole, in which reason is rooted, makes possible the creative advance. It is the organ of transcendence, that is, of possible transcendence. It opens to each actual entity, whether it accepts or not, the possibility of going beyond the actual givens. Transcendence, like its correlative "novelty," has a double meaning. In one sense every actual entity is novel; even when a new concrescence simply conforms to its past, it is a new occurrence of that conformation. Thus, too, every actual entity transcends the entire world out of which it concresces; it goes beyond "all that" to be its own particular self. Even the entity which repeats its past is transcendent in this way. But the possibility of introducing some new form of definiteness into the concrescence is an option, and when that option is taken up there is transcendence in a larger sense.

There are two ways of asking the next question I want to deal with. The first question falls within the requirements of the Whiteheadian synthesis: in all this business of prehensions, how does an actual entity "know" *what* to prehend (positively and negatively), and *how* to prehend its objects. The answers to the "what" and "how" are "subjective aim" and "subjective form."

A second way of posing the question is one that recurs frequently in the history of philosophy. Our immediate, crass contact with reality yields a double experience: there is identity or sameness, but there is also change. Admittedly, some philosophies have denied one or the other: Parmenides, change; Heraclitus, sameness. But most often philosophies have attempted to be explanatory of both. One of the two experiences—change or sameness—often arrests the attention more than the other and becomes a central concern. Then other perceptions get arranged around the requirements of the central concern. Sameness or identity was more fundamental in Aristotle. Something IS, and then it has its adventures. For Whitehead, the adventures are what IS. The possibility of change, for Aristotle, is always an indication of imperfection: if something can become better, then it isn't perfect; if it can get worse, that is not a perfect way of being, i.e., subject to decadence; if it can be other than it is, then it doesn't have all that it might have. Substance is the vehicle of sameness; and substance undergoes change. Change and movement are functions of substance. Being the same is an Aristotelian good. It is a dynamic good, of course, in that we can wish to change toward something better, so that the identity we wish to maintain might well require change, even drastic change. But the aim is to come to rest once again. Scholastic philosophy speaks of the starting point and ending point of a change as the *terminus a quo* and the *terminus ad quem*. I call attention to the word *terminus:* change is the interim condition while going from one resting place to another, one *terminus* to another. Admittedly, once one terminus is reached, it may immediately become the starting point for another change. Yet the changing always has the interim status.

What arrested Whitehead's attention and became his central perception was change, becoming, process. In contrast to Aristotle who dealt with change in terms of what happens to substance, Whitehead deals with sameness or identity in terms of what happens within process. Identity is a function of process. Any stoppage of process is a stoppage of reality. Becoming, therefore, is normative. The question is then: what, in the Whiteheadian system, accounts for our experience of sameness and identity? They are the notions of subjective aim and subjective form, and they are functions of process.

The psychic model again is useful. What we want to become in life determines to a great extent the decisions we make. There is a givenness to the actual world over which we have no control, yet we can control which of those givens we will be receptive toward. This point is not without ambiguity in Whitehead. One can ask whether the graded relevance that exists among the eternal objects, that is, in the structure of possibility, does not indicate which of the givens we will be receptive toward. In any event, we are free to accept in part or as a whole, with or without revision, the initial aim offered at the onset of each occasion of experience. And we can control *how* we come to grips with our world, for there are many ways of dealing with the same world. The aim which directs the overall becoming of a subject accounts for what the subject finally becomes, and that is "subjective aim." The subjective aim determines what is relevant to a concrescing entity, and therefore controls the prehensions which in fact constitute an actual entity. Subjective aim, therefore, is the function of process which accounts for the "whatness" of an actual entity; it is responsible for the shape which finally defines the particularity of an actual entity. To continue the psychic model, there is not only a defining shape which makes all men be men, for example. There is a style that develops, and that contributes further to identity. Two people who deal with more or less the same set of situations, even with very similar goals, will still each have his own style. *How* a subject deals with his world is his own unique way of experiencing. How data are experienced is determined by the "subjective form." In some places Whitehead speaks of subjective form in terms of affective tone, for subjective form has to do with how a concrescing entity enjoys the objects of its experiencing.

In connection with subjective form, something certainly needs to be said about the role of "emotion" in Whitehead's system of thought. As I have already pointed out, conceptuality is a factor in every actual entity. Yet in the root sense of the conceptual operation, there is no necessary implication of conceptuality as we understand it in conscious, human operations. Yet human conceptuality is but a more highly developed form of that kind of conceptuality which operates everywhere. The same thing is true of emotion. For Whitehead, "the primitive form of physical experience is emotion —blind emotion . . . In the language appropriate to higher stages of experience, the primitive element is *sympathy*, that is, feeling the feeling *in* another and feeling conformally *with* another." [54] An actual entity is constituted by its prehensions, by its feelings. When an actual entity is a datum for a concrescing entity, it becomes objectified to that other entity through one of its own forms, that is, through one of its own prehensions of a form—which is to say, through one of its feelings. An entity which is concrescing feels the feeling of another entity. In its simplest form, that is sympathy: feeling another's feeling. This theory is in opposition to Hume (to whom Whitehead is often in opposition) who holds that emotions are secondary and are derived from sense experience. The kind of emotion which Hume has in mind is not bare, primitive emotion, Whitehead holds, but rather "emotion interpreted, integrated, and transformed into higher categories of feeling." [55] *All* prehensions carry some emotional content.

In a psychological understanding of emotion, we understand emotion to mean *how* a person feels about something. Several persons can have a feeling for the same object, but how they feel about it is particular to each person. *How* things are felt is part of all prehensions. Subjective aim indicates to an occasion what is to be felt, what is pertinent. Each prehension is also clothed with subjective form—and emotion is a species of subjective form. Graduated emotional intensity can greatly facilitate the prehension. In the context of the previous statement, "intensity" has a particular Whiteheadian signification. Both the order of the universe and the growth it seeks are aesthetic. Process is in motion toward the achievement of a more intense aesthetic satisfaction, that is, simple harmony is not a resting place; a beauty that is grander, that embraces a great variety of detail in its harmony is the quest. (That is an aesthetic way of calling attention to evolutionary development toward greater complexity of forms and greater organic unity and operation.) In this context, Whitehead understands emotional intensity to accrue from the "profuse addition of eternal objects." [56]

Emotion, therefore, is a very primitive behavior found throughout reality. It enables one entity to feel the feelings of another and make them its own. Emotional intensity increases when the possibilities offered to a concrescence are manifold, when possibilities of growth are offered. Every prehension has a subjective form, which includes affective tone. There is always a way in which a datum is felt. Emotion pertains both to how the past asserts its presence in the now and to how an entity puts itself together in preparation for the future.

Let us now refer to the aesthetic model and to a living room which is to be furnished and decorated. The owner of the house who will do the decorating goes into a huge store which handles furnishings and art work. He has opted for French provincial. The salesman meets him near the entrance and learns that he is interested in French provincial. He points to that section of the store where French provincial furniture is on display, indicating it to the prospective buyer who sees it and heads toward it. His eyes are on that area, and as he passes through all the other departments, he does not even notice the other styles that are there. He reaches the desired area and with strong positive reactions, takes in all the furniture that is in the style that interests him. Thus far we have a subjective aim which in its initial stage says: a French provincial parlor. Negative prehension eliminates from his feelings all those items that do not bear relevance to his overall aim. He doesn't even entertain the possibilities of pieces of furniture in another style. It's not a matter of considering them and then saying no. He doesn't even notice them. For him, that whole store of furniture has been trimmed down to the one display area where he will make choices that finally determine the internal constitution of his room. As he looks around at the display furniture he begins to put together different possibilities in his mind. If he chooses this chair, then that lamp seems best. But if he chooses that chair, then this lamp seems best. With the one chair and lamp combination, one small table goes best; with the other combination, a table nearby would be out of place. The value of one piece of furniture or another is higher or lower, depending upon the whole ensemble which finally is chosen. He chooses a particular divan which he wants. This choice then influences other choices until the final result satisfies the gentleman. Before that moment of satisfaction, there is room for many possible arrangements. But as the room takes shape, that shape clarifies many of the choices. And while many pieces of furniture are appealing, not all are possible. So the attractions must be integrated. Sometimes that is difficult. Because one piece is highly desirable for its shape, and another for its color. A decision must be made. It may even be that as the man visualizes the room, he needs a piece of furniture to go in some particular place, as he pictures it, but of a somewhat different shape and size and color from any that are there. He sketches it and has it made to order. His initial aim has undergone a lot of rearranging and some modification—for the sketch he made, for example, has a certain Jacobean aspect, but it seems to fit into the context of the French provincial room, though that initial aim had to be adjusted to accommodate the novelty. In the process of putting such a room together there is a whole series of valuations placed upon this piece of furniture or that, depending upon whether it is viewed in this particular arrangement or that other one. Such valuations are subjective forms under which those items of furniture are experienced. If attention is paid to particular aspects of furniture such as the fine shape or the lovely color, that is somewhat comparable to a hybrid physical prehension, in which some form of definiteness is the focus from which the item is experienced. The mental construction of a Jacobean chair, which isn't like any real one he has ever seen, is comparable to a conceptual prehension where some genuine novelty is introduced which modifies the subjective aim from its original position. All in all, there is an intricate process of balancing the possibilities over and against each other, in terms of one's aim, until somehow the "whole thing" is put together satisfactorily. At the moment of satisfaction, that experience is a finished one, and it makes its content available to the beginning of a next "moment" of experience. If succeeding "moments" continue the defining characteristics of the preceding occasions, then a sort of historical unity is created out of these succeeding moments. Closer to Whitehead's terminology, one would say that there is an historic route through those successive drops of experience.

I put "moment" in quotation marks several times. For Whitehead, every drop of experience, i.e., every concrescence, has temporal thickness. But the actual private life of a concrescing entity doesn't follow clocks. There is no unit of reality more fundamental than an actual entity. There is no such thing as a half an actual entity that occupies half as much time is a whole actual entity. Logically it is possible to talk about the phases of concrescence, but there is no real temporal succession. In that sense, the example of the man in the department store choosing furniture is misleading. For "the whole business" of starting with an aim, doing commerce with a vast world of possible objects until the wares are small enough in number to actually consider, the balancing of likes and dislikes and preferences over and against each other, adjusting the aim, perhaps introducing some novelty, etc., etc., —all of this occurs in but a "moment" which has temporal thickness, but which doesn't have clear temporal succession within it. What we normally understand as time is the transition from one drop of experience to the next, but not the internal workings of a drop of experience, for an actual entity is, in the literal sense of the Greek word, a-tomic, that is to say, indivisible.

Whitehead singled out four notions which he thought were characteristic of his thought: the ontological principle, the notion of actual entity, that of prehension, and that of a nexus. Although the nexus hasn't been dealt with yet, it has been an unnamed factor in speaking of each act of concrescence.

> Actual entities involve each other by reason of their prehensions of each other. There are thus real individual facts of the togetherness of actual entities, which are real, individual, and particular, in the same sense in which actual entities and the prehensions are real, individual, and particular. Any such particular fact of togetherness among actual entities is called a "nexus" (plural form is written "nexūs"). The ultimate facts of immediate experience are actual entities, prehensions and nexūs.[57]

A nexus is a fact of togetherness, from either a spatial or temporal point of view. A number of specific items are held together in some kind of unity that makes them spatially thick —a molecule is thicker than an atom. There is also a togetherness of successive drops of experience, such as those which together make up the life of a butterfly or the life of a human being. That kind of nexus creates temporal thickness. Any fact of togetherness is a nexus, which may be as loose a fact of togetherness as a sandpile, or as intricate as that of living things.

Whitehead uses the term "society" for a particular species of nexus. There is a society when in a series of drops of experience, each new-generation event retains the same form of definiteness that characterized its predecessors. This is the historic route of occasions. The defining characteristic appears throughout the history of those occasions that constitute a society. The historic route of occasions emphasizes the temporal thickness—the fact of togetherness that unifies the drops of experience as they follow upon each other. There are also some aspects of a society that bear more upon the spatial thickness. There is a defining characteristic in virtue of which each datum that enters a concrescence belongs there. The defining characteristic imposes certain requirements that each constituent element must meet; in each element there are feelings of the common form that defines the nexus. (Whitehead says that the notion of defining characteristic is allied to Aristotle's "substantial form.") [58]

In choosing a word like "society" or an expression like "social order," Whitehead is again using a category named from life experience, though he adjusts and extends it to include forms of togetherness below the life level. However, he also deals with "society" in terms of evolutionary development, analyzing certain requirements for survival and certain others for the attainment of intensity of experience. This discussion of society in terms of organic evolution also has bearings upward for the structure of human society.

There is a two-fold pressure: to survive and to achieve intensity. Mere survival is mostly a matter of stability. The more that variable conditions in the environment do not threaten existence, the more stable is an organism. In regard to temperature variations, for example, cold-blooded organisms are more stable than warm-blooded organisms. The more special the requirements of an organism, the lower its survival potential. The highly unspecialized organism is much more stable and can survive greater changes in the environment in which it is situated. The unspecialized society is less intimately related to the specific details of its environment, which is why it can survive easily even when specific details of environment change drastically. "By reason of this flexibility of structural pattern, the society can adopt that special pattern when viewed as a whole." [59]

On the other hand, there is a much higher degree of intensity in a society which relates intimately to the various elements of its environment; which is more specialized in its specific operations; which, because it answers to the specific demands of a historical period, is more "timely." Such societies are more highly structured and better defined. But because they are more complex, they will be more deficient in survival value. "Thus the problem for Nature is the production of societies which are 'structures' with a high 'complexity,' and which are at the same time 'unspecialized.' In this way, the intensity is mated with survival." [60] (Whitehead's presentation of "society" will have bearing upon the development, later in this work, of a process understanding of that society which is the Church. The sacramental system is one of the means of mating intensity power and survival power.)

Up to this point, the description of an actual entity has been mainly concerned with its private life, its subjectivity: how its subjective aim directs its becoming, deciding what items from the structure of actuality and what elements from the structure of possibility are to be part of its becoming, then finding ways to integrate its prehensions of all those items and elements, and all of this issuing finally in a kind of satisfaction. It is at that moment of completion that an actual entity begins its public career, its "superjectivity."

An actual entity "is a subject-superject, and neither half of this description can be lost sight of for a moment." [61] If a concrescing entity must take account, via positive or negative prehensions, of the entire universe of data, then it stands to reason that once an actual entity has terminated its becoming, then it too is an historical fact. As historical fact it is "out there" in the universe of data for all other concrescences to consider in their becoming. It can serve for all time now as an object for future creativity. That availability forever to the future is the superjective character of an actual entity. Whitehead also refers to this condition as an actual entity's "objective immortality," i.e., for all time it never loses its availability to be an object to all further concrescence.

An actual entity, therefore, has a very genuine once-and-for-all character. At the instant that a concrescence terminates in its final satisfaction, it is truly finished in its active life; it is "intolerant of any addition." [62] That is its "once" character. As superject, it has a public life for all later process to reckon with. That is its "and-for-all" character.

The presence of one actual entity to another that is concrescing is a matter of its once-and-for-all character. Whitehead himself notes the contrast of his understanding of presence with that of Aristotle. Whitehead's position is based upon several points: that the whole universe is relative to every process, even if barely so or negligibly so; that the entire process that a concrescing entity experiences IS its reality; and that having a causal role in some entity's concrescence is the mode of presence:

> The principle of universality directly traverses Aristotle's dictum, "(A substance) is not present in a subject." On the contrary, according to this principle an actual entity *is* present in other actual entities. In fact, if we allow for degrees of relevance, and for negligible relevance, we must say that every actual entity is present in every other actual entity. The philosophy of organism is mainly devoted to the task of making clear the notion of "being present in another entity." [63]

He continues the contrast, noting that Aristotle's idea of one entity not being able to be present *in* another entity suggests the crude notion that one actual entity cannot be added to another *simpliciter,* i.e., solid substances can't be amassed and still have their own mass.

There is a sense in which the absence of some element in a concrescence actually conditions the concrescence: it is different in view of that absence; it would be other than it is were that item in fact a component. Therefore, even those items that were dismissed (by negative prehensions) were reckoned with. However, there is a sense of presence that corresponds more to the psychological model, and that is also one of the meanings of presence in Whitehead, that is, those elements which contribute to the real internal constitution of an actual entity. The weight of the Aristotelian heritage tends to make us think of presence in terms of proximity, or physical "hereness" and "nearness"—close enough to be perceived by one of the senses. There is an expression of Gabriel Marcel which, even though he is not speaking in a defined process framework, captures a Whiteheadian sense of presence. Marcel says that the "notion of presence corresponds to a certain hold that something has upon my being." [64] We are acquainted with our own many experiences of the "presence" of a situation or of a person far away that exercises far more influence upon us than nearer or here-at-hand situations or persons or things. A man's wife may be far more present to him at the office, as he ponders a decision, than a man at a desk five feet away. In Whitehead's perspective, our experiences are what constitute us, and the objects of our experiencing are made present in us as they exercise a certain hold on our being, or better, on our becoming. One actual entity becomes present in another actual entity through its role as a cause. The power of an actual entity is expressed in its becoming an object for other actual entities. The power of presence is effected by prehensions. That is their "vector" character, whereby the prehension facilitates the transfer of power from some other actual entity into the becoming of a new entity. Past occasions, i.e., actual entities in their superjective character, energize the new occasion in its prehension of them. That is still another way of describing the exercise of presence. In the Whiteheadian perspective, one actual entity has a real presence in another actual entity when it enters into that new entity's becoming. And although nearness or here-at-handness is often a condition of those entities that do in fact enter into the real, internal constitution of a new entity, the fact remains—and it cannot be over-dramatized—that *being a cause in another entity's coming-to-be is the essential notion of presence.*

In the presentation of Whitehead so far no mention has been made of God. Most of the material has been drawn from *Process and Reality*. This book represents the Gifford lectures at the University of Edinburgh in 1927–1928. And the Gifford lectures are concerned with the question of God. Whitehead's concern for God was never facile. His father was an Anglican clergyman. And Bertrand Russell reports that at one point in his earlier life Whitehead considered Roman Catholicism, being very much taken with Cardinal Newman. Lucien Price tells of a period early in their married life when the Whiteheads "had read a great many books on theology. This study went on for years, eight of them, I think he said. When he had finished with the subject, for he *had* finished with it, he called in a Cambridge bookseller and asked what he would give for the lot." [65] That was followed by a long period of what is perhaps described as agnosticism. In the last period of his life when he is concerned primarily with philosophy, he returns with a strong interest to the religious question. In *Science and the Modern World* (1925), Whitehead exhibits great caution in dealing with the God question:

What is the status of the enduring stability of the order

of nature? There is the summary answer, which refers nature to some greater reality standing behind it . . . My point is that any summary conclusion jumping from our conviction of the existence of such an order of nature to the easy assumption that there is an ultimate reality which, in some unexplained way, is to be appealed to for the removal of perplexity, constitutes the great refusal of rationality to assert its rights.[66]

A year later in *Religion in the Making* there is a somewhat softened attitude toward theology and an avowal of the importance of religious experience:

. . . you cannot confine any important reorganization to one sphere of thought alone. You cannot shelter theology from science, or science from theology; nor can you shelter either of them from metaphysics, or metaphysics from either of them. There is no short cut to truth.

Religion, therefore, . . . still brings its own contribution of immediate experience.[67]

In the course of the Gifford lectures the following year (*Process and Reality*) he is very clear in stating that philosophy must take note of the religious experience of man:

The chief danger to philosophy is narrowness in the selection of evidence . . . Philosophy may not neglect the multifariousness of the world—the fairies dance, and Christ is nailed to the cross.[68]

But Whitehead is still cautious. The one-world universe he describes does not allow a double set of rubrics, a natural and a supernatural. "The secularization of God's functions in the world is at least as urgent a requisite of thought as is the secularization of other elements of experience." [69] "God," therefore, "is not to be treated as an exception to all metaphysical principles, invoked to save their collapse. He is their chief exemplification." [70] Whether or not Whitehead succeeds perfectly in a description of God that does not fail against his categories is open to discussion, and there are some fine discussions available.[71] There are Whiteheadian scholars who have made refinements upon his natural theology.[72] Notwithstanding those critiques, which do not, by and large, make substantial alterations upon his natural theology, I believe that Whitehead succeeds admirably in his presentation of God. I say "succeeds," for I think that God, as he understands him, does not fail against the demands of the contemporary mind for a one-world reality; and at the same time God is essential for the real world as we know it.

Whitehead shares with Aristotle not only his empiricism, but some strong rationalistic strains. By the latter I mean the conviction that reality is together in an orderly way, and that orderly thinking can make revelations about it which are out of empirical reach. Whitehead holds that each concrescing entity has two realms to draw from: there is the structure of the real, i.e., the actual world that has already (be)come into existence; and there is also the structure of possibility, new forms of definiteness that might be given priority over the already existing forms. The structure of actuality takes in the world of actual entities. The structure of possibility Whitehead describes in the category of eternal objects. Every entity, as it comes into being, faces the structure of possibility. For reality is evolutionary in character, and that means that at some points along the line, new forms of being appear. Really new things turn up. Whitehead further holds that evolution is a history of creative advance. The path of that "advance" is, to be sure, strewn with failures and setbacks, but the overall configuration is one of creative *advance*. And that is the basis for insisting upon the word "structure" in the phrase, structure of possibility. An entity may face numerous possibilities in its becoming—but not all of them would represent an advance. Some possible new forms are more relative than others to an act of becoming, if that concrescence is supposed to be in search of a better self (which is what creative advance means). This presupposes an ordering among those forms of possibility—a structure of possibility—for some are more pertinent than others to a creative advance. This approach also seems to demand some kind of sensitivity on the part of each concrescence to those forms which relate most intimately to its possible betterment. There is a grading among the eternal objects which guides their respective relevances to the creative advance. And now comes the element of rationalism in Whitehead. We are talking about eternal objects, about a realm of possibility that is different from actuality. We are invoking the structure of possibility as one of the *reasons* why reality is the way it is, why it becomes as it does. The ontological principle holds that the whole of reality consists of actual entities, and that any reason for anything must derive from actual entities; there's no going behind actual entities for anything more real. If there is no actual entity, then there is no reason. The structure of possibility has been introduced as something explanatory of what is real, for an entity may decide to aim toward some new possibility in its becoming (i.e., a matter of a new element in its final cause). But that cannot be unless there is some actual entity whose character is to maintain the structure of possibility, and make it available. That there is such an entity is a conclusion of reason, but a rationalist holds that a conclusion of reason does indeed alert us to the character of reality:

Everything must be somewhere; and here "somewhere" means "some actual entity." Accordingly the general potentiality of the universe must be somewhere; since it retains its relevance to actual entities for which it is unrealized. This "proximate relevance" appears in subsequent concrescence as final causation regulative of the emergence of novelty. This "somewhere" is the non-temporal actual entity. Thus, "proximate relevance" means "relevance in the primordial mind of God."[73]

This aspect of God Whitehead calls his "primordial nature." God's primordial nature is his envisagement of all possibility—or better, his envisagement of the structure of possibility. There is an ordering of the forms of definiteness, not in the sense of any configuration that is envisaged ahead of time for the world. For each act of becoming is a free act, as a result of which the texture of reality is modified. Since the texture of reality is continually being modified by its on-going process, some possible form of definiteness that might at this instant be relevant, will in the succeeding instant not have much at all to offer to a present situation, in view of the recent modifications. At that point, some other form of definiteness may become more relevant to the possibilities of creative advance. The structure of possibility does not therefore impose itself in any way on the course of reality, except in the sense that given the decisions which have shaped reality up to this point, some possibilities make more sense than others—they are graded in their relevance. But that grading is part of their structure; it doesn't arise in terms of the immediate situation. It is there, in the primordial nature of God, and the immediate situation avails itself of structured possibility.

The fact that God envisages "the absolute wealth of potentiality" is not the whole picture. Reality is a community of inter-*related* events. "Thus by reason of the relativity of all things, there is a reaction of the world on God." [74] God prehends the real world as it happens. He knows the actual world. Whitehead calls this aspect of God his *consequent* nature for, to state the obvious, although God knows all that is actual, the exact shape of his knowing is *consequent* upon the particular shape of what comes to be. Whitehead maintains that the distinction between the two natures or aspects of God is "a distinction of reason." [75] That means that there is not first a primordial nature and then a consequent nature, even though we distinguish between them. The actuality of God, like the actuality of any actual entity, is constituted by his becoming. God needs the world for his own actuality; though it is equally and more primordially true that the world needs God to be actual. As Whitehead understands reality, there is no kind of a being which needs only itself to exist. God, therefore, "is not before all creation, but with all creation." [76] God is with creation in both his primordial and consequent natures; "but, as primordial, so far is he from 'eminent reality,' that in this abstraction he is 'deficiently actual' . . ." [77] His prehensions of the world are necessary for his actuality.

That God becomes is obviously at variance with the traditional doctrine of his immutability. I would like to make two brief reflections upon this. The first is that the Judeo-Christian religious experience alternately reports both upon the changelessness of God and upon his susceptibility to being prevailed upon, even though he had "made up his mind" already. The second point is that the theological elaboration of God's immutability bears the heavy impress of the Greek mind set in whose categories, for the most part, it was worked out. Process philosophy challenges some of the presuppositions upon which that mind set is based.

Whitehead held that philosophy must consider the full range of human experience in the derivation of its categories, but also that the test of the categories is their accuracy in the interpretation of experience. I feel that the religious experience of mankind is at least partly responsible for Whitehead's description of God. At many points man's religious experience of God indicates a certain divine dipolarity. In the Old Testament, God is sometimes understood as the changeless one, sturdy as the rocks and mountains (which were experienced as changeless at that time). He knows our thoughts and words before they are in our minds or upon our lips, so that he does not gain new knowledge as we think new things or speak new words—he is unchanged by what we do. Yet there are other aspects of God. Moses bargains with Jahweh over Sodom and Gomorrah and changes Jahweh's mind in the matter. Jonah is impatient with Jahweh because he lets his mind be changed by human penitence. The Lord of the Old Testament is sometimes understood as unchanging and utterly the same always, and yet also as a Lord of History, deeply committed to and involved in historic event, with something at stake in history for himself.

The devotion and the theology of Christians have continued to assert this kind of dipolarity. At the same time that academic theology has insisted upon the utter changelessness of God and the lack of real relations between God and creation, practices and devotion have approached God as one who can be prevailed upon to act, and to influence events in ways that he wouldn't have, had he not been prevailed upon. While the technical theology may have had an explanation of the meaning of a "votive Mass to ask for rain," it would not have been the same as what was in the hearts of those convinced that God would *really* relate to their prayers.

Christian theologizing has been heavily conditioned by the Hellenistic mind whose categories it drew upon. In Aristotle's metaphysics, the principal philosophical resource of scholastic theology, to be able to change is to be imperfect. God, therefore, who is perfect cannot change. God's unchangeability raises a number of problems. For example, when a man knows something he is modified by his knowledge. His knowledge is shaped by the objects he knows. The objects of man's knowledge, however, are not modified by the mere fact of being known. Scholastic philosophy has called a man's relation to the objects of his knowledge a "real relation"; the import of "real" being that he is shaped in some way by the object known, i.e., it is a cause, the effect of which is the particular shape of his knowledge. But the relation of an object to the one who knows it is a "logical relation," for there is no causal influence of a man who knows an object upon the being of the object. Only real relations, in scholastic philosophy, reflect a change. In this framework, God can have no real relations with creation, for that would mean that God would change, that he would become. Since he cannot have *new* knowledge, and since he does know creation, it must be (within this world view) that God already knows all that will ever come to be and thus acquires no new knowledge. That position rescues God from the problem of being involved in change. It creates another problem. Somehow or another if God knows all that will ever come to be, there is already eternally in existence the exact configuration of all that will ever be. Though God is saved from "becoming," it is difficult to salvage the reality of history; it is difficult to avoid making *our* experience of time and of free decision be but *our* illusion—for the exact configuration of all reality ever is, there is exact detail in the eternity of God's knowing.

Another disturbing implication of God's total changelessness is the problem of seeing how anything radically matters to God. If God has no real relations with creation, how can the life of any one man or even the destiny of an entire universe make any real difference? To make a real difference is to have a real effect. Charles Hartshorne has, perhaps better than anyone, dwelt upon the problems of the absolutely unchanging God; I strongly recommend his discussions of the knowledge, the love, and the compassion of God in his book, *The Divine Relativity*.[78]

It seems clear to me that religious experience has affirmed both that God is changeless and that he can still be moved, that his changelessness is needed as a ground for creation and that his real involvement with historic event is needed if religion is to make any real difference to man. It also seems clear to me that the absolute changelessness of God in any real way is a theological requirement only in the face of a world view which presupposes that change is in every event an indication of imperfection.

The conviction throughout process modes of thought, and I think a strong persuasion of much contemporary thought, is that becoming is normative; becoming is the story of every reality; where there is no becoming, there is not anything presently real. Becoming is not only *not* an imperfection; it is the very condition of being actual. Process is reality. This philosophical presupposition makes it easier for theology to explain the knowledge and love of God; and easier for religion to be grounded in the fact that history matters utterly to God, and so "it" (which is everything) makes a difference, whatever happens, it makes a difference.

An important religious (as well as philosophical) question to raise is, how is God *present* to creation? As we have seen already, the critical import of the word "presence" is that of causal efficacy. An entity is present to any actual entity by playing some role in that actual entity's constitution. The question of God's presence to creation is a question of how he acts, how he affects the course of creative advance.

Though Whitehead differs from Aristotle in some critical ways, especially in giving priority to becoming over being, there are many striking similarities. For each of them, the fact of order in the universe is an expression of God's activity *vis-à-vis* the universe. If there is order in the structure of actuality, as Whitehead would have it, then there must be order also in the structure of possibility which actuality expresses. The Whiteheadian treatment of this is sometimes under the heading of value. Every actual entity has an irreducible particularity or individuality. It has a value for itself. The "decisions" which shaped it were determined by whatever goal or value its subjective aim was in motion toward. The lineaments of order within every actual entity derive from the requirements of its particular pursuit of some value or another. Often, the psychic model of becoming underlies such a description. A conscious pursuit of value is not attributed to below-life realities. Yet somehow the molecules of a wheat stalk remember what they are about (albeit a physical memory), and because of what they are about the patterns of their functioning differ from the patterns of a rose bush. As we have already seen, the pursuit of value has a three-fold thrust: simply to be, in the first place; but to do it well; and to find new ways of improving, of being better. Again using the language of the psychic model, each actual entity is in pursuit of its own selfhood. It "knows" how to put itself together (to concresce). Because it "wants" to be the best possible self, it sometimes "makes decisions" that result in partial departures from its immediately past way of being. The thrust through which creation gropes "knowingly" for becoming a good self and a better self is the thrust through which God is *with creation*. "The purpose of God is the attainment of value in the temporal world." [79] The impetus in each event at its inception, which Whitehead calls "initial aim," is God's purpose. Inasmuch as an entity's aim is what directs (and therefore makes possible) its concrescence, in *Science and the Modern World* Whitehead called God the "Principle of Concretion." "Every actual occasion is a limitation imposed on possibility, and . . . by virtue of this limitation the particular value of that shaped togetherness of things emerges." [80] Thus Whitehead can also understand God as the principle of limitation, for every value is *this* value and not *that,* and as such imposes *this* set of conditions or limitations rather than *that* set. [81]

Each process is instigated by a subjective aim—the reason why there ever is any becoming. Each becoming is the actualization of some elements from the structure of possibility. The initial aim of every event, which makes possible the commencement of process, and which therefore makes reality

possible, derives from the structure of possibility; that is, derives from the primordial nature of God. The initial aim is
God's purpose at work, that each entity attain value, that
each entity strive for greater intensity, harmony, beauty
(which is to say that creative *advance* is the overall characteristic of process). This communication to each event of a
kind of process-toward-value-attainment is not forceful or
coercive. It is above all a persuasive influence in which God
enters the process as "a lure for feeling, the eternal urge of
desire." [82] In the attainment of value in each event God is,
therefore, self-expressed. The less the discrepancy between
the initial aim, which is for each entity to become its best self,
and the final realization, the more perfectly is God expressed
in the event. "Every event on its finer side introduces God
into the world . . . The power by which God sustains the world
is the power of himself as the ideal. He adds himself to the
actual ground from which every creative act takes its rise. The
world lives by the incarnation of God in itself." [83] It cannot be
emphasized too strongly that the derivation of an initial aim
from God does not remove the freedom of an actual entity. An
actual entity is always free to decide finally what it will become. This understanding of God's insertion into the creation
of the world involves him essentially—but in that he does not
communicate exact dimensions to what is coming to pass; he
leaves process genuinely free. His purpose—for each event to
become its best self—is part of the initial aim of each occasion; but then, as the occasion progresses, its own subjective
aim is reponsibile for its maximum achievement. When it
acts irresponsibly, there is evil: repression and inhibition of
high achievement. This primordial aspect of God's nature is
required for the upward and forward movement—the progress—of creation. God keeps a steady, though gentle and
tender, pressure upon the heart of the universe toward the
highest harmony:

The religious insight is the grasp of this truth: that the order of the world, the depth of reality of the world, the value of the world in its whole and in its parts, the beauty of the world, the zest of life, and the mastery of evil, are all bound together—not accidentally, but by reason of this truth: that the universe exhibits a creativity with infinite freedom, and a realm of forms with infinite possibilities; but that this creativity and these forms are together impotent to achieve that actuality apart from the completed ideal harmony, which is God.[84]

In his primordial nature God is infinite and complete. For he envisages all possibility, the full potentiality for the universe. And since it is a conceptual envisagement of potentiality, it does not depend upon actual realization for being: it is utterly complete.

Before passing to a discussion of the consequent nature of God, it might be well to call attention to the rational elements in the movement of Whitehead's thought about God. The structure of possibility, as well as the structure of actuality, is a contributory factor to the real. Possibility, by nature and definition, is unactual. Yet it is an explanatory element of the real. Since, according to the ontological principle, any reason for anything must derive from the actual (be in some way traceable to actual entities), Whitehead sees the rational need for positing some actual entity which envisages the structure of possibility. That structure of possibility must be somewhere, that is, in some actual entity, in order to be available to creation. The structure of possibility is in God. Every actual entity, as a necessary condition of being, must have put itself together according to some pattern of assemblage or another; it must have had some initial contact with the structure of possibility from which to derive an aim, a value to be in motion toward. Thus it is, therefore, that Whitehead is rationally persuaded that in its initial aim an actual entity encounters God in his primordial nature. In keeping with his categories, Whitehead considers this contact with God to be made via a hybrid prehension: God is "felt" (prehended) under the aspect of an element of his concepuality, that is, his conceptual envisagement of forms of definiteness (eternal objects).

Hartshorne's insistence on keeping a clear distinction between the abstract and the concrete is helpful in this discussion of God. Reason can give information about the abstract character of reality. Empirical evidence gives information about the concrete character of reality. A lot of disenchantment about "proofs" for the existence of God derives from the confusion of the proofs and provers. Rational proofs cannot make disclosures about the actuality of God, only about his abstract character. However, based upon abstract information, empirical evidence is then able to add concrete information. A rational "proof" can never, never touch the concrete, actual God. The failure of "proofs" to affirm that they do not yield God's actuality but only his abstract character has caused disenchantment with such "proofs": they leave us cold (and understandably so, for our religious sensibilities search out the actuality of God).

To say that God has a consequent nature as well as a primordial nature is still to make an abstract statement. The unfamiliar wordings might disguise the simple meaning: that everyone has an abstract character, but that to be real, it must be expressed in concrete ways. Every man is a real, concrete, *actual* man through his insertedness into historic event. While his reality might have been expressed in a million different historical settings, it is necessarily expressed, finally, in this particular setting rather than that. Every man has a consequent nature. That is still abstract. Only when we describe his engagement in the real world are we giving a content to his actuality. But we must wait upon the empirical evidence if we are to deal with the content of his consequent nature. For that is a matter of actuality, not of abstract character. It is an abstract characteristic of God that his purpose "is the attainment of value in the temporal world." [85] Further, "the 'consequent nature' of God is the physical prehension by God of the actualities of the evolving universe." [86] Concretely, then, God prehends the actual course of events; and since his purpose is for each occasion to become its best self, then it matters to him what happens. The knowledge that there is an actual entity in whom our own self-creativity is grounded (not tied), and that "it matters" radically to "him" what we do, is a constant "lure" to our own becoming. "Thus God in the world is the perpetual vision of the road which leads to the deeper realities." [87]

The model of human relationships is again a useful one here. Because of similar interests between myself and another person, there might be a myriad of occasions of experience that are common to us both, even though we may not know each other, e.g., the unknown person who sits next to me at the symphony, enjoying the same music which I enjoy. If in the course of events the two of us become acquainted, the event which we were already sharing (the music) can become a way in which we share in each other's life. Besides loving a Brahms symphony simply because I love it, I may also enjoy and love my friend's enthrallment over the symphony, which adds a new quality of intensity and zest to my enjoyment. The symphony which already mattered to me now matters to me even more because of how much it matters to my friend. The occasion of experience which a symphony is, is heightened considerably through my new element of consciousness about my friend's caring for this same occasion. While the occasion experienced is fundamentally the same occasion, it is nonetheless transformed by that new element in my consciousness. The experience is qualified by my consciousness that "it matters" to my friend.

"It matters" might be a good summary of the attitude of God, as Whitehead understands him, in regard to all process. Those events of history, whether our personal history or universal history, at which "it matters" most are the most significant occasions through which we can share in the life of God by taking them up into our experience, knowing that they are also events of God's experience, i.e., constitutive of the life of God in his consequent nature. Even though the defining characteristics of an event remain unchanged, the intensity of our experience of it can be altered greatly by our consciousness of how "it matters" to God. Because "it matters," our valuations placed upon occasions of experience can add to either our acceptance or rejection of them; can weight the contribution of an occasion of experience to our overall act of becoming.

The "it matters" of God touches reality first of all through his primordial nature, whereby each event at its inception has an aim or value in pursuit of which it is able to become. Though an initial value is given, the event remains free in its realization of the value, for better or for worse. Yet "it matters" to God as well as to the actual entity that it realize its best self. The "it matters" of God also touches reality through his consequent nature, through our realization that concrete, actual events do make a difference to him. "It matters" to us that "it matters" to him that all the adventures of our becoming are in pursuit of value. Religion is man's "it matters" in response to the "it matters" of God:

Religion is the reaction of human nature to its search for God . . . The power of God is the worship He inspires. That religion is strong which in its ritual and modes of thought evokes an apprehension of the commanding vision. The worship of God is not a rule of safety—it is an adventure of the spirit, a flight after the unattainable.

The death of religion comes with the repression of the high hope of adventure.[88]

In Whitehead's understanding of God, "the inclusion of God in every creature shows itself in the determination whereby a definite result is emergent," [89] and without that inclusion there would be no event. But this involvement of God in process, though fully necessary, is always persuasive, never coercive. God's persuasion works through his presentation of an ideal to an occasion. "He is the lure for feeling, the eternal urge of desire." [90]

"Tenderness" is Whitehead's choice for a description of God's consequent nature, how he receives into his own nature the creative advance of the world:

The image—and it is but an image—the image under which this operative growth of God's nature is best conceived, is that of a tender care that nothing be lost.

The consequent nature of God is his judgment on the world. He saves the world as it passes into the immediacy of his own life. It is the judgment of a tenderness which loses nothing that can be saved . . .

We conceive of the patience of God, tenderly saving the turmoil of the intermediate world by the completion of his own nature . . . God's role is not the combat of productive force with productive force, of destructive force with destructive force; it lies in the patient operation of the overpowering rationality of his conceptual harmonization. He does not create the world, he saves it: or, more accurately, he is the poet of the world, with tender patience leading it by his vision of truth, beauty and goodness.[91]

In one of the more often cited passages from *Process and Reality* Whitehead gives half a dozen antitheses about God and the World, each of which involves a shift of meaning, for example, "It is as true to say that the World is immanent in God, as that God is immanent in the World." [92] In concluding this short discussion of Whitehead's understanding of God, I would like to add a seventh antithesis: It is as true to say there is nothing new under the sun, as that everything under the sun is new. In the first case, there is never a new potentiality, since the entire structure of all the potentiality of the universe is in God's primordial nature. Yet, in the second case, every actual entity has a unique individuality that is not duplicated anywhere in the entire actual world. Since God's consequent nature is created by his reception of the newness of each unique entity into his experience, he is truly, in the celebrated phrase of Augustine, "ever ancient, ever new."

Finally, I want to discuss Whitehead's theory of symbol. There is a narrower and more technical development of symbol, through which Whitehead offers his solution to one of the questions that has plagued modern philosophy: how can man know reality. In this drama, the principal protagonists are David Hume and Immanuel Kant, especially for Whitehead, the former. Then there is the broader understanding of symbol as a factor in human culture and society. The analogue for the broader understanding is the more technical development.

British empirical philosophy, which got well on its way with Locke and Berkeley, culminated in the full blown skepticism of Hume. We know only our percepts (of things), and never the things themselves. The notion of causality has no empirical referent that could originate sense perceptions of it. Hence there can be no perception of causality. We can know our perceptions of color, shapes, tastes, etc., but we cannot know things, for we are not allowed to infer causality. For Hume, primordial data is sense data, and there is no way of going beyond sensa to know the things themselves, to posit their real existence.

Whitehead agrees with Hume that the world of sense perceptions is not the world of things. He calls this mode of experiencing or perceiving the mode of presentational immediacy: we perceive the sensa *as though* we perceive a world of contemporaneous things. But Whitehead diverges with Hume as to sense being the primordial mode of perception, and that divergence makes all the difference. Whitehead understands the mode of perception which he calls causal efficacy to be the primordial mode of perception. He does not need to find a way to assert causality in order to establish a real world of things which we really know. That, in a sense, is one of the Whiteheadian presuppositions.

The world which Whitehead describes is a world which is totally organically inter-related. That entire world enters causally into each new actual entity. "The whole world conspires to produce a new creation." [93] That vast web of causal relationships, or better, of causal relatings, is the activity which constitutes actual entities. And that vast web of causal relatings is the primordial mode of perception. There are two pure modes of perception, then: that of causal efficacy, and that of presentational immediacy.

Whitehead's understanding of contemporaneity enters as a factor in the modes of perception. The whole world that conspires to produce a new creation is the whole *antecedent* world. While an actual entity is in the process of becoming, its life is radically private. A concrescing entity does not itself become a possible object for other processes until it has concluded its own becoming, until it is no longer concrescing, but concrete. Two entities that are concrescing at the same time must do so in causal independence. For Whitehead, that is the essential notion of contemporaneity. Two concrescing

entities may share some of the same regions of space, yet they
have no causal influence on each other if they are true con-
temporaries. This means that there is always a split second
timing gap. We know people who are with us, for example, without realizing that we know their *completed* "drops"
of experience. But the successive drops of experience are, for
the most part, so close to the pattern of their immediate predecessors that the incredibly small time lag is not disruptive of
our conscious. functioning. If I would touch an iron whose
temperature is steadily rising, there would be that tiny time
lag between the first physical touch and the sensation of being
burned. At the time of the sensation, however the rising temperature would have gone along its way and be at a different
point, however small the difference. Yet we *seem* to be experiencing contemporary events through our sense percepta.
Yet Whitehead insists that it takes time, albeit infinitesimally
small, for the initial contact (causal efficacy) to be translated
into sense and register consciously (presentational immediacy). The epistemological question is how is it possible to
relate the perception of presentational immediacy to that of
causal efficacy; that is, on what basis can we hold that we
experience real things, and not just our perceptions of things.
Two pure modes of perception must have some points of
intersection, some common ground, if we are to be justified
in connecting the two modes. This synthetic activity which
connects the two modes is what Whitehead calls "symbolic
reference." Symbolic reference is possible because of two elements of common ground which the two pure modes of perceptions share. First there are the forms of definiteness, or
eternal objects, through which the actual world is objectified
for the concrescing entity in order for causal efficacy to function. Because of the subjective aim, there is already a principle of selectivity in operation through which some forms of
definiteness receive more attention than others. Yet already
in that primordial mode of dealing with the actual world,

that of causal efficacy, there is perception of the forms of definiteness which make the actual world what it is, which make it relevant (or irrelevant) to a concrescing entity, and through which the actual world is objectified and thereby functions causally in the new concrescence. There are also forms of definiteness through which perception in the mode of presentational immediacy operates, and which we experience as sense data. Whitehead holds that the forms of definiteness we know in sense perception are the same forms of definiteness perceived in causal efficacy. The forms of definiteness of presentational immediacy do in fact participate in the mode of perception of causal efficacy. There is the possibility that a form of definiteness which plays a part in causal efficacy may undergo a revision before presentational immediacy deals with it. And while there is no error possible in those two pure modes of perception, symbolic reference, which connects the two modes, introduces the possibility or error. Symbolic reference is a synthetic activity, and error is introduced as a possibility since the reference requires interpretation. "Thus, in general, human perception is subject to error, because, in respect to those components most clearly in consciousness, it is interpretative. In fact, error is the mark of the higher organisms, and is the schoolmaster by whose agency there is upward evolution." [94]

The second point at which causal efficacy and presentational immediacy intersect is that of locality. "Localizations, diverse or identical, in a spatio-temporal system common to both," are, along with common forms of definiteness, "the partial community of structure whereby the two perceptive modes yield immediate demonstration of a common world." [95] Taste is referred, for example, both to the mouth and to the food that is "there." Color is referred both to some external space and to the eyes by which it is seen. Though Hume would not allow the certainty of causal efficacy, Whitehead feels that he nonetheless affirmed it in saying that "if it be perceived by the eyes, it must be a colour; if by the ears, a sound"; for what else could "by" the eyes and "by" the ears mean if not agency, and how could he say that it "must" be a colour or it "must" be a sound were he not relying on a causality to produce the "must" on the basis of the "by." [96]

It has not been possible here to do more than give a brief sketch of Whiteheadian symbolic reference. But it is important because Whitehead holds "that all human symbolism however superficial it may seem, is ultimately to be reduced to trains of this fundamental symbolic reference . . ." [97] In the latter sections of his book, *Symbolism,* he treats the functions of symbols in some of the more popular (or anthropological) senses. Without trying to systematize his treatment of symbolism in the broader sense, I want to make a few characterizations which bear upon my later use of his treatment of symbolism in the broader sense for understanding Sacrament.

There are some points of similarity between Whitehead and Tillich or between Whitehead and Jaspers. They stress that a symbol is able to function as a symbol because while it is an element of our consciousness, it also participates in the reality to which it gives access. Such "participation" would be, in the Whiteheadian scheme, the points of intersection between the two pure modes of perception. Another way of making a similar statement would be to call attention to the fact that a past event shares in the making of a new event, and symbolic reference allows our human consciousness to see how the past and present reach into each other creatively.

There is another aspect of symbol which, though it is indicated in Whitehead, is more fully developed in Susanne Langer's *Philosophy in a New Key.*[98] The symbols which enable consciousness to see the penetration of the past into the present are detachable, that is, symbols can be elicited even when the event to which they refer is no longer spatially or temporally close. Yet through those symbols, the past can continue to invade the present since the symbols do indeed participate in the past. Societies use symbolism extensively in the maintenance of their identity, e.g., past events and the lives of heroes that embody aspects of a society's defining characteristics. Those events and heroes can serve as symbols, as the various rituals of a nation periodically celebrate a nation's identity through the symbols: July 4 and the celebration of Independence, Thanksgiving, the birthdays of Washington and Lincoln. Such ritual observances over and over again re-appropriate the defining characteristics in which those symbols participate. In personal lives, anniversaries and jubilees are rituals that serve similar functions.

Another very important function is in providing an interpretive key for experience. Not all aspects of some event which touches our lives are equally weighted. Not all aspects of a person who is our friend are equally important. We single out certain characteristics which mean very much and forget about other characteristics. And having singled out certain aspects, we let those important aspects become "handles" of a sort by which we take hold of a friend. Those "handles" are symbols which mediate our experience of our friend. The symbols are to the front in our perceptions of our friend, and other perceptions tend to arrange themselves around the central perceptions. For many children, for example, the "honesty" of George Washington is a symbol of the man and until there are more sophisticated symbols to capture him, a child's perceptions of George Washington will be in terms of his honesty, and the child will instinctively attempt to interpret events of Washington's life as manifestations of his cherry-tree honesty. Each of the Gospels works with a particular way of getting hold of the Jesus event, a symbol or

a combination of them (e.g., the titles of Jesus), and those
central symbols function as interpretative keys for each
evangelist to get a hold on the Jesus event. Symbols simplify
the data. They single out certain characteristics through
which an event is experienced. They provide a key for interpreting both the past event and the new event which appro-
priates the past through symbol. Because symbols determine
how we get hold of a past event, they influence the shape of
the new event. To one who is a devotee of George Washington,
it matters to the shape of the devotee's life whether he focuses
upon Washington simply as the honest man, as the politi-
cian, as the general and military strategist, or as the husband
of Martha. The situation is the same for the Christian as he
looks for the symbols through which he lets the life of Jesus
enter into the making of his own life. There are multiple aspects of Jesus. Since different symbols have access to different
aspects of the Jesus-event, as well as to different aspects of
the present situation to which the Jesus-event is related, it
matters immensely to the Christian and to the Church what
symbols they avail themselves of in their appropriations of
the Jesus-event.

A related aspect of symbol, as it functions in a society, is
that in communicating certain characteristics to the action of
a person in a society a lot of time-consuming deliberation can
be circumvented. Symbols foster the instinctiveness of certain ways of acting. There is a good and a bad side to this.
Tradition is full of symbols. The good side of tradition is that
it contains within it the fruit of an immense amount of human
experience. We have learned a lot, and our symbolic code
keeps the fruit of that learning in touch with living so that we
are spared from eternally starting from scratch. The negative
side of tradition and its symbolic code is that it may so easily
block access to new experiences. Or, as Heidegger has pointed
out, tradition sometimes even blocks access to the reality of the

experiences out of which it arose in the first place; it can block access, therefore, to the past. It must, therefore, be subject to challenge and to revision; vitality demands that:

> The art of free society consists first in the maintenance of the symbolic code; and secondly, in fearlessness of revision, to secure that the code serves those purposes which satisfy an enlightened reason. Those societies which cannot combine reverence to their symbols with freedom of revision, must ultimately decay either from anarchy, or from the slow atrophy of a life stifled by useless shadows.[99]

Symbols are critical to human existence. In the earlier and narrower Whiteheadian sense, symbolic reference does not occur except in human consciousness. It is the basis, albeit subject to error, of ontological realism: it connects our sense knowledge into the causal efficacy in which it is rooted. In the broader sense also, symbols help us discover meaning through the relating of past and present to each other. Symbols help situate the new in the context of the old. Because symbols are handles by which we can get hold of our experience, they facilitate our interpretation of experience. In both our personal lives and in our communal lives, symbols allow our experience to be significantly organized. Symbols, or better, symbolic codes, enable us culturally to contain and pass on the experience of the past as we move through the present into the future. Symbols, especially as they become ritualized, play a large role in the maintenance of a society's identity; they are effective in transmitting the defining characteristics of a society. Perhaps the highest compliment that can be paid to the function of symbol is that in the Whiteheadian framework, where "getting it together" is the fundamental description of all that is real, the play of symbol in the human enterprise (and there alone) adds new and poignant possibility to

the task of "getting it together" and of "keeping it together."
Like any dynamic capable of great good, this one too can also
work great harm—a staid symbolic code can "keep it together" long after "it" should have moved on to a new way
of togetherness. That is the risk of having the power of symbol at the disposal of human history to enable man to gather
together the fruit of his life experience and to offer it over and
over to the future.

WHITEHEADIAN CHRISTOLOGY

A constant in Christian faith has been that in Jesus God
has made a most special appearance among men, an appearance of critical importance to man personally and collectively.
What "of God" is present in and through Jesus, *how* the "of
God" becomes available, and *why* the "of God" is important
to us, are questions that have engaged the energies of many
human beings and sometimes of almost entire cultures for
centuries. Throughout the tradition theologies of the Divinity
of Jesus Christ, of the Incarnation, and of Redemption and
Salvation have been responding to the "what?" and "how?"
and "why?" questions. Every Christology is an attempt to deal
with those questions. No one of the "models" upon which a
Christology is constructed can exhaustively interpret Jesus.
And even within the New Testament itself, there are Christological statements that differ from each other.

More recently historical criticism has helped us to understand why Christologies differ, or, for that matter, why human responses to anything can differ so much in one place or
another, or at one time or another. We always experience
reality out of a perspective. The words we use and the grammatical structure have an implied perspective which conditions us from the earliest moments of consciousness. The
viable symbols of any era condition the perspective out of

which we operate. No perspective is definitive or absolute—
every perspective is *a* perspective. Eliot's J. Alfred Prufrock
was immobilized at the thought of how the next minute can
alter things, so why dare to disturb the universe when

> In a minute there is time
> For decisions and revisions which a minute will
>   reverse.[100]

Like many a contemporary man, Prufrock was aware of how
acutely our fundamental perceptions are shaped and conditioned by historical circumstances. Every grasp of reality is
historically conditioned and mediated through a perspective.
The grasp may be a genuine hold on reality, yet it is through
an historical perspective. We are increasingly aware of how
much a next moment of history will reverse or revise the decisions and the visions that at this moment mediate our contact with reality. Perhaps Prufrock, like his creator, had a
classical hankering after a greater stability of perspective
than what the contemporary sense of historical relativity
proffers to us. And he was unnerved. For similar reasons it
has been somewhat unnerving to the Church to admit to herself the historical relativity of all her perspectives, and as-
siduously to do her form-critical homework on her own
utterances.

Process Christology is an attempt to take a perspective,
i.e., process modes of thought, and attempt to get at the
"what," the "how," and the "why" of God's presence to history in and through Jesus. Whitehead does not have a full
treatment any place of his interpretation of Jesus, but there
are some scattered reflections. As he understands the persuasiveness and tenderness of God who desires everything's and
everyone's best good, he sees in Jesus a particularly apt God-
like event. Whitehead's insistence that reality is organically one, as we have seen repeatedly, means that no part of it

can fail against metaphysical first principles; it means that the
same basic categories obtain throughout. Therefore, when he
deals with Jesus, he cannot invoke any explanation that does
not conform to the natural inner-workings of reality:

> To speak with complete candor, I cannot place any of the
> events within that [Jesus' life] period as out of scale in
> type of happenings with analogous occurrences else-
> where.[101]

Yet, having made that proviso, he does see a sort of pre-
eminence in the Jesus event:

> I do hold, however, that the culminating points of the
> period embody the greatest expression of moral and in-
> tellectual intuitions which mark the growth of recent
> civilizations.[102]

Whitehead understands what Christians have claimed about
Jesus. And as long as Jesus is not explained as a metaphysical
exception, I think he fundamentally agrees with the claim
that in some way the Jesus event is the watershed divide of
history.

> The essence of Christianity is its appeal to the life of
> Christ as a revelation of the nature of God and of his
> agency in the world. The record is fragmentary . . . but
> there can be no doubt as to what elements in the record
> have evoked a response from all that is best in human
> nature. The Mother, the Child, and the bare manger:
> the lowly man, homeless and self-forgetful, with his mes-
> sage of peace, love, and sympathy: the suffering, the
> agony, the tender words as life ebbed, the final despair:
> and the whole with the authenticity of supreme
> victory.[103]

He affirms the historical criticalness of Jesus:

> Its [the life of Jesus] power lies in the absence of force.
> It has the decisiveness of a supreme ideal, and that is why
> the history of the world divides at this point of time.[104]

And through Christianity, the Jesus event maintains its relevance to history:

> There stands in the public view the persuasiveness of the
> eternal ideals, the same today as when realized in the
> Founder of Christianity.[105]

Whitehead has certainly not supplied a Christology himself. But there is clearly one rubric that any Whiteheadian Christology must observe: no explanation of Jesus can fail against the metaphysical first principles. No sooner did Whitehead's philosophical output reach the public than attempts were made to grapple with the theological implications. Lionel Thornton's *The Incarnate Lord* [106] was the first essay at a Whiteheadian Christology. It was published in 1928, before *Process and Reality;* it relies upon the Whitehead that was available through *Science and the Modern World,* and was not able to benefit, therefore, from the full Whiteheadian synthesis. Norman Pittenger has been one of the leading process theologians to grapple with Christology. His first major Christological work, *Christ and Christian Faith* [107] appeared in 1941. In 1958 he published his *The Word Incarnate.*[108] His *Christology Reconsidered,*[109] published in 1970, takes note of what some of the critics of the previous book have said. In some cases he makes alterations in view of the critics; at other points in the book he responds to critique. He does not depart from the main lines of *The Word Incarnate.* His 1967 book, *God In Process,*[110] deals briefly with the trinitarian question and has, therefore, a chapter on Christology. A Whiteheadian Christological formulation has recently become a principal concern of the process theologian,

John B. Cobb, Jr. As I have already indicated, I would like
to indicate the main lines of Cobb's developing Christology.
As I discuss Church and Sacrament later, I would like to have
a couple of possibilities to keep in mind as a "content" for
the Jesus-event which the Church continues and which the
Sacraments over and over again re-appropriate into the life
of the Church. It is for that reason also that I will indicate the
main lines of Teilhard's Christology in the next chapter. I
chose Cobb's presentation even though he has not (yet) dealt
with the topic in a book length work, because I think he has
thus far the Christology that is most finely hewn in Whiteheadian categories. The two principal sources are "A
Whiteheadian Christology," a chapter in the book, *Process
Philosophy and Christian Thought*,[111] and his discussion
of finality as to the Jesus-event in his book, *The Structure of
Christian Existence*.[112]

Cobb's Christology is his attempt to demonstrate how the
claim of Jesus might be understood within the world view
and the philosophical categories of Whitehead. It is not a
matter of substantiating or proving the claim. He writes as a
Christian, that is, as one who is in some way already grasped
by the claim. His purpose is to offer conceptuality in support
of the claim.

The conceptual tools he uses are the Whiteheadian categories and in some cases his own further projections of Whitehead's philosophy. The "claim" of Jesus he wishes to eluci-
date corresponds largely to the understanding of Jesus that
has emerged out of the theologians of the "new quest" of the
historical Jesus.[113] Basically Jesus claims a relation of extraordinary immediacy with God, intimate enough to experience God as Father and to confer upon himself the
authority to speak for God on his own:

Jesus was certainly a man conditioned by his time and
place. But he was a strange figure for any time and place.
His teaching and action involved an implicit assumption

or claim of authority that was different in kind rather than degree from the claim of other teachers of his time or of ours. The authority he implicitly claimed rested in himself rather than in received teachings or a fresh word from God. It was closely connected with a sense of relatedness to God such that he saw the response of men to his message and himself as decisive for their response to God or even identical with it.[114]

For Cobb, no understanding of Jesus can fail against the metaphysical categories. The one-world view of Whitehead makes that a requisite. That, by and large, is also a requirement of modern man if religion is to get a hearing. But beyond that, if the life of Jesus is to make a full claim upon us, it must be a claim that offers a life of relationship to God and man into which we can enter.

Cobb first treats how God is present in Jesus, which of course must be in terms of the dynamics through which God is present at other points of creation. He then develops a description of the personhood of Jesus, in which the presence of God to Jesus plays a central structural role.

The essential meaning of presence is that of causal efficacy: A has something to do with B's becoming, and A is thereby present to B. But there is a wide range of roles through which A is present to and in B. The role of A in B is partly determined by A and partly by B. There is something about a friend that conditions how he is a friend to me, but there is also much about me that determines how I let my friend enter into my life and be present to me. Or in terms of past occasions to my experience, if B represents an almost total break with what I was just doing, a new decision, then what I was just doing—that is, my "A" moment—plays a minimal role in my "B" moment. The presence of A is meager. But if A represents a decision that was just made, for example, to listen very carefully to what someone is saying, then

B, which is the succeeding moment is very largely determined by A. A has a large and highly effective presence.

God is present to every act of becoming in the first place through the initial aim which makes possible the act of becoming. In each instance, the initial aim is absolutely unique; it is for this precise act of becoming to be its best self. That best self will reflect both the individual act of becoming in itself and in its relation to the rest of the world. The actual world out of which any concrescence's best self emerges is different from every other actual world, and therefore is unique as it taps the structure of possibility. The initial aim does not impose its configuration on the remaining phases of a concrescence. The concrescence is responsible for what it does with the initial aim. If A is the initial aim, that is, if A represents what God offers, then the more fully B (the concrescence) keeps that offering of God intact in its own subjectivity, the more fully God is present. Full fidelity to the call of God in the initial aim means no discrepancy between the call and the attainment. And there is a cumulative effect in this. If my present act of becoming responds radically to what I understand as the summons of God offered to me as a gift, then my next moment has at its outset a large presence of God which conditions my new possibility. Cumulative fidelity to those successive aims offered means cumulative effectiveness of God's presence. The cumulative fidelity of Jesus to the call of God is a way of explaining the extraordinary presence of God in and to Jesus. Such fidelity could only be achieved with extraordinary awareness and deliberate human choices, that is, with consciousness of God's immediacy to one's act of becoming. And that is part of the claim of Jesus: the centrality and immediacy of God's presence to his very existence and his awareness of the fact.

Also, as Cobb indicates, the presence of God to a person is not restricted to the prehensive objectification of God in the initial aim. God can be prehended through a sense of his wider purposes and concern for the world; in New Testament terminology, God can be present through a life which is spent in building up his Kingdom. A sense of what the Kingdom of God requires is a sensitivity through which God shapes what a man is. Concern for the Kingdom of God is a mode of God's presence. The centrality and strength of Jesus' concern for the Kingdom of God is still another way of dealing with the presence of God to history in and through Jesus.

The mode of God's presence to, in, and through Jesus is not an exception to the modes in which God is present to other entities. But the call issued through God's presence, in each subjective aim, is unique in every case. And it is unique in Jesus. And there is a certain facticity about each instance of God's call and the ramifications of that call. Jesus sensed a meaning for all men in the shape of his life. He sensed the immediacy of God's presence to him which he understood as unique, as giving him access to God that was nowhere else available, and therefore as giving others access to God through him. Why? When all is said and done there is something ultimate about a decision that is made that is not further reducible, which is what freedom means. And that ultimacy counts for the decisions of God expressed in the initial aim offered to each moment of process, and it counts equally for the decisions a man makes as he works out the configuration of his responsibility to and for the call of God.

The second part of Cobb's treatment of Jesus concerns what other Christologies have understood as the "nature" question. One of the extremely valuable contributions of Cobb (in larger ways than just the Christological question, though there especially) is his rather close substitution of "structure of existence" for "nature." Though he doesn't use the expression "structure of experience," that would also, I think, come very close, and would perhaps reflect better the Whiteheadian framework. Every moment of process is a drop of experience, the experience of surveying the actual world and the world of possibility and from that welter of material "getting it all together." The experience of getting it together constitutes the existence of an entity. An entity does not first exist and then take note of the world and of possibilities; it's the very act of incorporating other entities, or aspects of them, or new possibilities, that is constitutive of the entity's existence. The structure of an entity's getting it together is determinative of what an entity finally becomes. Cobb is impatient with a too facile and too definition-full understanding of "human nature." To treat human nature as though the concept has a perfectly clear and stable content is to ignore the vastly different ways that men have got it together as men since the first inklings of humanity at the dawn of psychic evolution. The structure of human existence of Neanderthal Man has little in common with the structure of twentieth century human existence. It may well have more in common, over all, with the structure of existence of pre-human primates. Nor does the classical concept of human nature make sufficient room for man's on-going creation of human history; human nature is still being created by human decisions that perpetuate *this* structure of existence rather than *that,* and which tomorrow can still make other decisions. As he points out in *The Structure of Christian Existence,* the different ways in which different cultures have perceived themselves and out of which they have structured their psychic experiences are simply too variant to yield an encompassing concept of "human nature." The Greek Socratic approach to life involves a great emphasis upon rationality in the structure of human experience. Rationality loomed large in the self-perception and self-understanding of that period. A person for whom rationality is a dominant theme in self-understanding would easily experience his emotional life as a "problem" since it does not always align itself with the rational. Cobb sees the structure of existence as manifested in the prophetic periods of Old Testament history as one in which the Ethical is a central concern: responsibility of man before God, and the immediacy of God's concern with man's history. How the Old Testament Jews "got it together" differs drastically from how the Greeks "got it together." I agree with Cobb's reluctance to find some clearly defined "human nature" operative throughout the various structures of existence.

These considerations of the structure of existence in a wide cultural sense have their analogue in the life of each person. There are certain perceptions which are central ones in our self-perception, in our perception of the world; and those central perceptions are the keys to how we interpret experience. What a man means when he says "I" derives largely from those central perceptions out of which he operates and around which he gets his life together. A man's dominant way of understanding himself might be in terms of his role as husband, yet that same man's life would get put together quite differently if his central perception of himself were in terms of mayor, or of a hopeless failure. There is no way of weighting equally all those factors of our experience which contribute to the structure of our becoming. Some always emerge as dominant, which is to say that some contribute structurally much more than others, and that the dominant elements have a larger presence (effect more) in our psychic constitution.

Cobb asks what was Jesus' central perception. When Jesus said "I", what was the structure of his experiencing that gave content to the meaning of his "I"?

> . . . God's presence in Jesus played a structural role in the actual occasions constituting his personal life which it has played nowhere else. . . .

Here the contrast of Jesus with the prophets is most clear. He spoke on his own authority which was at the same time the authority of God. The "I" of Jesus, rather than standing over and against the divine "I," identified its authority with that of God. Among religious leaders of mankind, *this is a unique role*. It differs from the mystics and ecstatics as much as from the great Hebrew prophets. The "I" of Jesus was neither merged with the divine nor replaced by the divine. On the contrary, *it retained its autonomous existence, but in such a way as to identify its perceptions with God's* . . .

God's aim for Jesus was that he prehend God in terms of that which constitutes him as God—his Lordship, his love, and his incomparable superiority of being and value. This prehension was not experienced by Jesus as information about God but as the presence of God to and in him. Furthermore, and most uniquely, it was not experienced by him as one prehension alongside others to be integrated by him into a synthesis with them. *Rather this prehension of God constituted in Jesus the center from which everything else in his psychic life was integrated . . . the "I" of Jesus was constituted by his prehension of God.*[115]

A Christology must try to offer conceptualization for Jesus' claim of the immediacy of God to his experience, to his very being. A Christology equally implies that for some critical reason, what happened in and to Jesus is important for us today. Though Cobb offers a response to this area of Christology also, and a very fine one largely worked out with the help of the Whiteheadian perspective, I will postpone a discussion of the meaning of Jesus for the unfolding of history until the treatment of the Church in a later chapter.

3

TEILHARD DE CHARDIN
AND HIS CHRISTOLOGY

P ierre Teilhard de Chardin is the
figure through whom Catholic
thought has most been touched
by process theology. Indeed though, the touching of Teilhard has been principally through a kind of spirituality which
he has enkindled, and less through theology as such. And it
is perhaps seemly that it happened this way. Teilhard and
Whitehead share in a passion for a one-world view. Both
men are deeply motivated by the science in which their expertise operates. But Whitehead's passion for the unified
world view bounced somewhat off of Descartes' world of
two substances, and the empirical and idealist failures somehow to get subjectivity and objectivity out of their separated
realms. For Teilhard, it was the split between things of earth
and things of spirit that compelled his passion for a vision of
easy and necessary togetherness of those things. He was
bouncing off a spirituality which long stressed conflict and
incompatibility of earthly and heavenly:

The originality of my belief lies in its being rooted in
two domains of life which are commonly regarded as

antagonistic. By upbringing and intellectual training, I belong to the "children of heaven"; but by temperament, and by my professional studies, I am a "child of the earth." . . . I have allowed two apparently conflicting influences full freedom to react upon one another deep within me. And now, at the end of that operation, after thirty years devoted to the pursuit of interior unity, I have the feeling that a synthesis has been effected naturally between the two currents that claim my allegiance.[1]

There is a sense in which a chapter on Teilhard is superfluous in this work, because I could carry on my treatment of Church and Sacrament entirely with the Whiteheadian framework. The main reason for Teilhard here is that we are now rather comfortable with the Teilhardian world and with the Teilhardian language, once so strange, that helps describe it; and this Teilhardian world, as I understand it, is rather thoroughly processive.

I have said "rather thoroughly" processive, because—as has been pointed out often enough—there are points at which Teilhard does not seem to be "fully" processive. It does not seem to be the case, for example, that in Teilhard's understanding of God, God too is in some way in process. And some question whether there is not a finality about the Omega point which, having been attained, means that there is no longer any process. These, of course, are valid questions.

I believe that some of this processive inconsistency is due to Teilhard's not having a consistent process metaphysics to pressure his thought patterns. He had Bergson. Cuénot says that Teilhard thought to read (songé à lire) Whitehead's Science and the Modern World,[2] but there aren't any indications from Teilhard that he did actually read it. He was not a philosopher himself, and he knew that. He benefited not only from Bergson, but also from Blondel, from Cardinal Newman, and from Edouard LeRoy who was associated with the Modernist movement. He knew that his work was fraught with philosophical implications, and it was his intention earlier in his career to develop a philosophical synthesis, which he intended to call *L'Union Créatrice*. The title is clearly reminiscent of Bergson's *L'Evolution Créatrice* (and perhaps indicative of a point of divergence in their respective positions). He felt that such a philosophical base would have been helpful to him, for he foresaw being called upon to explain and defend himself.

Besides that, the air in the Catholic Church was still heavy from the Modernist crisis. Teilhard's work got under way just at the tail end of the bitter Modernist controversy, and the ghosts of the movement continued to haunt Rome and keep her edgy. One of the *bêtes noirs* in the Modernist cage was evolutionary and developmental thought. I would guess that the pressure from the Modernist controversy had something of a curbing effect—though not in a conscious way— upon Teilhard's development of process implications.

There are some amazing similarities between the fundamental visions of Teilhard and Whitehead. These I want to dwell upon, but not without acknowledging that there are some very different things about their respective approaches and visions. In this latter respect I would like to compare briefly their methodologies, for therein lies the reason for many of the differences. After that, I want to deal with the similarities and finally with the Christology of Teilhard.

Whitehead would begin with a phenomenological description of how things are, within a restricted area of investigation. The next step is to generalize that description and test out its broader applications. Those generalizations which are found to obtain throughout our descriptions of reality—which everywhere apply and which never fail of exemplification—are metaphysical statements.

In this description of philosophic method the term "philosophic generalization" has meant "the utilization of specific notions, applying to a restricted group of facts, for the divination of the generic notions which apply to all the facts." [3]

Since *The Phenomenon of Man* is Teilhard's master synthesis, it is perhaps the best place to see his methodology in action. That same basic approach, however, is characteristic of the endeavor of his life.

Based upon a scientific phenomenological examination of the universe and man as *thus far* developed, he describes what is *thus far* the case. His phenomenological description is from his experience as a paleontologist, and his description presupposes evolutionary development. Then, like Whitehead, he generalizes that description and upgrades the generalized categories to a metaphysical status.

But at this point, his methodology carries him beyond the arena where Whitehead works. For with the aid of his generalized description, Teilhard does an extrapolation to suggest where the evolutionary development, thus far enacted, must logically move in the future. His positing of the Omega point is the result of such extrapolation, and projection.

A further step in the Teilhardian movement is the result of his faith commitment. Revelation often, for him, confirms the validity of his extrapolation and projection. In this he certainly differs from Whitehead who, though clearly influenced and conditioned by Christian faith, does not operate with a specific faith commitment.

It is not always clear to me (nor, I think, is it to Teilhard) when Teilhard's faith commitment has backed up into the earlier phases of his methodological movement and gives some content there. Perhaps that would not even be too disturbing to him in the sense that at critical points he sees Revelation not so much as "new" stuff from the outside, but as a confirmation of the natural workings of things; in that sense, there might well be the feeling that Revelation is at some points a clue to the natural workings of things. Yet

Teilhard is conscious that the use of Revelation takes him beyond the purely scientific. Thus he makes the final section of *The Phenomenon of Man,* "The Christian Phenomenon," an epilogue, and sets it off from the body of the book.

Among those who fully accept the evolutionary nature of reality, there are yet different ways of understanding its dynamics. Whitehead, for example, understands that "(i) to live, (ii) to live well, (iii) to live better" [4] is the essential dynamic, and that living better necessitates the emergence of newness, or novelty, for "better" means something that wasn't the case before. And he understands the evolution of reason as the emergence of a very effective organ of novelty, which criticizes and directs the urge toward what is better: the forward thrust, or creative advance. For Teilhard, the controlling dynamism is *survival*. To survive is an internal preference in the nature of things. In man this internal preference is manifested in a "zest for life." (Zest is a favorite Whiteheadian word too.) Although we are dealing with unimaginable aeons of time, the survival of the universe is threatened in an ultimate way by entropy. Someday its energies will all have been exhausted. Its only way out, its only means of survival, is to deploy its energies in psychic forms, for those are not susceptible to the law of entropy. Spirit can survive in a way that matter cannot, ultimately so. It would seem therefore to be conformable to the nature of reality for man to be biologically capable of surviving beyond the restrictions of his physical body. Teilhard would understand the resurrection of Christ both as a confirmation of that biological possibility, and as a holding out of the possibility for man to take up. The following text, probably from 1951, is worth citing at length:

If biology is taken to its extreme limit in a certain direction, can it effect our emergence into the transcendent? To that question, I believe, we must answer that it can, and for the following reasons.

Although we too often forget this, what we call evolution develops only in virtue of a certain internal preference for survival (or, if you prefer to put it so, self-survival) which in man takes on a markedly psychic appearance, in the form of a *zest for life*. Ultimately, it is that and that alone which underlies and supports the whole complex of bio-physical energies whose operation, acting experimentally, conditions anthropogenesis.

In view of that fact, what would happen if one day we should see that the universe is so hermetically closed in upon itself that there is no possible way of our emerging from it—either because we are forced indefinitely to go round and round inside it, or (which comes to the same thing) because we are doomed to a total death? Immediately and without further ado, I believe—just like the miners who find the gallery is blocked ahead of them—we would lose heart to act, and man's impetus would be radically checked and "defeated" forever, by this fundamental discouragement and *loss of zest*.

That can mean only one thing: that by becoming reflective the evolutionary process *can continue only if it sees that it is irreversible, in other words transcendent:* since the complete irreversibility of a physical magnitude, in as much as it implies escape from the conditions productive of disintegration which are proper to time and space, is simply the biological expression of transcendence.

Evolution, the way out towards something that escapes total death, is the hand of God gathering us back to himself.[5]

The passage exhibits much of Teilhard: the observation of the urge for survival as a dynamic of evolution, the generalization of that into a dynamic that applies to the universe, the prognostic extrapolation about future directions, and—though it is not explicit here—I think there is operative his conviction that the resurrection of Jesus validates the extrapolation.

It is above all these last two phases of Teilhard's methodology—prognostic extrapolation and validation from revelation—that account for a number of differences between him and Whitehead. And it is also positions of Teilhard that depend upon those latter phases that some of his critics find unscientific, and in a strongly positivistic sense, that is surely so. In terms of Teilhard's presuppositions, it would not be. For, as we shall see later in discussing Teilhard's understanding of the supernatural, the Incarnation and Redemption are prodigious biological activities.

What is immediately striking as a similarity between Teilhard and Whitehead are their fundamental categories. As we have already seen, the category of the ultimate comprises, for Whitehead: creativity, the many, and the one.[6] For Teilhard the fundamental categories are: "plurality, unity, energy: the three faces of matter."[7]

Teilhard's category of energy is quite comparable to Whitehead's creativity. Both work with a world that has, in Teilhard's words, a "profoundly atomic character."[8] Whitehead says that "the ultimate metaphysical truth is atomism."[9] The "atomic" parts of the Whiteheadian world are actual entities, apart from which there is nothing. The real world is the result of the multifarious inter-relatings of actual entities. Creativity does the inter-relatings, that is, it brings off reality. The Teilhardian world is quite similar: "the stuff of tangible things reveals itself with increasing insistence as radically particulate yet essentially related, and lastly, prodigiously active."[10] That energy which relates what is essentially particulate is a matter of creativity, for, as Teilhard says in another place, "to create means to unite."[11]

Both agree, therefore, that the world is both radically particulate and essentially related. The unity of the universe probably looms larger in Teilhard than in Whitehead, yet Teilhard is never very far from the "granulation" of the universe in his thinking, whether granules of matter or of spirit.

Whitehead affirms over and over again the inter-relatedness of the entire universe. In fact, as we have noted, he refers to his system as the philosophy of organism. "An actual entity has a perfectly definite bond with each item in the Universe." [12] Teilhard says about cosmic corpuscles that "each of them can only be defined in terms of its influence on all around it. Whatever space we suppose it to be in, each cosmic element radiates in it and entirely fills it. However narrowly the 'heart' of an atom may be circumscribed, its realm is coextensive, at least potentially, with that of every other atom." [13]

There are some forms of togetherness of the particules of reality that are no more tightly bound than a sand pile. But there are other forms of togetherness which exist in virtue of all the particules sharing in some common defining characteristic, and contributing to and depending upon, in some way, the whole. This latter kind of togetherness Whitehead calls a society, a term which applies far below the level of human life. In a less defined way, but to refer to the togetherness of particules, even in a below-human-life context, Teilhard also uses the word society,[14] and in quite the same way, the word colony.[15] Teilhard also reflects Whitehead's distinction between the democratic society, where all particules have equal membership (such as a crystal) and a regnant society, where some particules have a more directive function as regards the whole society (such as the brain functions in life forms). Teilhard often speaks of the directive function in terms of centering. "By simple juxtaposition of atoms or relatively simple atomic groups in geometrical patterns, regular aggregates may be produced whose level of composition is often very high, but they correspond to no properly centered units." [16]

Both men strive to overcome the duality of matter and spirit which has marked both science and asceticism. Teilhard wants "to connect the two energies, of the body and the soul, in a coherent way." [17] He wants to take "spirit . . . [as] born within, and as a function of, matter." [18] Whitehead works at this unification through his understanding of the dipolarization of energy, which he deals with as physical and conceptual prehensions. Physical prehensions are the relatings that are conformal; they repeat the past, maintaining things as they are. Conceptual prehensions open the way for novelty, for movement out toward the new and better. Teilhard too maintains the dipolarity of a single energy: "Without the slightest doubt *there is something* through which material and spiritual hold together and are complementary. In the last analysis, *somehow or other,* there must be a single energy operating in the world." [19] Teilhard presumes "that, essentially, all energy is psychical in nature"; but hastens to add "that in each particular element this fundamental energy is divided into two distinct components: a *tangential energy* which links the element with all others of the same order (that is to say of the same complexity and the same centricity) as itself in the universe; and a *radial energy* which draws it towards ever greater complexity and centricity—in other words forwards." [20] Both men, of course, understand the advent of life and of consciousness as a triumph finally of conceptual operations (Whitehead) and radial energy (Teilhard).

"The fragments of the world," says Teilhard, "seek each other so that the world may come into being." [21] The storyline of the world's coming-to-be is the "Law of Complexification-Consciousness." That, more than anything else, is the central dynamic of the Teilhardian synthesis and is also a central concept at work within his Christology.

As the name of the "law" suggests, there are two dynamics at work, and they are inter-related. The first dynamic is stated thus:

> Historically, the stuff of the universe goes on becoming concentrated into ever more organised forms of matter.[22]

And secondly:

> To guide him through the fogbanks of life, man has an absolutely certain biological and moral rule, which is continually to direct himself "toward the greater degree of consciousness." If he does this, he can be certain of sailing in convoy with and making port with the universe. In other words, we should use the following as an absolute principle of appraisal in our judgments: "It is better, no matter what the cost, to be more conscious than less conscious." This principle, I believe, is the absolute condition of the world's existence.[23]

Even though these two short texts are from different works, they capture together the sense of the Law of Consciousness and Complexity. In rather graphic language (for the abstractions they are), Teilhard also speaks of the dipolarity of energy in terms of the "Without" and the "Within" of things, all things. The Without corresponds to what we experience largely as the physical aspect of things. The Within comes into evidence as it manifests itself in higher forms of existence, where there is some kind of "Centeredness." To continue with the graphicness, the Withouts must, as it were, come together and stick together organically in order to allow the Withins also to coalesce. It is the coalescence of the Withins that increases the centeredness which finally manifests itself as consciousness or spirit. Every increase in centeredness is effected *"by the intervention of an arrangement"* [24] on the part of the physical side, that is, through greater physical complexity. The following is probably Teilhard's best description of the Law, which appears in a Postscript to *The Phenomenon of Man:*

> Reduced to its ultimate essence, the substance of these long pages can be summed up in this simple affirmation: that if the universe, regarded siderally, is in process of spatial expansion (from the infinitesimal to the immense), in the same way and still more clearly it presents itself to us, physico-chemically, as in process of organic *involution* upon itself (from the extremely simple to the extremely complex)—and, moreover, this particular involution "of complexity" is experimentally bound up with a correlative increase in interiorization, that is to say in the psyche or consciousness. [25]

Teilhard is not as explicit as Whitehead in his insistence that process is reality, though it seems clear that for him the universe is not a state but a process, and he affirms in many ways and places that "the unity of the world is by nature dynamic and evolutive." [26] The clearest, most explicit and unequivocal statement is perhaps that contained in a letter written in 1951:

> Lately I have once more become aware that the whole nucleus of my interior outlook depends entirely upon and can be reduced to a simple transposition into dimensions of "cosmogenesis" of the vision which is traditionally expressed in terms of "cosmos." Creation, spirit, evil, God (and more specifically, original sin, the Cross, the Resurrection, the Parousia, charity . . .) *all*

these ideas, transferred to the dimension of "genesis," become coherent and clear in a way which is astounding.[27]

Every noun must have "-genesis" added onto it. Every "substance" must be translated into a "becoming." And that is necessary for a clear and coherent rendering of the universe as we have come to know it. In this text, Teilhard says that God too must have "-genesis" added on. His natural theology, as exposed here and there throughout his works, is never really explicated and refined. There are many reflections of a more or less traditional natural theology. But he is aware, even if his own natural theology never comes to grips head-on with the question, that fidelity to his basic presuppositions demands a process understanding of God also. To be sure, he never develops such a process God.

Reflecting his understanding of Whitehead, Cobb says that "the soul is not at all like a substance undergoing accidental adventures in time. It is constituted by its adventures." [28] Teilhard too says that a man builds himself, a self into which enters something from all the elements of the earth. "*He makes his own soul* throughout all his earthly days"; and that individual achievement is simply part of the larger reality: "the completing of the world . . . the world, too, undergoes a sort of vast 'ontogenesis' (a vast becoming what it is) in which the development of each soul, assisted by the perceptible realities on which it depends, is but a diminished harmonic." [29]

I would like to cite still another Teilhardian text, which seems to me (though it has not received a lot of attention) one of the clearest statements of a thoroughgoing process mind. It is a redefinition of "body," in a way that says "I *am* everything in the universe which in any way enters into my experience, my constitution." The outer edges of a man are not his skin surfaces where his body leaves off. His body is whatever in the universe is touched by and touches his process. Through the word "body," Teilhard in fact redefines "substance" into "genesis" and all that the becoming involves.

> Hitherto, the prevailing view has been that the body (that is to say, the matter that is incommunicably attached to each soul) is a *fragment* of the universe, a piece completely detached from the rest and handed over to a spirit that informs it.

> In the future we shall say that the Body is the very Universality of things, in as much as they are centred on an animating Spirit, in as much as they influence that spirit, and are themselves influenced and sustained by it. For a soul to have a body is to be ἐγκεκοσμισμένη.

> The action of the individual, it is true, radiates from an organic centre that is more specially mobile—from a group of lower monads that forms a more effective colony. But the sphere of immanent operation extends in reality to something that belongs to the whole universe.

> My own body is not these cells or those cells that belong *exclusively* to me: it is *what*, in these cells *and* in the rest of the world feels my influence and reacts against me. *My* matter is not a *part* of the universe that I possess *totaliter:* it is the *totality* of the Universe possessed by me *partialiter*.

And, as if any clearer statement were needed:

> To our clearer vision the universe is no longer an Order but a Process. The cosmos has become a Cosmogenesis. And it may be said without exaggeration that, directly or

indirectly, all the intellectual crises through which civili-
sation has passed in the last four centuries arise out of
the successive stages whereby a static *Weltanschauung*
has been and is being transformed, in our minds and
hearts, into a Weltanschauung of movement.[30]

That, in a word, is also the thesis of Whitehead's *Science and
the Modern World!*

As I mentioned already, there is not in Teilhard a systematic natural theology. And in this brief discussion of God in
Teilhard's thought, I do not want to imply that unconsciously
he subscribed to the dipolar God of Whitehead, with a primordial and consequent nature. But there are, to be sure, points
of striking similarity. And granted the many points of fundamental agreement in their respective world views, even to the
point of substantial identity in naming the basic categories, it
would be surprising if there were not important points of
agreement in an understanding of God.

For Whitehead, the primordial nature of God responds to
the fact that the structure of possibility—since it is essential
for things coming to be—must be somewhere, and that somewhere he identifies as God. For Teilhard too, nothing which
comes to be is possible if it "has not already existed in an
obscure and primordial way." [31] He does not, in the same
text, attribute that "primordial way" to an aspect of God. But
in a text, reminiscent of Whitehead's insistence that God is
with creation and not before it, Teilhard says that "God's
creative action is no longer conceived as abruptly inserting
its work into the midst of pre-existent beings, but rather as
causing to come to birth in the depths of things the successive
terminations of its activity." [32] There are two points to be
made here in showing a similarity to Whitehead. The first is
seeing the same kind of temporal atomicity in process as does
Whitehead. There are successive terminations in process, not
the steady flux of Bergson. And secondly, God touches the

coming-to-birth of each of those drops of experience that make up the stream of reality. Yet God does not do this in a way that detracts from freedom within creation. In the same text Teilhard says that "God . . . makes things make themselves."

Teilhard also sees the action of God as a kind of lure. With something of a dipolar sense of God, he speaks of evolution as "stirred by the Prime Mover Ahead." [33] And similarly, also with the sense of God as a lure, he prays: "Yes, O God, I believe it: . . . it is you who are at the origin of the impulse, and at the end of the continuing pull which all my life I can do no other than follow, or favor the first impulse and its developments." [34] There is also the notion that God touches a process in its first impulse (cf., initial aim).

There are many things in Teilhard's statements about God that manifest the Whiteheadian emphasis upon the tenderness and gentleness of God, who, with infinite patience, receives the action of the world into his own being, desirous of losing nothing which can be saved, of making the best even out of turmoil. Teilhard sees "Providence across the ages as brooding over the world in ceaseless effort to spare the world its bitter wounds and to bind up its hurts," thus, "the more we repel suffering . . . with our whole heart, the more closely we cleave to the heart and action of God." [35]

There is a sense in which the suffering of the world is unavoidable. It is a consequence of the freedom and the evolutionary nature of the world's working out of its history. While, in one way, every occurrence of evil could have been other if the structure of the process at that moment had been other, *statistically* it is the story of evolutionary groping that suffering and evil, mistakes and errors, do accompany the process. Such is the little-by-little and groping character of evolution. "The unavoidable counterpart of any success obtained in this way is that it has to be paid for by a certain proportion of waste products. Disharmony or physical decomposition in the preliving domain, pain among the living, sin in the domain of freedom. There is no order in the process of formation which, at all degrees, does not imply some disorder." [36] Teilhard insists that this understanding does not confer on evil an ontological status. And in an Aristotelian-Thomistic sense he is right. For there can be no ontological being which is a principle of evil, e.g., Manicheanism. But in the process approach, where the philosophical method implies generalizing from phenomenological descriptions, to say that some degree of disorder is always present in the process or formation is at least to give evil an ontological status as a *condition* of evolutionary reality.

The process approaches of Whitehead and Teilhard open the way for an understanding of man's participation in the life of God that makes him more available to man, it seems to me, than the traditional interpretations of sharing in God's life—I am tempted to say a more real sharing in divine life. Whatever in the universe touches me and is touched by me is my Body, that is, is really me. God's life in regard to creation is his impulse, communicated to every entity, that it realize its best self, that nothing be lost which is saveable, that the world's wounds be bound. That creative "work" *is* God's life, for the process *is* the reality (albeit, that the temporal process of any event is not exhaustively the reality of God). By participating in creative event, I can make occasions of God's life be occasions of my own life. And by adding consciousness to what I am doing, that participation becomes a personal sharing, a merging of my life with his. Teilhard writes:

> To begin with, in action I adhere to the creative power of God; I coincide with it; I become not only its instrument but its living extension. And as there is nothing more personal in a being than his will, I merge myself, in a sense, through my heart, with the very heart of God.

This commerce is continuous because I am always acting; and at the same time I can never set a boundary to
the perfection of my fidelity nor to the fervour of my
intention, this commerce enables me to liken myself,
ever more strictly and indefinitely, to God.[37]

There is a striking resemblance to the thought of Whitehead,
as Lucien Price reports his words from conversation:

God is *in* the world, or nowhere, creating continually
in us and around us. This creative principle is everywhere, in animate and so-called inanimate matter, in the
ether, water, earth, human hearts. But this creation is a
continuing process, and "the process is itself the actuality," since no sooner do you arrive than you start on a
fresh journey. In so far as man partakes of this creative
process does he partake of the divine. . . . His true
destiny as co-creator in the universe is his dignity and
his grandeur.[38]

There is perhaps a temptation to see this way of participating
in the life of God as merely mediated and indirect, as com-
pared with the "directness" of interpersonal relationships. But
if it's true that every experience of God is also an experience
of something else at the same time (and I believe that is true),
it is equally true that every experience of another person is
also an experience of something else at the same time. Our
inner selves express and manifest themselves in event, in the
various adventures which are our reality. We are always
within a setting, a milieu. While another may experience me
and may focus upon me, there is no way to catch me without
a setting. Further, we share in each other's lives as we learn
"what matters" to one another, and then make the "it matters"
of another into the stuff of our own lives. Empirically, we do

not "see" God as we see another person because, obviously, there is not a similar physical matter-body to operate upon with the sense of sight. Yet there are shared events with other persons that do not necessarily require mutual physical presence in the sense of "there" to be seen. It is enough that the "it matters" of one person become the "it matters" of another, who makes that be an event of his life because he knows that "it matters" to the other. All our sharing is where we make our individual "it matters" touch together. That is how we really share in each other's lives. And we participate thus in the life of God too.

Teilhard wanted a system of thought so unified that it would capture the unity of the Real. However, the continued use of "supernatural" in Teilhard's thought, even with his sporadic attempts to do something with it, is perhaps the closest thing to a seam in the seamless garment it was his ambition to weave. As I have indicated already, I think a big part of the reason is that in the wake of Modernism and its immanentist heresy, the "supernatural" became a theological untouchable. Instinctively and sometimes consciously, Teilhard had to walk lightly (cf., his repudiation at different points of Pelagianism, pantheism, immanentism, etc.). A second reason is that he had not worked out the full philosophical systematique that he would have needed to handle the intricacies of the "problem." As I indicated in the opening chapter in the discussion of Pelagianism, the early Christian theologies of the supernatural were elaborated with categories from the Greek world view, where the category of "nature" was very clearly defined and delimited. What a thing could do was determined by what a thing is: *agere sequitur esse*. Such an understanding of the "regular-what" of a thing determines what would have to be considered a "super-what," i.e., that which transcends the "regular-what." The same question looks very different when pitched in process modes of thought. For *every* entity is open to the appearance of something very new in its constitution. Not only is every entity open to transcending what it already is, there is in reality the impulse toward such transcendence. The theology-of-hope school speaks often about the *novum,* and reality is always open to the *novum.* Evolution is a long history of the appearances of really *new things,* of *novelty* not pre-contained in the immediately preceding causes, for the structure of possibility is there to be tapped as well as the structure of actuality. Since nature is not a fixed given in process modes of thought, there is *always* the possibility of transcending any given condition by extending it to include in its becoming what was not previously part of the becoming. There is the always-possibility of a *novum,* of extension into some real newness. The *novum,* it seems to me, is the category under which the supernatural must be situated in process modes of thought—although that makes the terminology obsolete (both super- and -nature). As Teilhard says, "grace does not force a man to enter another universe; it introduces him to an extension of our own universe." [39] It is in similar terms that he describes the faith experience (in his words, the "spiritualization which the 'true religion' represents"):

> Yet, precisely because this continual upward shifting of the limits of our possibilities seems to me to constitute an unbroken continuation of a natural property of evolution, I can no longer see it characterized by a break, amounting to the seamless veil of phenomena.[40]

What we have called "supernatural" does indeed represent an upward shift in the limits of our potentialities; the big difference is that reality is always open to such an upward shift, whereas in Greek modes of thought, nature did not allow such an upward shift. Nature had *to be* elevated to a new possibility, something it could not do for itself. The process approach does not destroy the gratuity of the supernatural; it

redefines and relocates it. Ultimately, the structure of all possibility is rooted in the primordial nature of God, in the
Whiteheadian analysis. But that structure is available, as it
were, from its constant, seething presence below the surface
of the real. And nothing is possible to any entity which God
has not primordially envisioned as possible and made available through the structure of possibility. "Whatever may be
the precise positive content of the term 'supernatural,' it cannot mean anything except supremely 'real,' in other words,
'supremely in conformity' with the conditions of reality which
nature imposes on beings." [41] As we shall see shortly in Teilhard's Christology, he endeavors to understand the Incarna-
tion-Redemption as "supernatural" within the understanding
of the term just suggested.

It seems to me, then, that "novel advance" is the critical
process category for explicating what has traditionally been
called "supernatural," and that elaborating upon the *novum*
of Christianity is the route to go in order to answer one of the
principal questions that motivated Teilhard throughout his
works:

> How exactly is the divine power to put the universe to-
> gether in such a way that it may be possible for an in-
> carnation to be *biologically* effected in it? [42]

The emphasis in the question I added, for I think that "biologically" makes the gist of the question clear: can we speak of
the Jesus-event in a way that does not break the seamless veil
of phenomena? Very shortly I shall return to that question in
considering Teilhard's Christology.

It is too bad—although it leaves us some sturdy homework
—that Whitehead and Teilhard were not mutually familiar
with each other's thought. I think the interplay between them
urges out some implications from their respective systems.

Their fundamental visions are so very close: the primary categories of one-unity, many-plurality, creativity-energy; the dipolar functions of energy, i.e., physical-tangential and conceptual-radial; the passion for a one-world rendering of all reality; the presence of God on the inside of on-going creativity, in a way that both makes reality possible yet leaves history radically free to work itself out; a teleological approach to evolution, expressed causally by Whitehead through "subjective aim" and aspects of his philosophy of forms (eternal objects, the structure of possibility), and by Teilhard in the inexorable workings of the Law of Complexity-Consciousness.

There are, of course, important differences between the two. Teilhard's strong faith commitment was always present to his scientific undertakings, and it is not always clear where the one leaves off and the other takes over. It would miss Teilhard almost entirely not to mention the fundamental role of faith in his life and work. He was keenly aware of the risk involved in the positions he took and of the uncertainty. Five years before his death he wrote: "Today I encounter still the risks to which he is exposed who finds himself compelled by inner constraint to leave the well beaten track of a certain traditional type of asceticism not fully human, in order to search out a way to heaven along which the whole dynamism of matter and flesh can pass by way of synthesis into the birth of spirit." [43] And only a month before his death, he reminded himself once more that his Omega remained "by nature an assumption and a conjecture." [44] One of the most poignant expressions of his faith comes in the final passages of *How I Believe:*

Certain though I am—and ever more certain—that I must press on in life as though Christ awaited me at the term of the universe, at the same time I feel no special

assurance of the existence of Christ. Believing is not seeing. As much as anyone, I imagine, I walk in the shad-
ows of faith.[45]

There is in Teilhard, to be sure, a very strong optimism.
Perhaps "hope" would be more accurate. In any event, it
wasn't a smug optimism. And he did not come by it easily.
Apart from his strictly scientific work, he never got a hearing
during his lifetime. And when he was honored by an offer
of one of the most prestigious academic posts in France, his
superiors did not allow him to accept it. If he does not lose
hope (and he does not), the pain and the chagrin sometimes
show through. For example:

In a kind of way I no longer have confidence in the ex-
terior manifestations of the Church. I believe that
through it the divine influence will continue to reach me,
but I no longer have much belief in the immediate and
tangible value of official directions and decisions. Some
people feel happy in the visible Church; but for my own
part I think I shall be happy to die in order to be free
of it—and to find our Lord outside of it.[46]

Teilhard was encouraged by several of his close friends and
trusted advisors to try to get *The Phenomenon of Man* published. This was his life work, the vision that he had labored
at for most of the previous twenty years. Disappointment over
the failure to get the work published must certainly be part
of Teilhard's depression referred to in the following excerpt
from a letter of Pierre LeRoy, a fellow Jesuit and friend, to
Max and Simone Bégouën (mutual friends of LeRoy and
Teilhard):

He bore with patience, it is true, trials that might well
have proved too much for the strongest of us, but how

often in intimate conversation have I found him depressed and with almost no heart to carry on. The agonizing distress he already had to face in 1939 was intensified in the following years, and sometimes he felt that he could venture no further. During that period he was at times prostrated by fits of weeping, and he appeared to be on the verge of despair. But calling on all the resources of his will, he abandoned himself to the supremely Great, to his Christ, as the only purpose of his being; and so hid his suffering and took up his work again . . ." [47]

In a life like Teilhard's, where scientific-consciousness and Catholic-priest-consciousness and Christian-consciousness so flow together, it is hardly possible to assess and weigh his Faith as a formative factor of his synthesis. Perhaps it is enough to know that it weighs heavy. While Whitehead did not operate with that kind of specific faith commitment, he still insisted that "religion . . . brings its own contribution of immediate experience," [48] and "it contributes its own independent evidence, which metaphysics must take account of in framing its descriptions." [49] "Philosophy may not neglect the multifariousness of the world—the fairies dance, and Christ is nailed to the cross." [50]

THE CHRISTOLOGY OF TEILHARD

There has been much excellent scholarship dealing with the Christology of Teilhard, especially Christopher Mooney's *Teilhard de Chardin and the Mystery of Christ*. It would be redundant, therefore, simply to re-present still once more the general lines of that Christology. My purpose here in dealing with the topic is to commend Teilhard's Christology to process undertakings. And that for two reasons: first, as I have indicated, the basic vision of Teilhard is a deeply process one, with the Law of Complexity-Consciousness as the central dynamic. And that central dynamic of Teilhard's understanding of how reality works is also the central dynamic explanatory of Jesus Christ and his relevance, or necessity even, to the workings of reality. The second reason for dealing with Teilhard's Christology here is his serious attempt to fit it within a one-world rendering, to understand Jesus, as it were, coming from the "inside out" and not from the "outside in." In this he is only *part*ially successful, but that part is strategic for process theology. A Christology must somehow deal with Jesus, the Christ, *vis-à-vis* man; and Jesus, the Christ, *vis-à vis* God. In terms of fidelity to a one-world or seamless garment understanding of Jesus, the successful part of Teilhard's Christology is his presentation of Jesus *vis-à-vis* man and creation. In his dealings with the "divinity" of Jesus, there is no systematic treatment. In this regard, he often reflects many of the Chalcedon-influenced traditional interpretations. And that has many elements of two-world understandings which neither the secular mind nor a thoroughgoing process interpretation is willing to do business with. If one grants that the Teilhardian synthesis bears a striking resemblance to that of Whitehead, then it might well be that the pressure of Whitehead's philosophical coherence on Teilhard's Christology would draw out some implications that would add consistency (though Teilhard, again with the pressure of the Modernist panic close to him, would perhaps have shied away from the implications). Conversely, it is interesting to muse what Whitehead would have done with Teilhard's Omega projection. In any event, the point of interest is Teilhard's understanding of Christ *vis-à-vis* man and creation. He simply did not grapple with the other problem. That's not where his motivating question was. Let us allow Teilhard to once again state his own question, and then move from there:

How exactly is the divine power to put the universe together in such a way that it may be possible for an incarnation to be biologically effected in it? That is what matters to me, and that is what I have tried to understand.[51]

The world is atomic in character, that is, it is particulate or granular. The becoming of the world is through that energy which over and over again arranges and re-arranges the granules. There is a configuration to all that arranging and re-arranging. The configuration is that more and more complex syntheses emerge. Those complex syntheses often display a very organic structure; there is much more interplay and mutual interdependence. The "parts" of an animal need each other more than the billions of granules of a mountain need each other. In those units marked by organic interplay and mutual interdependence, the life levels reveal degrees of centeredness. Human life and consciousness is the high point of such centeredness in creation, as far as we know. All of the stuff of reality has a Within and a Without. We have often identified the Within as spirit and the Without as matter. But that is too dichotomous. "The determinisms of matter are no more than the remnants of spirit's period of bondage." [52] Disunity of the granules of reality is what keeps the spirit in bondage. Certain highly organic and complex arrangements of matter are necessary for the spirit to break bondage. The "Withouts" have to get together effectively to enable the "Withins" to get together effectively. The Withins are the centers of all grains of matter, but they are not identifiable or effectively functional until a certain degree of coalescence when a large centeredness has been effected. The dynamic that urges the higher forms of togetherness, which in their turn touch off the presence of Spirit, is the Law of Complexification-Consciousness.

That Law first of all conspired to produce life forms. The earth, once lifeless, one day found its surface teeming with life. This envelope of life Teilhard calls the biosphere. The

Law, still at work within the biosphere, finally succeeds in seeing the emergence of human life and consciousness: the appearance of Mind. The earth, once without man upon it, now finds its surface teeming with Mind. That envelope of Mind Teilhard calls the Noosphere (*Noos* is the Greek word for Mind). History, since the development of the Noosphere, is marked by a more and more assertive presence of Mind and by a developing sense of the Personal. That, for the most part, is an attempt to describe reality as well as we know it at present. And at this point begins the Teilhardian extrapolation and projection.

Grains of matter, operating as the Laws describe, yield Centers which are, in their turn, grains of Spirit. They too should organize themselves more and more effectively into a system of centers out of which should emerge a new Center, some sort of super-Center, and also a new peak in the presence of the Personal. That super-Center, which Teilhard sees as the logical requirement of the Law's operation, is what he calls the *Omega*.

> By its structure Omega, in its ultimate principle, can only be a *distinct Centre radiating at the core of a system of centres;* a grouping in which personalisation of the All and personalisations of the elements reach their maximum, simultaneously and without merging, under the influence of supremely autonomous focus of union. That is the only picture which emerges when we try to apply the notion of collectivity with remorseless logic to a granular whole of thoughts.[53]

"Evolution is an ascent towards consciousness. . . . Therefore it should culminate in some sort of supreme consciousness."[54] "Because it contains and engenders consciousness, space-time is necessarily *of a convergent nature*. Accordingly its enormous layers, followed in the right direction, must somewhere ahead become involuted to a Point which we might call *Omega,* which fuses and consumes them integrally into itself." [55] In Teilhard's understanding, the very nature of reality is such that it must move inexorably toward that Omega point. For that, there is needed a distinct Center around which a system of all other centers may take shape. At this point Christian revelation confirms, for Teilhard, the conclusions which "remorseless logic" had already urged upon him. More than anything else, Christian revelation is, for him, the Christ of the Epistles, especially those passages which affirm a cosmic significance of Christ, and which give him a unifying role.

The unifying role of Christ, which is how things have been since the beginning (i.e., how reality works), is attested to explicitly in Ephesians: [56]

> He has let us know the mystery of his purpose, the hidden plan he so kindly made in Christ from the beginning to act upon when the times had run their course to the end: that he would bring everything together under Christ, as head, everything in the heavens and everything on earth (Eph. 1:9-10).

Similarly in Colossians:

> Before anything was created, he existed, and he holds all things in unity. Now the Church is his body, and he is its head (Col. 1:17-18).

> In him you too find your own fulfilment, in the one who is head of every Sovereignty and Power (Col. 2:9b).

The Christology of 1 Cor. 15 is in a similar vein, that the role of the Christ is to gather all creation together under him, and then turn that whole Body over to God, so that God may be all in all.

It is clear to Teilhard theoretically that for evolution to pursue its natural course, in other words, to be true to itself, it must have an Omega or Center. It is also clear to him from revelation that the Christic function of Jesus is to be such a Center. "Christ is perfectly comparable to the Omega Point which our theory made us anticipate (provided that he is disclosed in the full realism of his Incarnation), and he tends to produce exactly the spiritual totalization we were waiting for. . . . Without him the human sense and everything it hopes to achieve can only miscarry." [57] He writes that even as a paleontologist he believes that the vast movement of evolution, which nothing can stop, can achieve its consummation only in becoming Christianized.[58]

There are several meanings of Omega in Teilhard, and sometimes there is confusion when he does not indicate the precise meaning he has in mind. Omega, in one sense, means the Center that evolution needs if it is to move along in its natural direction, as all the grains of Spirit arrange themselves according to the Law of Complexification-Consciousness. Omega sometimes means Christ in his function as that Center. And at other times, Omega indicates the final state that is achieved in the unity of Christ and creation. These three senses are, of course, all inter-related.

Evolution needs an Omega point, a unifying Center, for its grains of spirit. That Center is offered to creation in Christ. That means also, therefore, that the meaning of Christ needs the fact of evolution which develops along the lines that it does pursue. "By disclosing a world-peak, evolution makes Christ possible, just as Christ, by giving meaning and direction to the world, makes evolution possible." [59]

Christ has a cosmic function in making evolution possible. The Law of Complexification-Consciousness applies throughout reality. ("From the beginning till now the entire creation, as we know, has been groaning in one great act of giving birth"—Rom. 8:22.) The conditions for life, at least in the forms with which we are familiar, are so narrow and special that it is not easy for life to break through. On the planet earth those highly specialized conditions have been met and creation has succeeded in breaking through to life. Earth is sort of the front edge of creation's breakthrough, and all creation is succeeding in the success upon earth. (Creation may be succeeding other places too—Teilhard does not rule that out. But it is something of which, at present, we know nothing.) Christ, because evolution needs him, has a cosmic function, therefore, in making it possible for the front edge of reality to continue to cut into the future. "Either nature is closed to our demands for futurity, in which case thought, the fruit of millions of years of effort, is stifled, still-born in a self-abortive and absurd universe. Or else an opening exists —that of a super-soul above our souls . . ." [60] Christianity is, therefore, "the most realistic and at the same time the most *cosmic* of beliefs and hopes." [61]

Those aspects of the Teilhardian Christology so far dealt with commend it readily to the processive theological enterprise. There are other aspects, as I have indicated before, that still bespeak some of the traditional super-naturalism; and that, notwithstanding Teilhard's avowal that grace doesn't mean crossing into some other world of reality, and that supernatural means preeminently real, which includes the natural disposition always to be open to expanded possibilities that transcend the present. Though I recognize some ambiguity as to the achievement of a one-world rendering of things, it is my judgment that the full coherence we might like to see there was hampered in the first place by Teilhard not having a coherent metaphysics to support him, and his work is shot through with philosophical implications; in the second place, there were the orthodoxy-fears (if not, at some point, orthodoxy-paranoia) that continually exercised theological constraint; and thirdly, there was the simple fact that it was Christ-and-man that arrested Teilhard's attention and was the arena of his creative impulse, and not Christ-and-God. I make these observations so as not to impose a one-world coherence upon Teilhard that is not perhaps there. But my interest is in those aspects of Teilhard's Christology that are rather more susceptible to process theology. And those are the aspects that I will continue to deal with here.

The "new things" that were successively the front edge of evolutionary movement were life in plant forms, then simple to greatly complex animal forms, then human life with its great organic complexity, but with mind or spirit. The main axis of evolutionary development, where the present front edge is to be found, is in mind and spirit. That is where the Law of Complexification-Consciousness now pressures reality to move forward. Christ has come to history out of history to be the Omega evolution needs to move forward. That is why Teilhard can see Christianity as the main axis of evolutionary movement. The point I want to make here is that an important part of Teilhard's Christology consists in understanding Christ and the Church in terms of the category of *Novum:* something really new happening to man. And that real newness depends upon man's decision to let Christ be his Center. The Church then is the locus of human decision-making that lets Christ give history the Centering it must have to respond to its "supernatural calling," and this in the Teilhardian sense of being most real and true to self, which is to expand man's possibilities of being One out of love.

That "one" is to mark a new presence in Reality, a new structure of existence, to use Cobb's fine phrase. The new being is an All—a system of centers united in and through and with a super-Center, Christ. That "All" is not just a collection, but an All with Personal unity: a new structure of Personal existence resulting from the living-out of the Law of Complexification-Consciousness. And Teilhard is quick to point out that the super-personal All does not absorb the individual personalities of the myriad of centers that make it up (that would rather be how an Eastern mind would think it). He uses the analogy of lovers who are most in possession of themselves at that very moment when they are ecstatically lost in each other. "In truth, does not love every instant achieve all around us, in the couple or the team, the magic feat, the feat reputed to be contradictory, of 'personalising' by totalising?" [62]

Teilhard has called the Redeeming Incarnation "a prodigious biological operation." [63] It was necessary that Jesus come from the inside out, therefore. It was necessary for him to have "sprung up as man among men . . . and then, from this point of vantage in the heart of matter, assuming the control and leadership of what we now call evolution." [64] And that is what gives Christ his meaning and his importance to us. It is what makes him be the Christ. "It is, then, in this physical pole of universal evolution that we must, in my view, locate and recognize the plentitude of Christ. For *in no other type of cosmos,* and *in no other place,* can any being, *no matter how divine he be,* carry out the function of universal consolidation and universal animation which Christian dogma attributes to Christ." [65] Teilhard will speak of the supernatural plentitude of Christ. But it must be taken again with the meaning he attaches: "the supernatural is continually being formed by a new creation of the natural." [66] "Cosmogenesis, moving in its totality through anthropogenesis, ultimately shows itself to be a Christogenesis." [67]

In keeping with this context, it is consistent to look upon Christianity as a phylum, that is, a new development at the front edge of anthropogenesis. "Considered objectively as a phenomenon, the Christian movement . . . exhibits the characteristics of a *phylum.* Reset in an evolution interpreted as an ascent of consciousness, this phylum, in its trend towards a synthesis based on love, progresses precisely in the direction presumed for the leading-shoot of biogenesis." [68] Teilhard insists, in *The Phenomenon of Man,* that man is unique in his moving out everywhere upon the face of the earth without branching off. He maintains his phyletic unity, so that when there is a movement forward, the front edge, as it were, grabs the rest and pulls it along. In a sense (something which he is now experiencing historically), man cannot have separate destinies. Historically now we are of a piece. We are *a* people. Our salvation comes to us together. And the main axis of man's spiritualization is Christianity.[69]

In the context of Christianity or Church, or perhaps best of all, in the image of the Mystical Body of Christ, let us recall Teilhard's description of "body," by which he means "my reality":

> My own body is not these cells that belong *exclusively* to me: it is *what,* in these cells *and* in the rest of the world feels my influence and reacts against me.[70]

We become Christ's body, we become *his reality,* in our acceptance of his influence upon our lives, that is, in our letting his reality be a constituent of our own becoming. And by the same token, he becomes our reality, just as we become his. Those are meant to be metaphysical statements about the *real* presence of Christ and us in each other's reality.

Teilhard's reflections on "body" are from a letter which he wrote to Père Valensin (in September, 1919) who in turn forwarded it to Blondel. It is quite possibly that text which Blondel had in mind when he wrote:

> We are literally made out of one another without ceasing to be our individual personalities. The problem of the Incarnation appears to me (perhaps even antecedently to every other philosophical question) as the touchstone of a true cosmology, of an integral metaphysics. . . . I

share the ideas and sentiments of Father Teilhard de Chardin in the face of the Christological problem. Before the broader horizons created by science we cannot, without betraying Catholicism, remain satisfied with a limited and feeble Christology, in which Christ appears almost as an accident in history, isolated like a stranger amid the crushing and hostile immensity of the universe.[71]

It is my conviction, to be sure, that a process metaphysics, such as propounded by Alfred North Whitehead, and such as is implied throughout the work of Pierre Teilhard de Chardin, offers the possibility of a Christology and an ecclesiology in which Christ does not come like a "stranger" but rather, is one of our very own and simultaneously God's very own, in a way that does not rupture, at any point, the one-world reality to which the contemporary world broadly and deeply subscribes.

4

CHURCH

A mood . . .

That's God there at the corner, two blocks ahead. The Beckoner. He whistles, and then with a sweeping gesture and a gleam in his eyes beckons me, "C'mon!" I go. I know from the other times he whistled that when I get to his "corner" he'll be whistling a couple of blocks further on, and that it'll be my corner now. It's funny about those corners that become mine. When I'm running ahead to the corner, I know that I am exploring new areas; and that is an adventure—the new areas are usually very rewarding ones to have come upon. Yet while I move through those new areas, I have the strange sense that I hold property deeds along the way—all along the way. My new adventures show me my own surprising estate. Except I don't apparently own all of it. For I run into people who also hold deeds along the way. Once while we were running along together there was some confusion (as there often is)—this time over the deeds. So we examined briefly the deeds to our holdings and found it

155

was a strange sort of surveyor who measured them out. The boundaries turned out to be not boundary lines, but feathered boundary edges that could shift like a water's edge on a sandy shore. That confused us, but made us feel more corporate in our holdings —on the borders of all our holdings we were with each other. That might have generated some real problems. Well, it occasionally did if we forgot the adventure of chasing after the elusive Beckoner who wanted to lead us through our own great estate. When we stopped and got involved along the way with our properties, we'd get impatient with the surveyor who did the feathered edge borders and on our own we'd set ourselves to straightening them out. And was that ever good for a fight or three or four!

However, since so much of our adventure was a "together" one, we found some real advantages in being incorporated in our quest. Of course that didn't solve everything. Sometimes we paid so much attention to the corporation that we forgot the adventure. A corporation is real, but it doesn't have eyes of its own. Each man's pair of eyes and ears was the only way the corporation could see and hear the Beckoner whom our experience had pretty well convinced us really cared well for us in insisting upon our adventure. One had the distinct feeling that his insistence upon our adventure was a pretty exciting adventure of his own.

By and large, in our bumbling way, we found that we could move along better together, though we still had to read the signs ourselves to know how to move on. Often enough the summons up there ahead comes in the dusk and isn't fully clear; or in the fog, when even strong light is diffused and scat-

tered. (Light in a fog has its own kind of loveli-
ness.) Even when the signs are clear, there's some-
thing less than total information. We get general
directions, orientations, suggestions. In the long
run, we must do the major part of the mapping out.
That is exciting, even if perplexing. And there's a
way in which our own mapping out influences the
Beckoner. He always shows himself somewhere up
ahead on our path, but our own work of mapping-
out our adventures greatly determines just where
our path will be (of course, he normally finds our
path without too much trouble). And this is good.

We find over and over again that we are much
better off when we opt to let the Beckoner play a
large role in our lives—not in the sense of having
life presented to us on the proverbial silver platter.
The pioneer's life is more demanding than the set-
tler's. To be a settler is to settle for less. To park on
the avenue is not to know what the hell an avenue
is for: an avenue is a coming enterprise, where
parking meters are really only pausing meters with
time limits, and violations for staying too long in
one place.

To tell the truth, we get unnerved easily by the
thought of not having genuine parking places.
Don't we need to stop? Can we bear up with always
leaving familiar ground and always moving into the
unknown? Don't we have to stop to gather our-
selves together? Well, in a way we find it's more
those thoughts that are unnerving than the facts.
The fact is that if we enlarge our estate by pushing
the front edge into the unknown a bit, that new
front edge is just a small piece of the new added on
to the old familiar estate. (Hardly ever does the
configuration of the territory make it impossible to

see familiar land. Proportionally, there's nearly always more of the familiar than the unfamiliar—it's most unnerving when our peripheral vision doesn't register side glances, or doesn't reach around for a peek at the rear.) And surely we do stop to consolidate ourselves. It's just that stops are the interstices between our journeys-beyond; we don't journey between stops. And that's more than words. The heart muscle keeps on going when the leg muscle pauses. And the heart reconnoiters throughout our dreams in sleep as well as awake.

Lately I have been much better off; that is, we have been much better off. One of our people seems to have an inside track on the Beckoner—like he lives with him as well as with us. He can talk about him like he just came from table with him. (In a good family, table sharing is where you really find out about each other's lives and dreams. As they say these days, it's a great "plugging in" experience.) Our Fellow (can we call him that) is quite aware of his own special relationship with the Beckoner—in fact he calls him much more personal names than that. Our Fellow really seems to know which end is up. We have the strong sensation that to follow our Fellow is to be "right on" with the Beckoner. It makes us feel actually a little more personal about the Beckoner, for we never did run fast enough to catch him at the next corner. In fact, someone once said his name ought to be "I will be the one who will be" (which a linguist once mistranslated as "I am who am"). Anyone whose name is Future requires that any companion has to be moving ahead and along to be with him. His name wouldn't be Future if he let any Present totally embrace him—like standing on any one corner long enough to be caught up with. His game of tag is that everyone else is "it." Except for this Fellow who seems to be "it" like us, but he has tagged the Future, and now we are "it" in relation to him. It is difficult to explain this Fellow. Some have said that he used to live with the Beckoner before he came among us. Others have said that he is truly Beckoner and truly Pioneer himself, without confusion. Still others have said that he is the Light, but that he shines with the Beckoner's own light; it's the Beckoner's true light, but it is also truly he (the Fellow) who does the shining. He shines. True light of true light. To be frank, he is a mystery to us. Yet a fact to us—and there is something simply irreducible about a fact: a fact is a fact is a fact, like the well known rose that is a rose is a rose is a rose. All those explanations we've put together about the Fellow are our attempts to understand him—each attempt says something, no attempt manages to say it all (no fact is susceptible to having "all" said about it). Even though "our" facts can't get hold of this Fellow by the ears, it's the kind of life he puts together and asks us to put together that makes sense out of him. Ultimately, it makes sense to be one with him, to pick his brain till we put on his mind. And being at table with him is about the best way any of us have found to pick his mind (and of course, it really puts us together at the same time). Sometimes when he can't be there, we still do the table thing in his name; and he still works on our sensitivities, still has a hold on what we do and are. Well if that isn't being "present" I don't know what is. (He has other ways of being present like that too, even if his physical matter doesn't turn up.)

We really feel full of hope at having this Fellow with us. We've incorporated, in fact. And while life is as fraught as it ever was with problems, there is a certain confidence we have now as we move into the Future, knowing that only in movement-into-a-Future are we true to ourselves, true to how reality goes in its heart, true to the Fellow and in the self-same fidelity true to the Beckoner whom the Fellow says to call Father. And believe me, life stays a high adventure.

In the early part of his book, *The Quest of the Historical Jesus*, Albert Schweitzer remarks that if you want to know what a man is like, get him to write a life of Jesus. You may not in the long run know much about Jesus, but you will know a lot about the man. That is most of all true for the Christian who has let himself be grasped by the Jesus-event. That event is so important, so large, that its understanding cannot but reflect how the Christian understands himself and his entire world. The fundamental categories with which we approach the living-out of our lives are going to be the hermeneutic for our interpretation of existence, its problems and challenges and rich rewards.

That is why it makes sense once again to undertake a discussion of God and Jesus Christ, of Church and Sacrament: for there are many today who live and think and experience out of a self-understanding and a world-understanding that have not previously been a theological and spiritual hermeneutic. So there is a new task. There is more at stake than that one world view follows upon another. That is true, but we also believe that our knowledge and insights accumulate; there is *new* knowledge, there are *new* insights. And for that matter there are new realities. But that is already a process conviction. There are new errors too; and our intuitions get tricked. There has been no roadbed of any march that hasn't had the "litter" of our groping ways. Yet we do, for the most part, feel that we see reality better from better vantage points. We expect our doctors to keep up with the medical journals. Theologians must also keep abreast. We should and do feel dis-ease with God-talk that makes God a stranger. My purpose in discussing the secularization of contemporary experience in the first chapter is to suggest how God must come off if he is not to be a stranger. How God comes off—that is, how *we* understand it—is greatly determinative of how Jesus comes off, for God is available through and in him. How the Church comes off will equally be greatly influenced by our understanding of Jesus, for the Church arises out of human responses to what Jesus is about.

There is always a risk in the theological enterprise. The risk is that it is easy to shape God and Jesus to our own image and likeness. The risk comes in the possibility of forging images that do violence to the realities they attempt to express. But on the other hand, there are no understandings of anything that are not mediated by the words and symbols we use; they are all we have. The risk seems less risky to the extent that theologians engage in their enterprise as a theological community where dialogue, critique, affirmation and challenge are the order of the day. It is equally healthy to reckon with the critique of those who may stand outside a faith commitment; for example, the Marxist critique of religion has had some very positive effects in pressures that its presence generates upon the Church to be more attentive to "this worldly" cries and aspirations.

The People of God, the Church, are bound to be colored in their self-understanding by their understanding of the God whose people they are. To a people whose theologians are presenting a picture of God as understood through the categories of Greek-influenced philosophy, God must be unchanging in all ways. The Church, his People, would carry the configuration of God, as communicated to it through

Jesus, its Founder. The following excerpt is from the first draft of *The Dogmatic Constitution on the Church of Christ,* prepared for the First Vatican Council:

> We declare, moreover, that whether one considers its existence or its constitution, the Church of Christ is an everlasting and indefectible society, and that, after it, no more complete nor more perfect economy of salvation is to be hoped for in this world. For, to the very end of the world pilgrims of this earth are to be saved through Christ. Consequently, his Church, the only society of salvation, will last until the end of the world ever unchangeable and unchanged in its constitution. . . . It is free and immune from every danger of error and untruth.[1]

In the Whiteheadian understanding of God (and that of modern sensitivities, generally), God, like all reality, is himself "becoming" (not becoming God, but God becoming). His becoming is linked with the world's becoming—he offers the world its possibilities of always becoming more than it is, the perpetual possibility for self-transcendence along with all the risk that moving "beyond" and into newness entails. Nor is God's offer of newness to the world merely a neutral offer—he lures and invites: he wants us to move beyond and forward, and he facilitates our transcendence by the structure of possibility through which new values are presented to us:

> He is that element in life in virtue of which judgment stretches beyond facts of existence to values of existence.

> He is the lure for feeling, the eternal urge of desire.

> God in the world is the perpetual vision of the road which leads to the deeper realities.[2]

That is Whitehead's understanding of God. For him, "religion is the reaction of human nature to its search for God." [3] Consequently, religion looks much like the God it worships, the God who is always calling man forth to be more.

> The power of God is the worship He inspires. That religion is strong which in its ritual and its modes of thought evokes an apprehension of the commanding vision. The worship of God is not a rule of safety—it is an adventure of the spirit, a flight after the unattainable. The death of religion comes with the repression of the high hope of adventure. [4]

Jesus, the Christ of God, came "to make all things new." He promised salvation, which is a form of safety, i.e., a history which is safe enough for man to become man before God. It is the spirit of man that is offered safety in salvation history. But Jesus never offered safety, as the world understands safety:

> Men will seize you and persecute you; they will hand you over to the synagogues and to imprisonment, and bring you before kings and governors because of my name . . . you will be betrayed even by parents and brothers, relations and friends; and some of you will be put to death. You will be hated by all men on account of my name, but not a hair of your head will be lost. Your endurance will win you your lives. [5]

Yet here and elsewhere in the Jesus of the Gospels, there is the promise of life: in abundance and to the full.

There are some general orientations of the Whiteheadian synthesis that it might be well to look at in reference to an understanding of Church, before making specific use of some of the categories.

Whitehead gives us a metaphysics of the individual-in-community, which should almost be one word, so intimate and inextricable are individual and community: reality is essentially social. Yet if we *had* to weight one a little more than the other, it would be in behalf of the individual. Actual entities are all that there is. A good example of that weighting is in Whitehead's discussion of order.

We are tempted to look upon the orderliness of the universe and feel that some overall order accounts for it. What we recognize as overall order is really a matter of the mutually inter-penetrating patterns of order generated by the order of each actual entity and each society of actual entities. And order in each of those cases stems from the final causality (the subjective aim) of each entity. Reality is an interlocked community of occasions. The interlocking—the overall order—arises from the way in which all the member occasions of a community order themselves to each other: almost like a community of friends which "happens" when a group of people who are brought together gradually establish a network of relationships among themselves. A sociogram, for example, is a way of trying to illustrate the pattern of relationships that obtains within a group. The graph is developed by lines drawn from one entity to another, representative of the modes of relating between the individuals. A line is drawn as some actual line of communication is established among the individuals; a pattern emerges. The general order of the universe emerges. " 'Order' is a mere generic term: there can be only specific 'order,' not merely order in the vague." [6] There is no such thing as an individual-not-in-community. Community and individual are fundamental. Yet there remains a certain "primordialness" (not in the sense of God's primordial nature) about the individual: every reason for anything has to do in some way or another with actual entities. That "primordialness" is reflected in some of Whitehead's remarks about religion.

It is clear to Whitehead that religion is a social phenomenon, that it is, in fact, one of the most potent formative forces there is in civilization. Religion is man's search for God. Yet "man," like "order," is a generic term. What makes "man" have meaning is that there are in reality individual men. If there is religion, it is because individual men search for God. At the same time that we say that, we have to utter the other half immediately, that each individual man is a-man-in-community. But "man's" search for God is exercised through the ears and eyes and hearts and desires of individuals. There's no such entity as a "community eye." That particular attention to the individual comes through in Whitehead's oft cited observation that "religion is what the individual does with his solitariness." [7]

> . . . solitariness is discernible as constituting the heart of religious importance. The great religious conceptions which haunt the imagination of civilized mankind are scenes of solitariness: Prometheus chained to his rock, Mahomet brooding in the desert, the meditations of the Buddha, the solitary Man on the Cross. It belongs to the depth of the religious spirit to have felt forsaken even by God.[8]

It would be a serious mistake to understand Whitehead's emphasis upon the individual as psychological individualism. The emphasis is more a matter of the ontological principle, that reasons for things are attributable to actual entities, to them alone, or there are no reasons. That in no way belies the essential social character of reality and of religion for that matter. But the shape of the social order is determined by the patterns of relationships established through the individual members. Social configurations are the result of decisions that have been made; but strictly speaking there is no "group mind." A decision is the business of an individual (albeit influenced by its relationality). Individual members of a society affect each other, but ultimately a decision is the very solitary business of an individual. When Whitehead insists that religion is not *primarily* a social fact, he is not denying that it is nonetheless essentially a social phenomenon. But if human nature searches for God and "finds" him, it is only because individuals have made decisions which set them on the quest, and because the interior spirit of man has made contact:

> Religion is the art and the theory of the internal life of man, so far as it depends on the man himself and on what is permanent in the nature of things.

> This doctrine is the direct negation of the theory that religion is primarily a social fact. Social facts are of great importance to religion, because there is no such thing as an absolutely independent existence. You cannot abstract society from man: most psychology is herd psychology. But all the collective emotions leave untouched the awful, ultimate fact, which is the human being, consciously alone with itself, for its own sake.[9]

To put the matter another way: individuals create society. True, society, in its turn, is creative of the individuals who make it up. But in a primordial way, it is individuals who create society; and the creative reality lies within the individuals whose decisions shape the society. Again, it is true that as a society is formed, it emerges with certain defining characteristics, and in a sense, that societal configuration transcends the individual. The maintenance of a society requires the repeated historical appropriation of its defining characteristics by individual members. Their process of appropriation constitutes the reality of the society. Yet even in this regard there is a basic responsibility that lies within the interior spirit of the individual, an irreducible dependency upon the decision of the individual. In the final analysis, society exists for the individual members, and not the members for society—though no member exists without it. That seems to me to be the basic import of Jesus' insistence that "The sabbath was made for man, not man for the sabbath" (Mk. 2:27). That does not denigrate the importance of the sabbath; it is a strong reminder though of a certain priority. If there is a point in all of this for our reflections upon the Church, it is a similar reminder of that same strong priority. Jesus had a following of which he was clearly conscious, and which he affirmed. It was a society. It was for those who were in it, and not vice versa. It was there, rather, to serve and to give; the acceptance of the service and the gift in its turn often required serving and giving. But the priority was and is clear.

Christianity has never been a private religion. It is essentially social, that is, societal. "Church," in fact, means "an assemblage." But it has not always been so clear that the society has fundamentally ministered to the members, and that members have *ministered to each other in society* rather than that they have *ministered to society*. Of course, that is not merely a Church problem; it is a human problem. Society always has the tendency to take on the priority we have been withholding from it in this discussion. It forgets that its power and authority do not originate in itself, as Jesus had to remind Pilate.

Whitehead's insistence upon solitariness at the heart of religious experience is certainly not a position of narrowness, as it would be if the import of it all were some kind of individualism. God is in the world, or nowhere, Whitehead holds. Nor is he spottily there; he is there and available in the world in its totality. Through his primordial nature he touches each event at the very inception of its self-creativity; his consequent nature receives the world into his own experience.

Created events are all occasions of God's experience, of his life. Man participates in God's life through his participation in creation. Deeper participation requires increasingly deeper abilities to "feel with" the world, to know where it is going and to share in the creation and affirmation of its movement. Wide sympathies with all the universe are at the heart of the religious experience. In a sense, it is in the very universality of concern that the sense of solitariness originates. "The reason of the connection between universality and solitariness is that universality is a disconnection from the immediate surroundings." [10] In fact, so essential is the world to an individual that he cannot find or attain his value until his own quest is situated within the larger movement of creation:

> In its solitariness, the spirit asks, What, in the way of value, is the attainment of life? And it can find no such value till it has merged its individual claim with that of the objective universe. Religion is world loyalty.
>
> The spirit at once surrenders itself to this universal claim and appropriates it for itself.[11]

The universal claim is present to Christianity through the summons to love all men so that "all may be one." Or even more startlingly (though the statement is so commonplace that we often lose the radical sense of it), there is the redefinition of neighbor, who is close not because of physical proximity but because he has a need to which I might respond, or I have a need to which he might respond. Wherever in creation there is a situation where "it matters" very much that something be done and there is the possibility that I may do that something, there is where my neighbors are. By the same token, my own needs put me, as it were, in Everyman's backyard. "Neighborhood" is wherever in the world something "matters" deeply. "Religion," to repeat Whitehead, "is

world loyalty." But it is in the solitariness of my own irreducible self-hood where I make, or do not make, the decision to exercise responsibility as co-creator with God.

Two issues arise from Whitehead's metaphysic of individual-in-community to which I have called attention. The first,
which is more of a matter of overall orientation rather than
of specific structure when thinking of the Church, is the
special emphasis placed upon the individual. The human
decisions which create process and shape history are decisions
of individuals. Society has no mind of its own—there are only
the minds of its individual members. It is, therefore, in the
interior assent of the individual that society itself is created.
That is equally true of the Church. The Church is created by
the responses of individual persons to the Jesus-event. There
are objective matters of fact about the Jesus-event, of course,
which shape our possibilities of prehending it as constitutive
of our own reality. And the fact that responding to the event
has demanded from the outset—and by the nature of the
event—a societal response also shapes how individual members make their commitment to the Jesus-event. Granted those
considerations as entering into the defining characteristics of
the societal response to Jesus that we call Church, in an
irreducible way the decisions of individuals are responsible for there being a process of an on-going appropriation of
the Jesus-event. In that context, the Sacramental system of the
Church is in the service of the interior life of individual
Christians, for it is through their decisions that a society of
responding Christians is created. Yet because we have a metaphysic of the individual-in-community, it is equally true that
the Sacramental system is in large measure creative of the
societal response, and that the Sacraments are as essentially
public as they are private; they are the domain of all the
community because through the lives they touch they create
the community. *The process is the reality*.

A second orientation that derives from the individual-in-community metaphysic is that "-in-community," that is, "in-the-world-or-nowhere," is where one can participate in the life of God. God participates in the creativity of *every* event, urging every event to the best possible achievement. Every event holds out to the individual the possibility of taking part, therefore, in God's business. This situates religious experience essentially within the field of action. This is what some have called the "cybernetic model" of religious experience. The field-of-action understanding of religious experience of a process world view is much closer to the Jewish understanding of God than to the ethicizing tendencies of liberal Protestant Christianity, which also is action oriented. The process world view understands that through action one can *really* participate in the occasions of God's own life; and that is a different slant than seeing fidelity to the Christian calling in terms of ethical "oughts" demanded by the New Testament prescriptions of love. I think that Harnack had a good insight when he suggested that the Greek Orthodox Church, the Roman Catholic Church and Protestant Christianity might best be understood not in terms of schism and reform, but as modes of appropriating the Jesus-event through different cultural experiences. The distinctions were perhaps demanded because of the inability to assess, at that time, the historically conditioned and relative way that each approach worked out its way of being Christian. In the Greek experience, man's self-perception has intellect in a central place, with other perceptions arranged around that one. The Greek approach to Christianity is manifest in the many early (and late, for that matter) religious furors over statements of belief, credal and dogmatic formulations. It would be hard to imagine Jewish culture handling the situation that way. The contemplative element is strong in the Greek approach also: the satisfaction that derives from the contemplation of truth and beauty. The Greeks have given us in our religion a taste for mind. One of the major Roman contributions was its system of jurisprudence. It took an immense administrative ability for one city to rule the entire Mediterranean world for so long, and an amazing system of law and justice. The requisite instincts for that undertaking the Romans either had or developed. In any event, the Roman Church has been something of a counterpart in Church administration. Its juridical instincts were to extend beyond the practical administrative work, however, to embrace also the kinds of statements and creeds that were inherited from Greek experience. That particular historical approach rested comfortably enough upon Latin experience. But as Christianity took hold of the Germanic cultures, they needed a more indigenous historical appropriation of Christianity, and they developed one. That, certainly, is not the whole story of the divisions within Christianity; but I think it is a larger part of the picture than has usually been recognized. An interesting and intriguing situation presents itself today: is science becoming a truly universal, i.e., catholic, experience; and if so, will the mind-set that it seems to be generating sooner or later transcend the vast network of cultural differences? One might cite the effects of Japan's acceptance of western science and technology, and the easier rapport between the Japanese and western mind. Whitehead would have been the last to confer upon his process systematization a definitive status. Yet at present it is perhaps the most comprehensive systematization of thought there is which reflects the scientific experience. It urges a world view that is radically One World, and says that God is part of that one world and can be encountered anywhere and everywhere through man's conscious entrance into the world's creativity. Many of those who urge ecumenism today are realizing that it is not in doctrinal dialogic but in shoulders together at a common task of service that they savor their common heritage. If inter-communion is a fact today (and it is, officially or not), those participating are not so much the theological discutants who have worked out mutually acceptable *explanations* of the Eucharist, but those Christians who have been *at work together* and who feel the need to celebrate liturgically the community that has arisen among them in their common task of binding up the wounds of the world, healing it and making it safe. It just may be that the cybernetic model of religion may yet catholicize religious experience in ways mankind has not yet known. Such would certainly reflect Teilhard's Noosphere-toward-Omega. It would also reflect Van Leeuwen's suggestion that possibly Christianity will become more widely available on the coat tails of science and technology, for they generate a world view that is more neutral and more universal than previous historical appropriations of the charism of Christianity. The task is for the Church to work out her own self-understandings in the larger and authentic (as far as she can determine) categories of secular experience. Process modes of thought—and this, of course, is the main persuasion of the present work—open new understandings of man's participation in God's own life, through commitment to sharing in the creation of history, through sharing in the desire of man, alone and together, that each future truly transcend each present. If such a program appears melodramatic, let us be reminded by Ernst Bloch that *"ultimately* it is necessary to *overshoot* the mark in order to reach it."[12]

If one were allowed but a single statement in which to characterize Whitehead's philosophy, it would surely have to be that *process itself is the reality*. Thus too, the Church's becoming is its reality; it is not a receptacle-like some*thing* or some*place* into which one enters. It is an event that one takes up. *Being* a Christian is a result of a constant kind of *experiencing* which makes the Jesus-event play a constituting role in one's own becoming. Church is a society of Christians, that is, of those whose becoming maintains an on-going presence of the Jesus-event. The Church has a powerful interest, therefore, in the dynamics of "Christians becoming," for its life depends upon them. Sacramental life has been one of the major dynamics since the beginning of the Church. Hereafter I will use "Sacrament" with an upper case "S" to indicate specifically that system of Sacraments that we have come to call the seven Sacraments, though they clearly fit into a much larger category of sacrament: there are many sacraments of God's presence in Jesus, who is himself a sacrament of God; the Church itself is sacrament. The Sacraments, i.e., the Sacramental system, are central to the process which is the reality of the Church; they are, in a major way (there are other ways too), creative of that society which the Church is.

If thus far I have generally stressed the importance of the individual in society, I have done so for two reasons: first, there is the fact that in an ultimate way, if a society exists and propagates itself it is through decisions which individuals make, for there is no conceptual pole in a society other than in individuals; and secondly, because there seems to be quite a natural tendency for human societies to forget where they came from and for whom they exist—they exist for man and not man for them. Nationalism, which has been called a form of love that hates, is a case of forgotten priority. Inquisitions, which have made human life subservient to theological formulations, are also examples of priorities gone awry. All of that is a matter of priority, and only that. Reality is essentially social, intrinsically organismic:

There is no entity, not even God, "which requires nothing but itself to exist."

According to the doctrine of this lecture, every entity is in its essence social and requires the society in order to exist.[13]

If religion, generically, is the search of human nature for God, then organized religion, with which the history of man is laced, is but the essentially social character of that search. The Church is such a societal response to man's search for God, a societal response in which the Jesus-event is a central determinative factor. I would now like to look at Whitehead's description of a society, and then try to indicate how in that particular society, the Church, the Sacraments have functioned to continue the Jesus-event as determinative of man's relation to God and to fellow man.

I will first cite fully the text from *Process and Reality* in which Whitehead gives his definition of "society." And then I will take each of the three parts and reflect upon the dynamics of the Church being a society.

A nexus enjoys "social order" where (i) there is a common element of form illustrated in the definiteness of each of its included actual entities, and (ii) this common element of form arises in each member of the nexus by reason of the conditions imposed upon it by its prehension of some other members of the nexus, and (iii) these prehensions impose that condition of reproduction by reason of their inclusion of positive feelings of that common form. Such a nexus is called a "society," and the common form is the "defining characteristic" of the society. The notion of "defining characteristic" is allied to the Aristotelian notion of "substantial form." [14]

Let me simply point out, before continuing, that while the notion of "defining characteristic" is allied to Aristotle's notion of "substantial form," there is a most important difference. "Substantial form," as the expression itself indicates, is a category within substance philosophy, where the form makes something be what it is, and the "what it is" in its turn determines what a particular substance can do: *agere sequitur esse,* and substantial form determines the *esse.* For Whitehead, the "defining characteristic" is the characteristic of an *event,* of an occasion of experience; and since experiencing is the reality, whatever characterizes eventfulness characterizes reality. Thus, in counter distinction to the allied Aristotelian notion: *esse sequitur agere.* And that is more akin to existentialist presuppositions than to Aristotle.

A common element of form in each individual . . .

A first pre-requisite for a nexus to be a society is that all participating members share a common element of form. I do not want to enter into a detailed discussion of the "what" of that form for, as I indicated in the preface, my focus is upon the dynamics that make a society and how Sacramental life is a foremost dynamic of the Church's existence. But this much at least must be said, that Christians share a conviction that the Jesus-event is important to them and to the world. They see certain configurations in the Jesus-event that they want to be configurations of their own lives. When I speak of the conviction that the Jesus-event is important, I am using "important" in a rather specialized Whiteheadian sense. In a looser sense there are non-Christians who see the Jesus-event as important because of the sheer weight of its impact on history, past and present. All philosophies have certain starting points, certain notions which are central. All experience needs some point of view from which to view and assess its manifold data. Such "starting points," or "central notions," or "points of view" which govern interpretation: all of those are "important." Things that are important, in the Whiteheadian sense, give clues to the meaning of the whole. It is in this sense that a Christian is a Christian: the Jesus-event is important to him. To a greater or lesser degree, he interprets his experience in the light of the Jesus-event. In the Jesus-event he finds a clue to the meaning of his existence. In a Christian's own process of becoming, the Jesus-event, if it is truly important, contributes configuration to the pattern of assemblage according to which he puts together the events of his existence. The Jesus-event shapes his becoming and therefore is in some way present in him and part of him. Recognition of the importance of the Jesus-event would, therefore, would be "a common element of form illustrated in the definiteness of each of its included actual entities," as regards the Church.

> *The defining characteristic of a society emerges in an individual through certain conditions imposed upon him in his prehension of those who are already members of the society . . .*

Whitehead is, of course, setting down the requirements of "society" in a much more generic sense than what we mean by "human society." Our focus here is upon human society, specifically the Church; but this more specific meaning is in touch with the larger sense of social order in Whitehead's thought.

I want to call attention to three aspects of this particular requirement, for its bears upon how a new member is initiated into a society, how he keeps on being a member, and how he in his turn, once he is a member, is also an occasion of experience for others, which experience is on-goingly constitutive of the society.

Those individuals who are already members of a society all exhibit the defining characteristic of that society in the "pattern of assemblage" according to which they shape their existence. That defining characteristic is at least partly responsible for each member being what it is. The "what it is" (i.e., the facticity) of any actual fact dictates certain conditions upon any occasion that would make a positive prehension of it—to prehend it as it is, for what it is, means that its "what it is" must be respected in any prehension of it. If some individual makes a positive prehension of a member of a society in any really significant way, that defining characteristic which makes the prehended occasion be what it is (which includes its societal membership) then enters into the becoming of the individual making the prehension. As this happens repeatedly in a network of relationships with members of a society, that defining characteristic then emerges, creating a new member of a society.

Once an individual has become a member of a society, the defining characteristic maintains its hold on him through conditions that continue to be imposed through his prehensions of members of the society. Once he is a member, this includes his prehensions of his own past occasions, for if he affirms his past then he must affirm what made it what it was—and that imposes on him conditions out of which the society's defining characteristic continues its presence as a factor in his becoming.

An individual who has become a member of a society is himself a creative force in that society's life. For just as the defining characteristic emerged as a formative element in his own becoming, through conditions which were imposed in his positive prehensions of members of the society, so now also he is a source of those same imposed conditions when others are postively related to him, and the membership of others in the society is created and enhanced as they prehend him.

What is stressed particularly in this description of a society is not so much the defining characteristic, but the dynamic role of the inter-relating, especially the assertiveness of certain conditions surrounding the prehensive activity, conditions out of which emerges the defining characteristic.

Membership in a society means that an individual has appropriated for himself that defining charac-

teristic which the society has made available to him . . .

Let us recall how Teilhard redefined "self" in his redefinition of Body. The Body (the self) is not the matter that belongs exclusively to a man's soul. Body is not that part of the world that is totally mine. Body is, rather, the totality of the world that has become partially mine. It is what has become mine because I have made it part of my own becoming—I have allowed it a participation in my self-hood. Though Whitehead did not develop that thought at the same length as Teilhard (at least not under that image), he too has affirmed that "the Human Body is that region of the world which is the primary field of human expression." One of the images under which the Church has long been understood is that of "Mystical Body." In a processive world, it is possible to understand Body in that context in a much more literal sense. Whatever in the world an entity prehends positively enters into its own internal constitution: becomes Body. In process thought, that *must* be taken literally: we *are* the occasions that constitute our becoming. We *are* the adventures of our process. To become that society which is the Church is to allow the Jesus-event into our becoming. It is to have found the Jesus-event "important," and to have responded positively. It is to have opted in some "important" ways to have put the occasions of our own becoming together according to the patterns of assemblage that respect the Jesus-event, patterns of assemblage which are discovered in the various configurations of the Church's life.

In terms of the Jesus-event, both in its historical originality and in its historical reappropriations by and through the Church, there is a double aspect of becoming and being the Body. The first, which I dealt with just previously, is that when a person lets the Jesus-event into his own becoming, he makes it into his Body, his own self-hood. He lets it be part of the total universe of events which enters into his own real, internal constitution. The Jesus-event becomes causally efficacious—which is to say: Present. The Jesus-event is made present by the person who lets it be part of him. That is one aspect of Mystical Body, namely, letting the Jesus-event which one finds present in the Church become present in oneself. The other aspect, equally necessary for understanding the societal nature of Church, is that a person can become Body to another when his own life is an influence on the other. In Whiteheadian terminology, one can be a datum for another's becoming, one can be positively prehended into another's real, internal constitution through some objectification. A member of a society functions to propagate the life of the society. Since each member, which enters into the definition of being a member, emBodies in his own life the defining characteristic of a society, he in his turn makes available to the society its own life. The society's life is present in him and he "presents" it continually back to the society. In fact, the defining characteristics are nowhere present societally if they are not present in individual members. The society *is* society by its own emBodiment of members. There is a reciprocity between individuals who emBody the society and the society which emBodies individuals, and that double dynamic is inextricably inter-related in the life of a society. EmBodiment, like ancient Rome's Janus, has a face for each direction.

There are many ways in the Church in which emBodiment takes place. With obvious simplification, I will divide those ways into two: liturgical and non-liturgical, liturgical being the public official life of the Church. And taking liturgical even in a somewhat restricted sense, I intend that to mean the Sacramental life of the Church. In no way do I want to limit the dynamics of the Church's life to the Sacraments. Yet the Sacraments historically have been and are the privileged occasions of community life in the Church. I would like to relate Sacramental life to the discussion of Church presented thus far. And let me say that from this point on when I speak of the Christian, this implies for me Church. I am sure that there are those to whom Jesus is important who do not understand themselves to be Church. But historically Christianity has always had a societal dimension, and I doubt that a purely private "Christian" (if there is such) is an authentic response to the New Testament, by which I mean both the life of Jesus, and the community which knew him to be the Christ in their response to him.

The Whiteheadian sense of importance is that what is important somehow is important because it supplies some clues to an interpretation of the whole, the way certain events within an historical period provide a basis for understanding the whole period, or the way particular events in a person's life reveal a person's whole orientation. If the Jesus-event is important to human lives, then it should touch life frequently and at principal junctures, for the essence of Christian existence is the on-going re-appropriation of some of the configurations of that event into the configuration of present process. The Sacraments could hardly claim to touch life exhaustively, but they do spread themselves out over the span of existence: birth and new life, maturity and responsibility, suffering and death; the celebrations of community goodness and life, and of the presence of Jesus to and in and through that goodness and life; the fact of failings and sinfulness as moments of sorrow and realignment and redemption; marriage as the calling of the vast majority of men and women; and priesthood, as the calling and "ordering" of those who preside over the entire community's exercise of its priesthood. A person is not a Christian by virtue of having *at one time* allowed the Jesus-event into the structure of his own existence. Process is reality. The reality of the Christian depends upon the continuing presence of the Jesus-event in the structure of his becoming, and Sacraments are the Church's principal means of insuring and facilitating that continuance.

The presence of the Jesus-event to and in the structure of the Christian's existence does not and surely cannot imply a steady conscious appropriation of it. Being wife and mother or husband and father means more than the fact of having accepted once a spouse, or having fathered or given a child birth. It implies a whole pattern in how one puts his or her life together—yet that, like being Christian, cannot possibly mean a steady consciousness of that pattern. But it is important that at some junctures there be such a conscious appropriation. Our lives normally do not change all that much from one moment to the next, nor from one day or week to the next. And as is the case with most living things, we reappropriate from one second to the next the patterns of assemblage according to which we have been putting our lives together. If from time to time, therefore, the importance of some event (like marriage, motherhood and fatherhood, becoming Christian) enters into the patterns which form the structures of our existence, then we are shaped by our emBodiment of that Importance. But since there is no automatic meaning of what it means, at any given moment or juncture in life, to be Christian (or to be father or husband), we are required consciously to work out the structure of our Christian existence. If the Jesus-event is to be a constitutive object in our becoming, there must be some aspects of it through which it becomes objectified to us, and there must be some way in which we take it into our self-hood. The event must be related to the particularities of our experience. The Sacraments facilitate both of those items. Not only does each of the Sacraments objectify the Jesus-event from a different perspective, but each has the possibility of adding further specification as the Jesus-event is related to the particularities of a person or situation of community.

In this chapter I have been speaking of the Jesus-event and its importance to a Christian, but without attempting to specify the ground of that importance. As I have indicated already, my intention is to deal more with the dynamics that pertain to a society being a society, and the role of the Sacraments in that dynamic. At the close of the last chapter, however, I indicated that I would refer again to Cobb's thought, especially interpretations that relate to a "content" of the structure of Christian existence. I want to do this now, not as an attempt to define the "content" of being Christian, but as I did with the two Christologies, to have "a" content to keep in mind while discussing Church and Sacrament. I do, of course, think that Cobb's perspective is an excellent one.

Jesus brought back both a renewed and a new sense of the immediacy of God's presence. In the Old Testament there was a keen sense of the immediacy of God to Hebrew history. But that was frequently in the context of getting ready for the final liberation, the Messiah who would free Israel. That sense of immediacy was mostly lost in the mainstream Judaism of Jesus' time, which was Pharisaism. In Jesus there is the sense once again of the immediacy of God. In fact, there is a double sense of the immediacy of God's presence. First, Cobb holds, that a sense of the immediacy of God's presence to and in Jesus is such as to constitute Jesus' central perception of himself, a perception around which and in conjunction with which all the activities of his life were understood and lived out. That sense of God's immediate presence to and through him was so central as to constitute the principal meaning of the word "I" when Jesus uttered it. And in the second place, Jesus preached a new immediacy of God's presence to history. History was no longer to await a further period: the Kingdom of God is at hand, it is now breaking in upon the world already, and Jesus ushers in the breaking-in of this Kingdom. The immediacy of God's presence to Jesus is integrally related to the immediacy of God's presence to history through the presence of God's Kingdom *now*. Through the presence of God to Jesus and through Jesus there comes a new sense of the mean-

ing of God's love which we are asked to accept in relation to
ourselves, and which we are asked to make operative in history. This love is a defining characteristic of God (not the only
one) in which Jesus participated and in which we are called to
participate. We have been accepting in this work that the ultimate meaning of presence is to be causally efficacious, to have
a real effect; in Marcel's description, presence is what takes
hold of our being. To change that but a little: presence is
what takes hold of our becoming. The presence of God to
Jesus and to the world comes about when we allow the defining characteristic of his love to define the shape of our love.
Christianity is a call to a personhood that is shaped by a way
of loving. That call is above all exercised in and through
Christian community, that is, Church. And again it is the
Sacramental structure of the Church's life which is a principal
means of expressing that call and responding to it.

Cobb, then, says that Christian existence is "defined as
spiritual existence that expresses itself in love," [15] and that
means a particular understanding of love. Love is a way of
relating to something (one) of intrinsic value. There may
also be at times elements of instrumental value—but response
to that *alone* is not love. Self-love and love-of-another are
closely related, and both—if they are genuine love—are responsive to intrinsic value. We need to know that we are
loved in order to have our intrinsic value affirmed; therefore
we *need* the love of other human beings to believe in ourselves, and that confers a certain instrumentality upon their
love in our own experience. Is it possible not to need the love
of others in order to believe in our own intrinsic worth? The
answer is a simultaneous Yes and No.

Jesus affirms over and over again the essential lovableness
of man by God. It is a love which frees us from needing to
be loved by anyone else to know that we are loved, and frees
us to love more largely than ever. For having been assured

of our own worth in a radical way, we can love even when love is not returned, for that love is not *needed* by us in order for us to believe in ourselves. The prodigal son, the shepherd with the lost sheep that is found: these tell man that his failures are not ultimate, but that his value is. The sinful son prepares in his heart his protestations of his sinfulness; but his Father does not even respond to these protestations. His acceptance is immediate and so is the celebration. Sin abounds but grace super-abounds, Paul reminds us. The sense of worth must transcend the sense of sin; otherwise the sense of sin is debilitating beyond measure. It is in this sense, where a sense of sin has pre-empted a sense of personal worth, that Whitehead has called the sense of sin "the worst blight that ever fell on man." [16]

That is the sense in which God's love, as manifested to us through Jesus, assures us that since we are radically lovable, and since each man is too, our own worth is not up for grabs when love is not returned. That makes it possible for the Christian to move into the midst of un-love, and to function there lovingly. The Christian is radically free to love others because of each man's intrinsic value, independently of whether or not that man loves him in return.

> You have learnt how it was said: You must love your neighbor and hate your enemy. But I say this to you: love your enemies and pray for those who persecute you; in this way you will be sons of your Father in heaven, for he causes his sun to rise on bad men as well as good, and his rain to fall on honest and dishonest men alike. For if you love those who love you, what right have you to claim credit? Even the tax collectors do as much, do they not? And if you save your greetings for your brothers, are you doing anything exceptional? Even the pagans do as much, do they not? You must therefore be perfect just as your heavenly Father is perfect.[17]

It would be only half the picture to acknowledge that our essential lovableness before God, as revealed by Jesus, does in a sense free us from the needs of particular loves in order to have our self-hood affirmed. The other half of the picture is that we need to experience that God's love is indeed such a love as has been described. In Jesus that defining characteristic of God's love is manifest, both in theory and in practice (as I will indicate in a moment). Today, the locus of that defining characteristic of God's love is meant to be in Christian community, so that it is Christian community that assures a person of his radical lovableness. If that kind of love is not present in Christian community, then it is not available as a datum of experience, and cannot transform the life and love of mankind. Christian community is the Sacrament of God's love—and in that sense we do need the love of others to know that we are radically lovable even before God. We need the presence of God's way of loving operative within Christian community to be able to introduce God's way of loving into the configuration of our own patterns of loving. (Penance, as a Sacrament of reconciliation, participates in that larger sense of the Church's Sacramentality of God's love.)

The cross is the ultimate revelation of the kind of love that Jesus understood as divine love, and it is also a soberingly realistic comment upon such love. The ultimate way in which a person can deny the intrinsic worth of another is to take his life from him; it is a final despair of finding more value there than worthlessness. Religious and civil society conspired to take Jesus' life from him; he prayed for their forgiveness, "Father, forgive them; they do not know what they are doing" (Lk. 23:34). Those who love with the kind of love asked for by Jesus are exposed to more hatred and ridicule and persecution than those who do not love that fully. It is an unprotected and therefore highly vulnerable love that loves not only within a safe periphery where love is returned.

To love where love is not returned means the capacity for absorbing hatred and hostility out beyond the safe periphery. The cross of Jesus is the ultimate expression of an unconditional love, an unconditioned capacity to absorb hatred in order to love.

I said earlier that one element of the defining characteristics of those who are Christian is a faith in the importance of Jesus. Another element now, which is a refinement of Jesus' importance, is the special revelation of God's love: namely, that man is loved by God, and that nothing can change man's radical lovableness before God. Man has the power to render his own lovableness impotent by not accepting it—that is perhaps the one unforgivable sin, in Tillich's words, to refuse to accept acceptance. Once a man has accepted acceptance, he is empowered in the direction of a universal love.

That says much about the Church's character. Jesus is the symbol of God's love, the kind of love we have just been discussing. Jesus participates in God's way of loving with an immediacy of emBodiment in his own loving; God's way of doing things, his plan, his logos, became flesh in Jesus. God is available in Jesus, with a particular way of loving as a principal symbol through which God continues to invade and inundate history. The Church is man's attempt to take that defining characteristic of Jesus' love, which redeems man from any ultimate condition of sinfulness, and to continue to make it available to history through its own emBodiment of it. There is a natural enough tendency for man to base his love of others and his society with others upon what people hold in common, and upon the mutual affirmation that all men need. Those values are not denied in Christian love, and they are indeed operative. But that is not the whole story. We are called to transcend those limitations—to love within them but also to love beyond them. God's love, which is made visible in Jesus' love, affirms that before him every man is found lovable.

That faith means that no one can be written off as unlovable (including ourselves) and that if at times lovability has low visibility it may well be a matter of *our* visual-ability and *our* love-ability.

Psychologically we would easily recognize that it is expansive (as well as expensive) to love what is different, what is new, what is confrontational, what threatens our comfortableness with the familiar (in addition to loving what is easy to love). Some of the process thinkers would feel that not only is such love psychologically healthy, it is the very basis of evolutionary development. That would mean that God's love, as revealed in Jesus, is the paradigm for how reality's heart ought to beat. And that is the thesis of an article, "Evolutionary Love," published by Charles Sanders Peirce in 1893. He finds the Johannine development of love to be the model of evolutionary love, without which evolution at this stage cannot continue (his emphasis on "mind" presages Teilhard):

> The philosophy we draw from John's Gospel is that this is the way the mind develops; and as for the cosmos, only so far as it yet is mind, and so has life, is it capable of further evolution. Love, recognizing germs of loveliness in the hateful, gradually warms it into life, and makes it lovely.[18]

In support of his position he cites a remarkable passage from Henry James, insisting upon a love which transcends the natural desire to love what is like ourselves:

> It is no doubt very tolerable finite or creaturely love to love one's own in another, to love another for his conformity to one's self: but nothing can be in more flagrant contrast with the Creative love, all whose tenderness *ex*

vi termini must be reserved only for what intrinsically is most bitterly hostile and negative to itself.[19]

In Whitehead, this insight comes through strongly and even metaphysically in his treatment of beauty (for all order is aesthetic). The creative advance is motivated by a striving for the greatest possible beauty, for the most intense aesthetic experience. When all of the parts that go into a whole are characterized by a lack of anything that inhibits their being together aesthetically, that is a minor form of beauty. Such beauty largely depends upon the conjunction of "likes" as the basis of harmony. But greater beauty is achieved by variety of detail and effective contrasts between the elements. Such an arrangement is not a mere juxtaposition of different items; not mere tolerance of differences; but feelings of acceptance and integrations of contrasts into a satisfying whole. A society, like every reality, achieves some level of beauty. A "minor beauty" society is much easier to bring off. Its defining characteristic emphasizes common elements that fit together easily. It is much more difficult for a society to put itself together when what is asked for as a defining characteristic is that put itself together on a basis of common support of the particularities of members. In Whiteheadian terms, it is more difficult to achieve a beauty that involves variety of detail and effective contrast. What that probably best translates into for society is some form of "pluralism." Pluralism is more than a co-existence of differences—or, at best, that would be a very meager expression of it. It is an affirmation also of the values of the differences, and it involves an integration of differences not on an "in spite of them" basis, "but because of them." As I pointed out in the previous chapter on Whitehead, such an approach to "putting to together" requires a much more effective network of inter-relatings, like the room whose decor is worked out with a great variety of colors and styles, rather than simpler color coordination, etc. Pluralism is perhaps not enough in itself to be the whole defining characteristic of a society, certainly not of that society we know as the Church. But the nature of Christian love seems to demand it as *an* element of the defining characteristic, for we are not to write off anyone because of differences; we are asked that no one be found unlovable for no one is unlovable. And love is a positive relationship, a positive prehension of something(one) of intrinsic value. While I still have not treated Sacramental life specifically, I would point out here that Penance and Eucharist are both dynamics that can be very much in the service of the kind of community we have been describing.

Teilhard's understanding of what reality is about (complexification-consciousness working toward the Noosphere and Omega), of Jesus as important for the world finally to become itself, of the Church as the front edge of the Church's becoming: these process interpretations also seem to demand the kind of Church structure we have been describing where a love operates which excludes no man, where the presence of Jesus (his causal efficacy) enables man to transcend his narrow loves which would embrace only what affirms him back. Perhaps it is only at this juncture of history that it has become clear to us that man *must* transcend his narrow loves if he is *even to survive* as man, much less to thrive as man. More than thirty years ago Teilhard saw that the conception of "nation" that has characterized civilization up to this point is becoming obsolete—"nations" are too small to take care of history at this point; they are tumble-down huts:

> In order to avoid disturbing our habits we seek in vain to settle international disputes by adjustments of frontiers —or we treat as "leisure" (to be whiled away) the activities at the disposal of mankind. As things are going now it will not be long before we run full tilt into one another. Something will explode if we persist in trying to squeeze into our old tumbledown huts the material and

spiritual forces that are henceforward on the scale of a world.[20]

The Second Vatican Council, in its pastoral constitution on the Church, also acknowledged that the evolutionary development of the world has brought it to the point where nations can no longer think of themselves as having a private history, and that we must therefore reconceptualize many of our understandings in order to accommodate this new fact. That seems to me to include a reconceptualization of Church, and how Church puts itself together, in terms of evolutionary thought.

History itself speeds along on so rapid a course that an individual person can scarcely keep abreast of it. The destiny of the human community has become all of a piece, where once the various groups of men had a kind of private history of their own. Thus, the human race has passed from a rather static concept of reality to a more dynamic, evolutionary one. In consequence, there has arisen a new series of problems, a series as important as can be, calling for new efforts of analysis and synthesis.[21]

One of the results of such analysis and synthesis, within the document *Gaudium et Spes* itself, is a reconceptualization of the notion of common good, and with it some implied reunderstandings of the nature of authority. In a more static approach to society, common good is going to be thought of very much in terms of corporate goals which transcend the individual goals. In substance approaches to philosophical analysis, there is naturally more emphasis upon the givenness of society's constitution. For a long time the Church resisted social teachings that appeared to be fostering an injurious individualism. It seems now in retrospect that many of those teachings were the beginnings of new understandings. Jeremy

Bentham attempted a social philosophy which tended to see the common good as the sum of individual goods; and since individual goods sometimes were in conflict, the common good was that which was able to embrace particular goods most broadly. The social doctrine of Luigi Taparelli [22] represents a still greater departure from static conceptions of society and a move toward the individual. He based his social doctrine upon the individual who has certain God given rights and who is also intended concretely to live socially with men. He places much more primordiality upon the *individual* who is in community than does Whitehead, of course. But the social teaching of men like Bentham, Taparelli, and Rosmini later drew the antagonism of the Church which steadfastly resisted formulating common good in terms of individual goods, for that seemed to belie what was understood to be the essentially transcendent (*vis-à-vis* the individual) character of common good. *Mater et Magistra* of John XXIII and Vatican II's *Gaudium et Spes* have moved a long way in re-interpreting social structure, common good, authority, etc. Common good is seen in terms of a *set of conditions* which favor individual fulfillment. This approach is not a denial of the importance of common goals in a society's make-up. But a large aspect of the common good is the set of conditions which best opens the way for individuals to work out those goals, but to work them out with a growing sense of inter-dependence. The combined sense of the human enterprise as a process, a new intensity in human inter-dependence, and a very contemporary concern with individual fulfillment—all of these are factors which are reflected in the definition of "common good" as "the sum of those conditions of social life which allow social groups and their individual members relatively thorough and ready access to their own fulfillment." [23] Man-in-community is a unity which cannot suffer mutilation of either aspect. But "man" has a primordialness:

Man's social nature makes it evident that the progress

of the human person and the advance of society itself
hinge on each other. For the beginning, the subject and
goal of all social institutions is and must be the human
person, which for its part and by its very nature stands
completely in need of social life.[24]

Let us see now how this approach affects an understanding
of authority:

Many different people go to make up the political community, and these can lawfully incline toward diverse
ways of doing things. Now, if the political community
is not to be torn to pieces as each man follows his own
viewpoint, authority is needed. This authority must dispose the whole citizenry to the common good, not me-
chanically or despotically, but primarily as a moral force
which depends on freedom and the conscientious dis-
charge of the burdens of any office which has been
undertaken.[25]

Several things are noteworthy in this description. First, there
is the affirmation of the pressures of contemporary life to
affirm and foster different ways of doing things. Secondly, the
role of authority receives an increasing accent upon its function as an overseer of the disposition of energies toward the
common good, namely, toward *a set of circumstances* which
allows decisions to be made at lower levels about how fulfillment is to be achieved, so that those different ways of doing
things may exist effectively side by side.

In this last discussion I have wanted to indicate that within
the Church itself there are some new formulations about
the nature of reality. There are affirmations of the evolutionary
nature of man and history which call for re-interpretations in
a dynamic framework. These re-interpretations touch critical
areas of social doctrine, such as the common good and the

function of authority. The role of authority places more emphasis upon a kind of facilitating function so that unity may come about at the same time that a greater and greater diversity is found within it. The new word "plurunity" has come into vogue in some quarters as a replacement for "conformity." Experientially as well as theoretically, it becomes clearer that Christian love—somewhat in the terms in which it has been briefly dealt with here—disposes men to dispose themselves so that plurunity may be realized, that is, so that all men can love each other and yet respect a great variety of ways in which man can be man.

The current emphasis on "collegiality" in the Church, with the frequent references of early Christian history as a paradigm, is an attempt to respond to re-interpretations of the role and function of authority. (I frankly think that collegiality is much more a contemporary response than it is given credit for.) The more an authority is called upon to be a facilitating presence among the diverse ways in which members of the society in which it functions work out their own expressions of identity within the society, the broader exposure to society must authority have. Collegiality helps spread authority out to give it that broader exposure to "where the action is." That this should be the case in the Church today is hopefully a response to new understandings of self and of the world which the Church serves. Hartshorne has called attention to the fact that the way God is understood influences how the Church understands herself and how she translates her self-understanding into comportment (Merleau-Ponty, I think rightly, sees comportment as a mode of thought). An immutable and almighty God easily translates into an authoritarian and highly dogmatic Church: *semper eadem*. The processive God of Hartshorne is one who receives the world into his love and understanding in a supereminent way. He relates perfectly and really with the world as it is. His love and knowledge are perfect responses to the

world *as it is*. The decisions that shape history are free decisions, and God waits upon those decisions to know and love
the history which they create. The perfect receptivity of
God is his best credential for being the Lord of history. From
the paradigm of such a God and such a reality, Hartshorne
arrives at what he calls "the metaphysics of democracy":

> The politically, and I am confident theologically,
> sounder principle is rather this, that he who is most
> adequately influenced by all may most appropriately
> exert influence upon all. The best ruler is an intermedi-
> ary in the universal interaction, able to moderate and
> harmonize actions because all that is done is done also
> to him, whose reactions to this action absorb and trans-
> mute all influences into counterinfluence, integrative and
> harmonizing in tendency . . .[26]

Many aspects of the contemporary situation are responsible
for urging collegiality upon the Church's *modus vivendi*. The
same situations contribute to the necessity of a genuine
pluralism, whether theological, liturgical or governmental.
I want to stress that a process world view makes similar suggestions. The Church—like every reality—is a process. In
the heart of the creative advance there is a yearning for higher
and more intensive forms of unity. Teilhard describes this
movement in terms of a law of complexification-consciousness.
Whitehead often does it in aesthetic terms. Jesus prays that
all men might be one, not just loosely one, but a unity that is
characterized by the same immediacy that marks his own
oneness with the Father. The tendency toward a certain dogmatism in the Church's history has made pluralism very difficult. The development of that dogmatism is an understandable one. The Greek influence has for centuries levied a strong
intellectualizing pressure on how Faith is understood, so that
dogmatic formulations and credal summaries have been of

capital importance. Also, basic epistemological presuppositions have not been in acceptance of an evolutionary understanding of the world. Cardinal Newman's *Essay on the Development of Christian Doctrine* was a beginning, but a beginning mostly negated by the reactionism of the Modernist controversy. Also, the awareness of historical relativity is relatively new upon the scene. Past ages have simply not been able to sense how historically conditioned *every* statement is. They have not realized how a world view is *a* perspective on reality and can make no more claim than that. Each man (each culture) must appropriate the Jesus-event within the perspective out of which he knows himself and his world. It becomes clearer how the conditions in which dogmatic formulations are worked out influence the formulation (a conditioning beyond that of the world view involved). There are formulations from the Council of Trent, such as those concerning Faith, which are clearly a reaction to the Reformation. And they stress the aspect of Faith that seemed to be challenged by the Reformation. The statement may not be false, but the stress may result in an unbalanced statement:

> This example brings out another fact: that a one-sided formulation may be true, but may have the effect of a lie by its distortion of emphasis. Such distortion does not stand in its character of a truth, but depends upon those who are affected by it. So far as the makeup of an individual mind is concerned, there is a proportion in truth as well as in art.[27]

Restructuring the role and function of the Holy Office in recent Catholic history is a first step in an approach to allow for greater pluralism not only in belief but in articulations of belief (which I understand as both verbal and ritual). I think that a further case for the necessity of pluralism in the structure of the Church is to be found in Whitehead's discussion of the development of organisms in evolution. An organism is, of course, a "society" in the Whiteheadian sense; but I think it is clear that the discussion also applies to "society" in the more common acceptation of the word, i.e., human society, or for our interest also Church.

In the following discussion "society" means a "notion of society which includes subordinate societies and nexūs with a definite pattern of structural inter-relations . . . Such societies will be termed 'structured.' " [28] In this sense, a human being is a society in which, for example, the various organs are subordinate societies. The human organism as a whole provides a favorable environment in which those subordinate organisms can function—which it must do, of course, because it needs the effective functioning of those subordinate organisms.

First, let us note that a society may be structured very simply or very complexly; secondly, that every society requires a wider social environment in which to exist. The relation of a society to its wider environment will affect the simplicity or complexity of its structure.

A society is more or less "stable" in relationship to its environment. The better able a society is to endure the changes that occur within its environment, the more stable it is. The more detailed a society's requirements are, the more specialized that society is. A cold blooded animal is more stable in regard to the temperature of its environment, a warm blooded animal more specialized. The more aspects on an environment with which a society interacts, the more specialized it is.

The unspecialized society can survive more and larger changes in its environment. The defining characteristic of such a society will generally involve a very simple structural pattern; it "is apt to be deficient in structural pattern, when viewed as a whole." [29] An unspecialized, loosely structured society will be high in survival value. But "in general an unspecialized society does not secure conditions favourable for intensity of satisfaction among its members." [30]

A specialized society, on the other hand, is low in survival value, but will involve a greater intensity for its members. If a human society is founded for a very specific purpose, that high specification will normally mean a close engagement in the particularities of the larger society in which it functions, i.e., its environment. Because it is so highly specific and so "attached" to the details of its environment, a specialized society favors intensity of satisfaction for its members.

Both intensity of satisfaction and survival are desirable values for a society, but they are at odds with each other for complexity of structure is in the service of the one value, simplicity the other. "Thus the problem for Nature is the production of societies which are 'structured' with a high 'complexity,' and which are at the same time unspecialized. In this way, intensity is mated with survival." [31]

As a society the Church meets the same challenge, to maintain itself in existence and to occasion an intense life in the membership. The gradual ability to mate survival with intensity develops in organisms with the evolution of intelligence. There are two ways in which structured societies have learned to meet the problem, both of which apply to the Church's experience. In Whiteheadian categories, those two ways are "transmutation," and "conceptual reversion."

If a traveler should stop in a town along his route, for a meal or perhaps overnight, or even several days as a tourist along the way, he will gather certain impressions through which he knows that town. His knowledge of the town will be much more general than that of the man who lives there. The visitor who walks down a main street will not have gathered into his impression the same detailed knowledge as the townsman. The townsman knows people along the way, knows buildings, knows where the side streets lead, etc. The townsman is more engaged in the specifics of the town, his involvement with it is more intense and more detailed. In a sense, when the visitor understands how the town puts itself together, he has substantially the same data at his disposal as the townsman (in the sense of the being physically there). But he simplifies the data for himself in order to get a manageable general impression by which to know the town. Something similar happens when a public figure is caricatured in an editorial cartoon in a newspaper. The caricature picks out certain features of a man's face which are a tip-off his identity, and then builds a whole face around those details with which the face has been generalized. If the case of both the town and the face, a vast number of details are passed over in favor of a few striking features which are allowed to function for the whole. We do this constantly in our knowing. With an item as simple as a chair, we generalize it through its shape and color and perhaps by its position in the room. If we tried to know every chair by fixing upon its every detail, we could hardly get on to the business of living. In pulling out several of the most telling details we simplify something so that we can know it more easily: we make an abstraction so that the object becomes manageable for us. In Whitehead this is the category of "transmutation":

> It ignores diversity of detail by overwhelming the nexus by means of some congenial uniformity which pervades it. The environment may then change indefinitely so far as concerns the ignored details—so long as they can be ignored.[32]

In other words, although a society wants to aim at a strong engagement with the world in which it exists, and an intense interaction with it, if it is to survive it must be careful to construe itself in the broadest possible terms. The more detailed is the understanding of "defining characteristic" the less leeway does a society have, and therefore the less survival

power. A society must understand itself in terms of its interaction and intensity in the world in which it operates, but it
must transmute its self-understanding "by eliciting a massive
average objectification of a nexus, while eliminating the detailed diversities of the various members of the nexus in
question." [33] But it is precisely the "detailed diversities" that
occasion intensity in the immediate occasions, as each member in his own way seeks to meet the challenges of the "new"
as they turn up in history. A structure which has been trans-
muted for the sake of survival does not, by its nature, give
clues to how immediacies are to be dealt with. This aspect—
the intensity—of a society's life calls for the operation of another Whiteheadian category, that of "conceptual reversion."
The Jesus-event is important to life. That means that the
Christian attempts to bring that event into frequent contact
with his life and the Church's life. The Jesus-event and history
engage each other in the on-goingness of daily reality. And
only in the internality of that on-going moment can the Jesus-
event contribute to the configuration of history. But structures
of responses to immediacies are too particular to enter into
the structure of the defining characteristic. Two things happen when the Jesus-event and contemporary history confront
each other. One is that when we see the present version of
what is going on in history, and then confront it with the
Jesus-event, we often find that we must try to re-shape history
—that is, take the version of it we have found, and do a reversion that is faithful to our understanding of Christian love.
A second thing that happens when Jesus-event and history
confront each other is that we often see the Jesus-event in a
new light; we do a re-version of the Jesus-event in terms of the
world view which our histories condition in us. In a sense,
each Christology is an historically conditioned version of the
importance of Jesus. We are dealing here with conceptual
reversion. A society which wants to offer possibilities of intense life to its members must provide occasions and dy-

namics for the operation of the category of conceptual reversion, that is, it must make provision for contact between the
Jesus-event and immediate situations so that new appropriations of the Jesus-event can be made in terms of the new challenges which history proffers.

A society which wants to survive and to live intensely must
constantly be on guard not to over-structure itself in its defining characteristics, for that can over-particularize the large
sense of its meaning as a society. And it must also be careful
not to get too detailed in whatever dynamisms it has to take
care of conceptual reversion, or else spontaneity in daily
appropriations of the society's life-intuition will be hampered.

The Sacramental life of the Church is its means, par excellence, of conceptual reversion. Each Sacramental experience is a possible initiative "to receive the novel elements of
the environment into explicit feelings with such subjective
forms as conciliate them with the complex experiences proper
to members of the structured society." [34]

I would like to do a little Monday morning quarter-backing
on Church history. And it really is Monday morning quarter-
backing for we have perspectives today (such as that of historical relativity) that we could not expect to have been op-
erational in an earlier era. And surely the next era will do its
Monday morning critique of our Sunday afternoon game.
Dogmatic formulations are an attempt to capture somehow
the essential kernel of a belief. Dogmatic formulations have
been imposed upon the entire Church and with a sense of
finality. Acceptance of such formulations has been understood
to enter into the defining characteristics, for a person who did
not accept them was anathema: outside the Church. The realization that every statement is historically conditioned, that
every statement reflects certain presuppositions that derive
from a world view, that every statement is *a* perspective—
that realization should engender a reluctance to make content statements with finality. "Nature" and "substance," terms

used frequently in dogma and theology, reflect basically the Greek world view. They are understandings that make eminent good sense within that framework. But what they have in fact done is impose a framework which is just one possible perspective, The nature/person Christological formulation of Chalcedon and scholastic theology's Transubstantiation explanation of the Eucharist so canonized a particular framework that new theology in a new framework became almost impossible. My point here is this: such formulations must and should take place. But they pertain more to the intensity dynamism than to the survival dynamism. Formulations, because they are an attempt to come to grips with the Jesus-event in terms of a particular perspective, are a matter of engagement of the Jesus-event with on-going history. That is an intensity dynamism. And no historically conditioned statement should be made to enter its contents into the defining characteristic of a Church who believes in its vocation to survive to the end of time. That of course is an ideal. The Church will always be articulating her self-understanding and will always be making historically conditioned statements. At this point, a process thinker would want to remind the Church that its reality is its process, and that it would be better for the Church's survival potential to try to delineate its defining characteristics in event-categories rather than substance categories. A first such characterization would be that the Jesus-event is "important" to process (but attempts to state the basis of that importance should perhaps not enter into the defining characteristics). A second such characterization would be that the principal dynamics for the interpretation of Jesus' "importance," and the assimilation of the Jesus-event into on-going history, are the Church's Sacramental system. I will treat each of these for a moment. (There are other elements of defining characteristics—such, I believe, as some manifestation of visible unity—therefore, I am not trying to make any kind of exhaustive description of the Church's defining characteristics. That would be the folly of attempting a verbal formulation with finality.)

To say that "faith in the importance of the Jesus-event" is a defining characteristic is to say much, as long as "importance" is understood in the Whiteheadian sense. For it means that human life intends to take the Jesus-event most seriously in the configuration of its own reality. One of Norman Pittenger's Christological statements in this regard is worth citing at length:

> Every interpretation of the meaning of human experience, every metaphysic, every understanding of the world in its totality, must by necessity start from some particular stance—or, better put, must find in some particular "important" point a disclosure of the significance of the whole. Furthermore, the fact taken as "important" not only gives a clue to the totality of experience; it also provides new occasions for future creative advance—for it is in terms of that which is taken as "important," that action in the direction of fulfilment of subjective aim or purpose will be undertaken.

> Now is it the contention of Christian faith that *the* important fact in history is the appearance in the world of Jesus of Nazareth. He is not the *only* important fact; yet he has been for millions and he is becoming increasingly for more millions, even if they are not in any sense avowed Christians, a fact which is central to the interpretation of the human enterprise. Whitehead once said that Jesus is the "revelation in act" of that which Plato —and other thinkers—have "discerned in theory": namely, the truth that persuasion not compulsion, love not force, is central to the creative process of the universe. It is this which has given Jesus a central place; and it is from this centrality, this "importance" in our under-

standing and in our living, that the evaluation of Jesus himself, his significance in the total scheme of things, his continuing impact on successive generations of men and women, takes its rise.[35]

This approach to Christology sees Jesus less as a revelation of *what* man is (though something of that too), and more as a revelation of how process goes at its heart, a "how" that Christian love supports and reinforces, a "how" that lets man become all he can become.

To follow through briefly with another of Pittenger's reflections in the passage just cited, the Jesus-event—because it is "important"—"provides occasions for future creative advance." It is here again that the Sacraments are functional in making the Jesus-event present to the particularities of the creative advance. The Sacraments provide occasions for adaptations of events in terms of what Christian loves indicate as a pattern that favors their best potential. The Sacramental experience—providing as it does the occasion of conceptual reversion in the historical appropriation of the Jesus-event—is the organ therefore of the intensity of Christian life.

This again is Monday morning quarter-backing, but a lot of intensity in Christian life has been inhibited by the over-specification of the Sacramental experience at too high a level. The Eucharistic celebration was for centuries specified in the minutest detail of word and gesture, the homily or sermon providing the sole occasion for the introduction of spontaneous reference to contemporary circumstances. (And of course the same is largely true of the other Sacraments.) The high level structures of a society should try to restrict themselves to the "massive average objectification" while leaving "the detailed diversities of the various members" at the level of their diverse involvements. That principle of operation is what we would perhaps today call the principle of subsidiarity, that is, that no decision should be made at an upper level which can be made at a lower level. Psychologically that is sound for the life of a society, for it asks that decisions be made at the lowest level possible. An authority should not ever make a decision that it could reasonably ask someone at a lower level to make (higher and lower refer, of course, to where in the structure the authority is situated). This policy means that more decisions are made by more individuals; there is a greater participation in more people's creative involvement in the life of a society; the responsibility for the society is taken up by more people, who cannot be bystanders or passive members. In a word, the principle of subsidiarity fosters greater intensity throughout the body of a society. As a principle of operation it would help to mate survival with intensity.

I have made numerous references in this chapter to Sacramental life in the Church, with the intention of developing a discussion of Sacrament in the next chapter. Before passing to that chapter, I would like to gather together some of the process reflections upon Church, to whose life the Sacraments are vital.

First of all, process is reality! The world is a process of creative advance. At each moment reality is called to become more than it was before—and the issuing of that summons is one of the functions of God in the world. He is a call to transcendence. The love of God in which we are invited to participate is a love that keeps us open to transcendence. God offers the world the high hope of adventure, the quest for further perfection and fulfillment.

Christian faith believes that in Jesus there is a revelation par excellence of the love of God and the design (Logos) of God. The events of the life and death of Jesus show a configuration of human life responding fully to the summons of God. God touched history very powerfully in Jesus, and he continues the presence of that special appearance in the appropriation of the Jesus-event in the life of the Church. The

Church, because it presents God to the world over and over again through a constant re-appropriation of the Jesus-event, is a reflection of God at work in the world; the Church is a sacrament of God at work in the world, especially through Jesus. The Church, like God, must issue man a summons of transcendence, a high hope of adventure; a quest and a hope and a promise.

That summons operates above all in the structure of Christian love, as made explicit in the life of Jesus. It consists in such a radical belief in being loved by God that man can experience himself as fundamentally lovable, notwithstanding his sinfulness. In knowing himself as lovable he is called to leave his sinfulness behind, and to open out in love. That implies a belief in the fundamental lovableness of every other person as well. There is an intrinsic worth in every man to which a positive response is always possible, and which is always demanded of the Christian. If a man is not radically in touch with his own worth, he needs the love of others as an affirmation, and he finds it difficult to love when love is not returned, for he cannot sustain such a negation. The Christian is specifically asked to sustain that negation, to absorb non-love—that is the meaning of the Cross.

The Church believes in the importance of Jesus; Christians, that is, find in the Jesus-event a clue to the meaning of their existence, and a central clue at that. They intend to let their lives be shaped by the inclusion of the Jesus-event as an occasion of their experience. It is principally in the life of the Church that the Jesus-event continues its presence, and it is from and in the Church that men hear of it and learn to let their lives be touched by it. Lives-being-touched-by-Jesus is the process which constitutes the actuality of the Church. The Sacramental life of the Church is the main dynamic through which the Jesus-event continues to take-hold of the lives of men. Through the Sacraments the Church is creative of the Christian and the Christian is creative of the Church. The

Christian emBodies the Church, and the Church emBodies the Christian. They are each other's life and self, not exhaustively but yet *really* and importantly.

Instead of understanding the Church as a place or thing or substancely understood society, it is seen to be an event whose process is its reality. Its identity is a function of its process and not vice versa. Both that fact, and the particular kind of process which the Church is, contribute most of its defining characteristics. A process model of understanding suggests to the Church that it keep its own understanding of its defining characteristics in the largest terms possible. First of all, that favors its survival and its wide availability. It also respects the historical relativity of every utterance. Past attempts to arrive at final, canonized formulations have mostly succeeded in imposing a world view (as well as developing an insight). And that inhibits survival power, for world views are only *a* perspective; they change and develop; and there are other world views besides. Secondly, as little prescriptive work as possible should be done at higher levels of structure; the more that can be done at the points of contact in life, the greater will be the intensity. There has been a tendency to over-prescribe at higher levels, with a consequent loss of relevancy at lower levels, both in articulations of belief and in ritual. When liturgical prayers are given word for word, they can hardly be expected to reflect the immediacies of the situation and to facilitate precise accommodations of the Jesus-event and contemporary history to each other. Perhaps it is enough to stress *that* the Jesus-event is important—i.e., that the Christian construes the meaning of his life and constructs its particular shape with the Jesus-event as an important occasion of experience; and also *that* the Sacraments are an official means of interpreting the importance of the Jesus-event and of appropriating it with immediacy and particularity (in the next chapter I will address myself to the elements of "ritual sameness" that are needed to maintain Sacraments as societal experience as well as private. Because the Sacraments are the privileged means through which the Church's defining characteristics are transmitted and communicated, some form of ritual identification is necessary and helpful).

The kind of love which Christian love shows itself to be is one that does not insist upon immediate compatibility as a basis for loving—it is able to embrace great differences, and to love even where love is not returned, or where perhaps hatred even is the response. It has a conviction of man's intrinsic worth which transcends differences and absorbs hatred. The structure of existence which emBodies that kind of love, as well as a structure which has tried to refrain from very exacting specifications in its defining characteristics ought to manifest a rather strong pluralism in its membership.

Many of these things that I am speaking about are now happening in the Church, or are beginning to happen. Sometimes they are welcomed and sometimes they are met with chagrin. I would hope that a theoretical basis for understanding many of these trends would facilitate the present evolution in the Church's understanding of herself, and the evolution of new elements in her comportment in the world.

5

SACRAMENT

A s I indicated in an earlier chapter, there are some critical ways in which the classical Hebrew mind approximates process modes of thought more closely than our more accustomed languages and modern cultures. There are no tenses as such in classical Hebrew, such as our past, present, and future. It is only possible to state an action in such a way that it is presented as completed or as not completed. Take the following sentences, for example:

I was speaking to him.	*I spoke* to him.
I am speaking.	*I will have spoken* to him by
I shall speak later.	evening.

Even though the sentences in the first column would suggest past, present and future tenses to us, the verbs would be the same in each case in classical Hebrew, for they are all stating an action as going on, or not completed. The two verbs in the second set of sentences would also be the same—completed action—though they would seem to us to be past and future perfect. In Hebrew they are both stated as completed.

When God gave his name to Moses (Ex. 3:13-15), he used verbs in the forms that indicated non-completed action: *Ehyeh asher ehyeh.* It is difficult to find a translation adequate to the sense of the verb "to be" in a non-completed sense. "I am who am" misses that important nuance. "I will be who I will be" is too casual to get the nuance. "I am in the process of becoming the one who I will be" is far too clumsy. But the last two are closer than "I am who am." Partly, this is a ploy to avoid giving a name. For a Hebrew, to name something is to have a power over it. (Adam named the animals before there was anyone else around to converse with—so the names were not first for communication sake.) And one cannot get power over God. But there also seems to be another sense to God's self-characterization. He has revealed himself to the Hebrews consistently through history. Through particular historical events he became their God and they became his people. Historical event constituted the relationship between God and his people; it was creative of him as their God and of them as his people. The lack of finality in God's naming of himself has the sense of: keep an eye on *what happens*, and you will find out who I am and what I am. Yahweh identified himself already to Abram through an exodus event: "I am Yahweh," he said to him, "who brought you out of Ur of the Chaldeans to make you heir to this land" (Gen. 15:7). The great Exodus out of Egypt became the historical event, par excellence, through which Yahweh was identified to the Hebrews, and through which they found their own identity as God's people: "It is I, Yahweh your God, who have brought you out of the land of Egypt so that I may be your God, I Yahweh your God" (Num. 15:41). The yearly ritual celebration of the Passover was a much more real Exodus event than the English word "commemoration" could possibly convey. It was a continuation of the event by which Yahweh *was still becoming* their God and they *were still becoming* his people, and the yearly Passover executed the continuation.

When children questioned their elders about the meaning of the ritual commemoration, they were not told: "This is to recall what happened to our ancestors." Rather: "On that day you will explain to your son, 'This is because of what Yahweh did for *me* when *I* came out of Egypt'" (Ex. 13:8). The event was not completed once and for all. It continues to take hold of each man's life; and since God identifies himself in terms of his historical action, he was not able to tell Moses exactly who he was, for his identity is a matter of a continuous taking hold of the Hebrew people. Therefore, watch history to find out who Yahweh is. The Hebrew people were who they were because of Yahweh's action in their lives. His taking hold of them through their history was the originating point of their identity. It was *the* "important" event. It shaped their present and its promise lured them into their future.

Ritual and Sacrament in the Catholic Church are in continuity with the Old Testament experience, as New Testament experience should be. The identity of the Church derives from the Jesus-event, which continues to shape Christian lives in the present and whose promise lures them into their future. The New Testament summons, however, is a call beyond the cultural limits of a single people. The new bourne is the outer edge of wherever man is.

The deepest sense of "presence" is that of causal efficacy. Whatever takes hold of one's becoming and in some way enters into it—that is what is present. Or, stated from the other side, whatever one's becoming takes hold of and lets be part of its own experience—that is what is present. Prehensions or feelings effect presence: "they feel what is *there* and transform it into what is *here*." [1] Physical proximity may be a factor and often is in effective presence, but it is not of the essence. The essence is "taking hold," and that means from whatever quarter. There is no deeper sense of presence than that. When we speak of the presence of the Jesus-event as creative of the Christian and of the Church, we are speaking of the fact that there are lives which in private and corporate ways have been significantly taken hold of by the Jesus-event. My concern in this chapter is with the *way* in which Sacramental life effects the fact of Jesus' presence.

Using the process categories of Whitehead, I would say first of all that a Sacrament is a positive prehension of the Jesus-event. The Jesus-event is felt *there* and made to be *here*. Something must be said about the "there" of the Jesus-event, that is, about the locus of its availability. During the historical life of Jesus, community was already touched off in the response of men to him—by positive prehensions of him. There had to be things about Jesus that made sense to the community that formed around him. Those "things about him" that made sense were "how" Jesus was objectified for his community of followers. The community arose as "the things about him" that made sense were introduced into the patterns of living of a community of men; the "things about *him*" also became "things about *them*." Thanks to modern biblical scholarship, we can appreciate today the extent to which the Gospel accounts of Jesus are expressions of early Christian communities, so that the accounts of him are often equally accounts of them. Different accounts fix upon different "things about him," and sometimes they fix upon the same things about him from different perspectives; and still other times the various communities were quite close to each other in their prehensions of Jesus. In any event, the Scriptures have become a privileged locus of Jesus' availability; they are what religious historians often call the "classic revelation." To state the obvious, the Gospels are not autobiographical. They are the reflections of those who had one foot in Jesus' life, another in the world of that time, and a human experience that resulted from where their feet took them. And the life of the Church continues to reflect that pattern. The Church has one foot in the Gospel and another in the contemporary world, and it creates a life out of where its two feet take it. The foot in the Gospel is "the things about him" that make sense and are prehended into a pattern of on-going experience. The Church, therefore, as well as the Gospel is a "there" source of things about Jesus from which an individual can feel what is *there* (the Jesus-event) and transform it into what is *here*. Forms of definiteness of the Jesus-event are *there* in the New Testament and in the life of the Church, which means, of course, in the lives of its individual members and in its history (tradition).

At the level of *knowing* human awareness, the past invades the contemporary scene with its presence through symbolic reference. Symbolic reference is possible when a form of definiteness participates in both a past event and a contemporary one. As Whitehead has indicated, symbols always require interpretation. They are subject to error. They can misfire. Care is necessary for symbols to do what men want them to do. A Sacrament will not make the Jesus-event present if the symbol's form of definiteness is not truly there in the Jesus-event as well as here in the contemporary occasion. The combination of the New Testament, tradition and the life of the community seems to guarantee the Sacramental signs as offering forms of definiteness through which the Jesus-event can truly be made present; yet there remains the possibility of error—of a mistake—in which case the Jesus-event is possibly not made present. The symbol, through which a Sacrament effects the presence of the Jesus-event, must be adequately interpreted (the Church has a vested interest, therefore, in supervising the intuition that guides interpretation). The Jesus-event cannot create the Church if it is not appropriated for what it is. If a Sacrament is to "work," its symbol must really participate in the Jesus-event by its own grasp of a "form of definiteness" that is really there in the Jesus-event; the symbol must be correctly interpreted; and the form of definiteness which the symbol emBodies must then be emBodied in the real internal constitution of the Christian's life. It is that em-

Bodiment which creates a life into a Christian life. It is along these lines that Whitehead interprets the sense of *ex opere operato,* a theological expression frequently used in discussions of Sacrament:

> But the expressive sign is more than interpretable. It is creative. It elicits the intuition which interprets it. It cannot elicit what is not there. A note on a tuning fork can elicit a response from a piano. But the piano has already in it the string attuned to the same note. In the same way the expressive sign elicits the existent intuition which would not otherwise emerge into distinctiveness. Again in theological language, the sign works *ex opere operato,* but only within the limitation that the recipient be patient of the creative action.[2]

To clarify the presence-making dynamics of the Sacraments, I want to elaborate upon several of the items involved in the preceding discussion. Each Sacrament involves some basic symbols. The history of the Church's use of these symbols in the appropriation of the Jesus-event seems, I believe, to validate the Sacramental symbols as being authentic vehicles of forms of definiteness of the Jesus-event. This, I also believe, is more a pre-suppositional matter in the Church's faith than an issue of scientific historicity (which is in no sense a denial of the historical base of the symbol). There are certainly many symbols through which the Jesus-event can be appropriated; they can be authentic carriers of forms of definiteness of the Jesus-event, and in this sense there are many Christian sacraments (with a small "s"). But "s"acraments, though they are useful and necessary and good, are not part of the official symbolic code of the Church's "S"acraments. And while sacraments are appropriations of the Jesus-event, they are not creative of the Church in the way that the symbolic code of every society sustains and nurtures the life and identity of that society. A society cannot maintain itself without its symbolic code. And I have suggested that perhaps the fact that the Sacramental system has been and is the main societal dynamic of the Church's emBodiment of Jesus' presence ought to make us understand the Sacraments as part of the essential symbolic code, that is, as taking part in the Church's defining characteristics. (The many ways in which Sacraments have been theologized and practiced should prevent us from trying to say anything very specific about the Sacraments when we speak of them as being part of the defining characteristic of the Church—when I speak of Sacraments in terms of defining characteristic, I want to insist upon a very wide sense of the *fact* of Sacraments characterizing the *process* by which the Church maintains the presence of the Jesus-event. The actuality of the Church is its process; the characteristics of its process are the characteristics of its actuality.)

Symbols require interpretation in order for them to make their yield. The same item might be symbolic of several differing things. The particular item that functions as symbol may itself involve several forms of definiteness, and before it can function as symbol in a particular instance, it must be interpreted so that the pertinent form of definiteness is clear. A misinterpreted symbol may in the long run be creative of a very desirable effect, or it may miss the point and create adverse effects. And even though in the first place the effects might be good, what happens is simply not Sacrament. The efficacy of the Sacrament, therefore, depends upon a correct intuition at work in the interpretation of the symbol. This has been understood in various ways. The spirit of Jesus must be authentically at work in order for the symbol to serve really as Sacrament; the symbol can only be Sacramental when his spirit informs our intuition. A symbol is manifold until the spirit of Jesus makes Sacrament of it. In the absence of the historical figure of Jesus, his spirit has maintained its availability to history in the Church. In fact, "availability" is too neutral a term: Jesus' spirit has been creative of the Church. One would expect, then, that the intuition through which our interpretation makes Sacrament out of symbol would be found in the Church. In our tradition we have spoken of the necessity of thinking with the mind of the Church as a condition for the validity of Sacrament: *sentire cum ecclasia.* I hope the sense of this is clear: it is no mere juridical requirement; it is the condition under which any symbol is able to make present that in which it participates. The various symbols of a symbolic code cannot be creative of a society unless they function with that society's intuition as to their interpretation. Sacraments, because they are important parts of the Church's system of symbol, can only carry out their functions when experienced with the mind of the Church. That derives from the nature of symbolic experience.

A society's principal creative symbols are usually set within a ritual: a family's way of celebrating its birthdays and anniversaries; Bastille Day in France; Thanksgiving Day in the United States; the liturgical calendar of feasts in the Church which represent the life of Christ and of Christian heroes, and of course the Sacraments. In religious history, ritual has maintained the life of the myths through which a society kept in touch with its origins and knew its identity. Mircea Eliade says that a common trait of myths is that they narrate sacred history.[3] They tell of "beginnings," of what happened *in illo tempore* when the world came into being, or an island, or a particular kind of human behavior, or an institution. Myths relate the identity-source of a people: the Hebrews were who they were as a people because Yahweh led them out of Egypt and became their God. In ritual some aspects of the myth are re-enacted, re-presented: the Paschal meal; the Eucharist. The ritual presentation is intended to be more than simply a recall. It is meant to continue the historical act in which a society originated, in order to maintain the society's identity. In

Sacramental ritual there are many similar points, of course. The Jesus-event is the *in illo tempore* which for a Christian is both the originating source and the on-going source of identity. Because each of the Sacraments is *societally* creative, there needs to be a ritual sameness through which elements of the Church's identity might be touched wherever and whenever there is a Sacramental experience. That is a survival dynamic. In addition to the Sacramental symbol proper (such as the breaking of the bread and the covenanting cup of the Eucharist), there are additional symbols which the Church might want to insist upon because they make available the "intuition" out of which the principal Sacramental symbol is to be interpreted. These latter symbols are more closely related to particular historical and cultural conditions (e.g., the tradition of Gregorian chant). Yet these latter symbols too are still related very much to the survival dynamic; they intend to give guidance in the interpretation of the Sacramental symbol.

In each Sacramental experience there is need also for intensity dynamics as well as survival dynamics. The intensity dynamics are concerned with the immediacies of appropriating the Jesus-event. The intensity dynamics are of extraordinary importance as presence-making agents. If the symbol is validly "at work," that is, if it really participates in the Jesus-event and has been faithfully interpreted, it still remains for the concrescent occasion to positively prehend the Jesus-event through the symbol which has made it available. The form of definiteness from the Jesus-event contained in the symbol must relate to the concrescent occasion as a value in order to be prehended into a new occasion's real internal constitution. For that is the point at which the Jesus-event is causally efficacious and is therefore *PRESENT*. The Jesus-event presents itself through symbol to a new occasion of experience. The new occasion says: "Yes, I understand your importance. The symbol which bears you suggests how you are important. And now at this moment I understand your particular worth so much that I make you part of me. You are present to and in and through me now." Since the essential notion of "presence" is that of causal efficacy, real presence is not a matter of "here" or "not here." There are many degrees of presence.

The availability of the Jesus-event through Sacrament is only part of the Sacramental experience—a necessary part, but only part. Equally requisite (still only a part, though also a necessary part) is the decision of a new occasion of experience to let the Jesus-event take hold of its becoming. The degree to which the taking-hold of the Jesus-event is "important" reflects the degree of presence. This marks an important contrast between Greek thought and process thought, and therefore between a lot of traditional Sacramental theology and process theology. Greek modes of thought, while certainly giving due assessment to efficient causality, tended to stress the physical "thereness" of a substance as the sense of presence. Therefore the Real Presence of Jesus in the Eucharist had to be understood in terms of his "substance" being "here," that is, transubstantiation. In the Whiteheadian perspective, feelings (positive prehensions) take what is *there* and transform it into what is *here*. It is my conviction that this is the most real sense of presence, of which effective physical presence is an instance. Especially in the Sacramental discussion, this perspective lends itself to understanding the transformative nature of Sacramental experience. This perspective also emphasizes strongly what the "recipient" must do to allow presence to happen. And because the "there" of the Jesus-event is in a major way in the configuration of the community life within the Church, the community has a large role also in making Sacramental presence be real. Baptism, for example, is doomed to be ineffectual if the one baptized is not really introduced into a community where Christian love is operative. To be baptized is to be received into the Church. But Church is not a place or a thing. The actuality of the Church is its process: the Church is an event in which the Jesus-event takes hold. Effective Christian community is necessary (again, not the only necessity, but a real one) for baptism to "work," for entering the Church is entering an event where Jesus is important. Where there is not that process, there is not the actuality of the Church; there is no event into which one can enter.

I have said that the availability of the Jesus-event is a necessary condition for Sacraments to work. "Availability" is perhaps too weak or neutral a word. In a strictly neutral sense, every event that has ever transpired is available to future process. That is Whitehead's theory of "objective immortality." Christian faith is saying more than that about the Jesus-event. To understand the Jesus-event as important is to see more than neutral availability in it. A concern for the future is often a motivation in our actions. Events can aim at being relevant to the future; they can want to be events such that the future will want to take them up and make them present. We are like that when we have something to say that we think is important, and we say it with the hope that our utterance will "go out there" and change things. Such an utterance commends itself to future event much more than drinking a cup of coffee or sleeping. The utterance holds (or feels it does, at least) something which the future needs. When Christian faith affirms the importance of the Jesus-event, it is saying that Jesus is not simply available, but that he is disposed to enter into history. That is the sense of the beautiful French word *disponibilité:* not simply available, but leaning forward out of an impulse to be taken up. The Jesus-event is *disponible.* While other events may settle comfortably into the nest of accumulated past history, the Jesus-event sits on the edge of its chair, and Sacraments bring it to its feet.

In these last pages I have tried to stress the organic interaction of multiple factors in Sacramental life. A first requisite is the Jesus-event itself, which for some reason or another (every Christology develops those reasons) is important and therefore commends itself to the future. There are then certain symbols which participate in the Jesus-event and which the Sacraments use to let the Jesus-event into new occasions of experience. Sacramental occasions are creative of the Church's existence. As a society, therefore, the Church is concerned that the symbols are properly interpreted for they can only be effective if they do indeed make available forms of definiteness that are in the Jesus-event. The symbolic code which functions within a society is essential to the life of the society. The society must guard the intuition which interprets symbolic expressions and must also make it adequately available. Various elements of ritual assist in the interpretation of the symbols with the intuition of the society: *sentire cum ecclesia.* The life of the community is a locus of the "there" of the Jesus-event which a Sacramental experience transforms into a "here" in the life of a member. The member, through his own emBodiment of the Jesus-event creates Church and continues the presence of the Jesus-event in his own life and in the life of the Christian community. What I hope emerges from this characterization in process categories is a sense of the importance of the intensity dynamics, that is, the importance of those factors concerned with and surrounding the new occasion of experience in which a Sacrament takes part.

The Church faces the challenge which confronts every society: to mate survival with intensity. Whitehead understood the categories of "transmutation" and "conceptual reversion" to offer the possibility of mating survival and intensity. These two categories suggest implications for the Sacraments. There should and must be some elements of ritual sameness in the Sacraments, so that each experience is rooted in the Church and is recognizable as such. The Church is present in being a "there" where the Jesus-event is. It is present through its guidance of the interpretation of the symbols of Sacrament.

And the Church itself is re-created through every Sacramental experience. Yet the category of transmutation must function in regard to those elements of ritual sameness which are to obtain in Sacramental life. Of course that does not issue in any very precise guidelines, only in the persuasion that ritual sameness must be an element of the Sacramental experience. But the directives which construe it should be highly generalized (a massive average objectification). Intensity requires that there must be great specification at the level of the individual experiences where history and the Jesus-event engage each other. For that is where conceptual reversion operates. It is at that point that we re-do our versions of our own becoming, so that in the re-version the Jesus-event is able to contribute to our real internal constitution. We do re-versions of our lives in order for the Jesus-event to take hold of us so that we might emBody it. At the points of contact with on-going event there must be room for easy adaptation to the particularities of the occasion. In a lot of the Church's past history there has been an over-emphasis upon elements of ritual sameness, to the detriment of a keen sense of "relevancy" in individual experiences. In the Catholic Church, where cultural differences were even transcended by a universal language and a common music, there was an easy and immediate sense everywhere and at all times of the Church's identity. That this was the case, of course, is the result of another way of trying to understand reality and of interpreting the being of the Church. Two words which in our generation have become by-words are "relevant" and "meaningful." In fact, they have almost become trite; but nothing becomes trite until its insight has urged its repetition almost *ad infinitum*. These words are not mere fad words; they are symbols of many of the larger longings and desires of man. They are not just popularized ideals. Philosophies have taken them up, and so have theologies. "Relevancy" and "meaningfulness" are symbols of much of today's self-understanding. It would be easy enough to indicate factors that have given rise to that. But the point is that there is a large movement of feeling in the Church also that reacts to any religious ritual which is not meaningful and relevant. In another world view it might have been enough to say that any ritual is worship and gives glory to God. That is not persuasive today. It is a kind of life that gives glory to God, if we want to speak in that framework. Worship must generate a kind of life. Ritual, therefore, must have much in it that reflects the immediacies of the contemporary situation and suggests the meaningfulness and relevancy of the Jesus-event which it celebrates. In process categories, when we speak of the quest for meaning and relevance we are dealing with the dynamics of intensity. According to our self-understandings today we would find ritual both in the past and the present (though less so) over-determined.

As was the case when I discussed some of the process implications for an understanding of the Church and found movements in those directions, so too with Sacramental life. Many of the more recent trends are not yet officially sanctioned at either upper or lower levels, though common practices. The trends have to do largely with increased intensity. Though there are only four approved Eucharistic canons, many variations are in fact in use. There is a developing freedom in the selection of texts for the Liturgy of the Word, drawing equally from Scripture and from what used to be called secular sources. This sort of thing I would interpret in terms of the desire to create a more direct and immediate confrontation between the Jesus-event and the exigencies of the contemporary event. The use of contemporary "secular" music is another instance of the same thing. My point is not, I hope, to belabor the obvious phenomena; but rather to suggest that the process framework makes sense out of the phenomena. If the Church is understood in a process framework, many of the things that are happening are what one would expect to happen; though the same phenomena are often experienced as a threat within understandings of the Church pitched in the Aristotelian-Scholastic framework. For the tendency to structure the Sacraments in such a way that elements of ritual sameness are highly generalized (though immediately recognizable) serves the Church's will to remain Church—that is, to survive. And the tendency to require adaptation in *each* Sacramental experience so that it applies with particularity to the introduction of the Jesus-event into new occasions, that tendency is in the service of intensity. A Sacrament takes Faith in the "importance" of the Jesus-event (a defining characteristic) and implements the Faith in new acts of becoming through which the Jesus-event is made present. That is of course a statement of occasions in which "conceptual reversion" can operate in the on-going creation of the Church. The Sacraments are the Church's own best means of meeting the challenge of every society, every organism: to mate survival with intensity. (And of course there are other ways in which that challenge is met, such as periodic Councils and Synods; there too conceptual reversion can operate.)

A Sacramental experience is a positive prehension of the Jesus-event, mediated through symbol. The function of the symbol is critical in the making-present of the Jesus-event. Before dealing with the function of symbol, I want to make two prefatory observations about Sacramental symbol.

First of all, I think it is important to see the symbols as *events,* and *not things.* (I hope to make this clearer, by way of demonstration, when I discuss the Eucharist.) Sacramental theology has often characterized Sacrament in terms of matter and form. Sacramental validity required both matter and form. Matter and form, I take it, are an analysis of an event: not just some kind of thing (e.g., water at baptism), but also how it is used (e.g., water is poured as words are spoken). In Sacramental symbol, therefore, we should expect an *event* to emBody a characteristic form of the Jesus-event, the ingression of which into a new event effectively makes present anew the Jesus-event.

A second prefatory observation is that the event which functions as the Sacramental symbol is normally a whole related coterie of symbols: actions, words, ritual embellishments (setting, music, etc.). A Sacramental expression "mainly clothes itself in the media of action and of words, but also of art." [4] The event which is the symbol is a combination of multiple elements that must be integrated. The form of definiteness from the Jesus-event which the symbolic event emBodies is not simply there or not there. If it is there, it may be there with many degrees of accessibility. The accessibility of the form of definiteness does indeed affect the accessibility of the Jesus-event in the Sacrament. There is not just *ex opere operato*. There is *ex opere bene operato, ex opere optime operato, ex opere male operato, ex opere pessime operato,* and all the possible in between nuances. The composition of the Sacramental event makes a large difference overall in the effectiveness of the making-present of the Jesus-event. It takes a keen sense of ritual, a keen sense of the contemporary situation and a keen ability to "compose" to make a highly effective Sacramental experience. Or, to put it differently, it takes a deep and integrated understanding of the Jesus-event, a remarkable sense of the contemporary (not a fadish "being with it") scene, and an intuition into how the one might well participate in the other. Or, to put it still differently, we might use the word "sympathy." There are degrees of sympathy, the ability to feel-with. For a Sacramental symbol to be greatly effective, the event must manifestly feel-with the Jesus-event, manifestly feel-with the exigencies of the new occasion, and manifestly feel some of the possibilities of integration. (If there is an immediate practical application, it might be the strong reminder that the one who presides over a community's Sacramental experience carries a strong responsibility for how he puts the experience together, for that makes a big difference in how much Presence of the Jesus-event is able to be evoked into the creation of history.)

An actual entity's "experience is its complete formal constitution." [5] A Christian is one who experiences the importance of the Jesus-event both as a value and as a formative occasion in his own act of becoming. No past event enters in its totality into another's act of becoming. A past occasion has something about it (something much or something little) that commends it to the new occasion. The "something about it" is the way that it becomes an object for another's experience, and under which it becomes present. (A "something about it" is a form of definiteness.) Each Sacrament involves the use of symbol to emBody something about the Jesus-event. The symbol must also be able to participate in the new occasion; it affords a perspective through which the new occasion of experience can see itself. Because the symbol has a foot in both the past and the present, it can help to walk the Jesus-event into the new occasions of our experience. That then is one of the functions of a Sacrament: it looks at the Jesus-event and looks at life, then through a symbol it objectifies the Jesus-event for the Christian's subjectivity into which its presence is summoned. The Jesus-event is vast, and our lives are vast in their scope. That is too large an arena, too vague. The effectiveness of the Jesus-event in history requires the relating of particularities of the Jesus-event to the particularities of history. Sacraments facilitate that. The "importance" of the Jesus-event needs to be implemented; importance translates into creativity or it becomes unimportant. Sacramental life is a translation of the importance of the Jesus-event through symbols which touch important configurations of the Jesus-event and of new event.

Sometimes when we try to express a rather poignant experience we say: "I find it easy to identify with that," or, "I can really feel with that." In a sense, there are moments of that in *every* experience. We take notice of certain occasions when something about them commends them to our notice. That, in fact, is what makes some things stand out against a background of a thousand other things: a special feeling for them. Special feelings isolate special things and present them to our experience in larger ways. There is, in fact, as Whitehead interprets experience, an emotional tone to every piece of commerce that an occasion has with its world. For every object *that* we feel, there is also a *how* to our feeling; a way in which we feel its presence. This is the category of subjective form, which we have seen already and should look at once again, for symbols generate emotional responses. That too is one of the roles which Sacraments play in the life of the Christian and the Church.

I would stress, of course, that the emotional engenderment of symbols can be abused as well as used for good. Emotions can stir us to a response that we might not make otherwise—sometimes we can be stirred to an immediate response, and we suspend all the deliberations that would otherwise have been required to get us there. Martial music can make a nonfighter fight. Protest music can overcome a squeamish response. Hate music can generate hate. And there are love songs. Symbols are powerful means of generating those emotions which foster and create the life within a society; they foster the acts of individual members to take up that pattern of life which forms the society:

> But in fact the symbol evokes loyalties to vaguely conceived notions, fundamental for our spiritual natures. The result is that our natures are stirred to suspend all antagonistic impulses, so that the symbol procures its required response in action. Thus the social symbolism has a double meaning. It means pragmatically the direction of individuals to specific actions; and it also means theoretically the vague ultimate reasons with their emotional accompaniments, whereby the symbols acquire their power to organize the miscellaneous crowd into a smoothly running community.[6]

Many prehensions go into a concrescence. Each prehension

has a subjective form, that is, its own emotional tone. Each emotion is a response to some quality or another (forms of definiteness, eternal objects). The many emotions have to be integrated in the course of the concrescence. They are involved in the valuations placed on all the possible occasions which a concrescence can admit into its becoming. Heightened emotion tends to weight the prehension of one datum over another, giving it a larger overall role in the concrescence. Some feelings emerge out of the welter of feelings and are heightened in value. Those become more central feelings, and other feelings can be arranged around them; a pattern of assemblage emerges making an integration of feelings possible. Emotions are important in the determinations by which some of the occasions of experience in our actual world have a large presence in the real internal constitution of our selfhood. The emotional elements of Sacramental experiences are not merely accessory. They play essential roles in the development of the pattern of assemblage of events in a man's life whereby he is Christian. Emotional tone enters essentially into the dynamics which make-present the Jesus-event. Because of the influence of Greek modes of thought on so much of our accumulated theological heritage, it is helpful to remind ourselves from time to time that in this process understanding we take the deepest meaning of *presence* to be causal efficacy: the fact that something takes hold of our becoming, enters into it and shapes it. The emotional elements that operate in a concrescence are essential to the taking-hold process by which the Jesus-event *is* present to us. What may perhaps seem to be a "psychologizing" of Sacramental presence within an Aristotelian framework, is indeed an "ontologizing" of it in process modes of thought. (And certainly one of the remarkable features of Whitehead's systematic thought is the presence of emotion in his metaphysical scheme.) There is no other mode of presence than that of causal efficacy. Some kind of physical near-at-handness may well be a factor. Proximity frequently conditions what things influence us most. But it's the influence ultimately and not the proximity which is the conclusive fact of presence. Emotions are critical elements in the creation of presence.

I have singled out two of the important functions of symbol in a society, functions which the Sacramental system of the Church fulfills. The first is that symbols make accessible through the forms and patterns which they emBody the creative inspiration which shapes a society—be they heroes, holidays, feast days, flags, faces, sayings, songs, or Sacraments and their emBodiments of the Jesus-event. And the second is that emotions aroused within the Sacrament are an integral part of the Sacramental experience, ontologically.

Before I make some brief reflections on the three Sacraments of Initiation, I would like to return to the starting point of this work. In my description of context within which the theological act is pitched today, I chose secularization as the best overall description of this context. Secularization's deepest single conviction is perhaps that there is but a single world of reality: there is only one book of rubrics, and all reality follows it. This presents a radical challenge to religion whose tradition has most of the time embraced a two world understanding, sometimes in terms of natural and supernatural, at other times in terms of reason and faith, etc. If the one world rendering is valid, then there are two choices for handling "supernatural" phenomena, as described in an earlier world view: one is to achieve a unified world view by simply discarding the whole supernatural package; the other choice involves re-understanding and re-interpreting many of the traditional articulations of religious belief. I feel that the one-world conviction of secularization is a valid one, and that process modes of thought seem to hold out some exciting possibilities for re-interpreting God, Jesus and the events and meaning of his life, and the modes of his presence which are constitutive of the life of the Church and its individual Christians-in-community.

Another of the secularization convictions is that man is indeed responsible for the creation of his own life and of history. Process modes of thought offer an understanding of God which implicates him deeply in each moment of the world's self-creation, but which yet leaves man finally free in his decisions. Jesus and the events of his existence are important to our understanding of God, how his love is at work in the world, how men might so put their lives together, personally and corporately that the world becomes its best self—a fact in which God finds deep satisfaction as well as man. The Jesus-event, which brought God-at-work-in-man to us continues its presence in the Church. Within the Church, the Sacraments have been and are privileged ways in which the Jesus-event takes hold of us and our world. The Sacraments really work, but for that to happen there must be both the *disponibilité* of the Jesus-event *and* the large participation and cooperation of man, that is, the Christian and his Church. The paradigm of God being everywhere at work in the world (from the inside out) at the same time that man bears full responsibility for it, works also as a paradigm for the Sacraments: the Jesus-event is *there* and is *disponible,* and there could be no Sacramental life without it; but man bears a full responsibility also for making the Sacraments work—and they must work for there to be Church.

I would like to look briefly now at the three Sacraments of initiation: Baptism, Confirmation, the Eucharist.

BAPTISM

One of the most remarkable chapters in Antoine de Saint Exupéry's *The Little Prince* is built around a discussion between the fox and the little prince about what it means "to tame" someone.[7] The little prince encounters a fox in the woods, and he asks the fox to play with him:

"I cannot play with you," the fox said. "I am not tamed."

"Ah! Please excuse me," said the little prince.

But, after some thought, he added:

"What does that mean—'tame'?"

.   .   .

"It is an act too often neglected," said the fox. "It means to establish ties."

" 'To establish ties'?"

"Just that," said the fox. "To me, you are still nothing more than a little boy who is just like a hundred thousand other little boys. And I have no need of you. But if you tame me, then we shall need each other. To me you will be unique in all the world. To you, I shall be unique in all the world. . . . My life is very monotonous," he said. "I hunt chickens; men hunt me. All the chickens are just alike, and all the men are just alike. And in consequence, I am a little bored. But if you tame me, it will be as if the sun came to shine on my life. I shall know the sound of a step that will be different from all the others. Other steps send me hurrying back underneath the ground. Yours will call me, like music, out of my burrow. . . ."

The fox gazed at the little prince, for a long time.

"Please—tame me!" he said.

"I want to very much," the little prince replied. "But I have not much time. I have friends to discover, and a great many things to understand."

"One only understands the things that one tames," said the fox. . . . "If you want a friend, tame me . . ."

"What must I do, to tame you?" asked the little prince.
"You must be very patient," replied the fox.

. . .

So the little prince tamed the fox. And when the hour
of his departure drew near—
"Ah," said the fox, "I shall cry."
"It is your own fault," said the little prince. "I never
wished you any sort of harm; but you wanted me to tame
you . . ."
"Yes, that is so," said the fox.

. . .

"Men have forgotten this truth," said the fox. "But
you must not forget it. You become responsible, forever,
for what you have tamed."

It comes very close to the import of Baptism to sense that
it is an act of "taming." The French word which "taming"
translates perhaps carries still a little more weight than our
English word. *Apprivoiser* has the root word for "private" in
it. Private contrasts with public, in the sense that when someone is tamed, he is no longer public domain, but he now
"belongs" to someone. One who is tamed "belongs" with the
one who has tamed him. There is also in "private" the sense
of one's home; we use the expression: "in the privacy of
home." Taming also carries that sense, of giving one access
to the privacy of our home. It is a deep level of sharing, of
taking someone in not as a mere guest, but as a member of
the household. A guest comes and goes. To be of the household is *always* to have a home. It is *permanent*. "You become
responsible, *forever*, for what you have tamed." It also means
"to establish ties," ties in both directions. Because there are

willing ties, the two need each other. The new membership that results from the taming is transformative; it is an introduction into a new way of living, a new way of putting a life together, a way intended to make more sense out of life: "But if you tame me, it will be as if the sun came to shine on my life." But taming, of course, takes a long time once it has begun, so "you must be very patient." It is not the work of a mere moment, it takes a life!

> Then I heard a loud voice call from the throne, "You see this city? Here God lives among men. He will make his home among them; they shall be his people, and he will be their God; his name is God-with-them. . . . The world of the past is gone." Then the one sitting on the throne spoke: "Now I am making the whole of creation new" he said. "Write this: that what I am saying will come true." And then he said, "It is already done. I am the Alpha and the Omega, the Beginning and the End. I will give water from the well of life free to anybody who is thirsty; it is the rightful inheritance of the one who proves victorious; and I will be his God, and he a son to me."
>
> Rev. 21:3, 4b-6

The Sacrament of Baptism initiates a person into a new community which holds out to him a new life, a new structure of existence. It is a structure of existence in which the Jesus-event is important. He may understand its importance, for example, as an ability to love everywhere, even though love is not returned, based upon his knowing that he is loved radically by God. He may understand its importance in that it makes available to him a new relationship to God as he enters into Jesus' own relationship to God: "I will be his God, and he a son to me." He may understand its importance in that the presence of sin in the world fetters him from becoming his full self, and even from knowing the full possibilities that are open to him, and he finds in Jesus a definitive revelation of man's original potential before God. He may understand its importance in that man, by the very nature of the dynamics of evolution, needs a spiritual Center, and Christ is precisely that Omega, desired and needed by man. He may be a child who does not yet understand any of those things, but because he is effectively inserted into a Christian community he partakes in its life and is caught up in the structure of its existence. No matter which of the ways the Jesus-event is understood to be impotarnt, the *important* thing is that it is *important*. A structure of existence in which the Jesus-event is important is one in which Jesus plays a central role in the determination of the meaning of existence: a Christian structure of existence.

Baptism introduces a person into the Christian structure of existence through a rite of initiation in which water is a primary symbol which the concomitant words help to interpret. The Sacramental symbol carries at least several "somethings about the Jesus-event" through which the Jesus-event is actualized. Passing into water and emerging out of it (which was the early use of water) signifies emergence into the new life of Christian promise. Water is also the symbol of washing and cleansing. Sin loses its hold and we are made clean; our acceptability to God, notwithstanding our sinfulness, radicalizes our lovableness above our sinfulness. We are bought out of our sin. However, it cannot be emphasized enough that for Baptism really to work, the community into which a person enters must really have within it the configuration of new life, of the structure of a Christian way of living—if that is not the case, then the symbol is false. It may "say" something about the promise of Jesus, but it does not in truth offer the promise. The symbol may participate in the Jesus-event with its promise of new life; but that is not enough. For the new life offered must also be in fact *there where* it can be entered into. The symbol has to have a foot in the past and a foot in the present if the promise is to be real. I would like to use one of the paradigms that has frequently been used to characterize the effects of Baptism, namely, the context of original sin. In recent theology, original sin has come more and more to be understood in terms of the presence of sin in the world (original sin is not, of course, a Scriptural expression; it is a theological formulation).

Every time that a man is given a choice he is free to choose the right or best thing, and to avoid the wrong or lesser thing. Theoretically, he need never make the wrong choice. But our experience of human nature tells us that even though we *might* make the better choice each time it is present, statistically we do sometimes make the lesser choice. There is no theoretical necessity of failure, but there is a statistical necessity, a necessity that originates in human freedom. Because man is man, he sometimes fails, a failure that has its origin in the nature of freedom. As Teilhard has pointed out, it is also failure that is rooted in the groping way in which evolution moves to work itself out.

Therefore, the very fact that we are born into a human community means that we are born into a world where the presence of human failure is on all sides. There is, of course, the constant presence of goodness, but a goodness dimmed by the presence of failure, or sin.

A child is born into the slums where family life rarely exists, where stealing is an ordinary means of acquisition, where prostitution is a common business, where even physically there is hardly the sight of beauty anywhere. That child, like every human being, always has the option of making right choices. But living in the midst of distortions of life, it is certainly most difficult for that child to have a clear understanding of human dignity or an adequate image of the real potential for full human life that he harbors within him. In the Whiteheadian framework, we would say that such a child's actual world does not offer to it the objects of experience from which to prehend the qualities of human life that it has need of.

Because we are born into a human community where there is the constant presence of failure and sin around us, we are somewhat like the slum child. The distortions of human life that failure presents make it very difficult to understand what our potential really is for a full human existence before God and man. And it is even harder to believe in a constant summons to self-transcendence, for there is not a milieu in which it seems to be offered or to be achievable.

One of the ways in which the importance of the Jesus-event has been formulated is that the community of his followers believes that Jesus is a definitive revelation of man's original potential for human existence—which involves a relationship with God. In being such a man, Jesus retrieves man from the morass of distortion surrounding him, and he makes available to man, through the very patterns of his own existence, the possibility of becoming a new man. Jesus is understood to be like us in every way, save the distortion.

His followers attempt to build community where men can live, retrieved from the full effect of failure present in their world. To do this they work constantly to keep their own pattern of living in touch with the pattern of life they find in Jesus. And in being a structured community, they hand on from one generation to the next their accumulated experience of a community trying to live in terms of its classic revelation. They have learned from Jesus that it is the very same movement which puts men deeply in touch with each other that—if men but make symbol of the movement—also puts them most deeply in touch with God. ("And the king will answer, "I tell you solemnly, in so far as you did this to one of the least of these brothers of mine, you did it to me' "—Mt. 25:40.)

Jesus made claim to a privileged grasp of God—a grasp

which, as Cobb pointed out, became a central perception to his own identity. His followers, trying to pattern their relationship with God after his, also claim a privileged relationship with God, a grace which summons the community and each of its members to their highest perfection—which is the work of unfettered love.

Baptism takes the entrance of a new member into such a community and makes symbol and Sacrament of it. The very fact of taking up life in such a community as I have been describing is to come under its influence. It is to come under its influence in two ways: first, there is the entire community, the ekklesia or Church; and second, there is the immediate assembly or community. Contact with the Church is through this smaller community which participates in Church and is the proximate presence and experience of Church. For the most part, the new member will draw life, understanding, and experience from the smaller community, although it is Church which has made Sacrament out of his entrance into that immediate community.

The rite should of course be different depending upon whether the new member is an adult or a child. But reception into the community is no less real for the child who is not even aware of the fact. He lives in a family and in a community, and by his very being there he is necessarily influenced by their mores, their ethics, their love. He begins to be formed immediately by the ideals and feelings which shape the patterns of living in which he finds himself. For that is the actual world out of which he, for the most part, draws the "stuff" of his own becoming. His fundamental understandings are given him by the community in which he finds life. His own sense of identity is shaped by those around him. If membership in a community retrieves or "redeems" him from a situation in which his sense of his real potential would be impossible, then from the beginning of his life within the folds of the community he is already coming to life in terms of the classic revelation in Jesus about the meanings of existence—a revelation that continues its emBodiment in the community itself. Baptism introduces a member into the on-going emBodiment of the Jesus-event.

If the "fact" of Baptism is the taking up of a new life in a new community, then the "act" of Baptism requires the presence of a real community that receives the new member into membership and into immediate participation in the life of a real here-and-now group of people, i.e., community of Christians, who make the Jesus-event present through their lives.

And that comes back to the reason why I began with the discussion of taming in *The Little Prince*. The real people who will form the actual community of a new member should certainly be present at a Baptism—chief members from among them symbolize them in the godparents. That actual community of people must become responsible for the new member; they must accept the ties that are established; they must embrace the new member, not in the vague as "some" new member, but in the particularity of "this" new member who is a unique individual with his special needs, his special contributions. From Baptism on, the new member and the Christian community have need of each other. If he does not learn Christian love through them, he cannot be caught up in it. If the Jesus-event is not living in them, it will not be "there" to take-hold of him. And he in his turn must let the Jesus-event that is there take hold of him; in doing that he enters into the defining characteristics of the Christian community. He creates the community. The community needs him to have life, to survive and to do it not "merely" but intensely.

Because for Baptism to work, a real community must take up a real responsibility for the new member; he becomes an occasion of their experience; they must help him in the particularity of his pattern of life to appropriate the Jesus-event. Each one's appropriation is unique, and the community must help its members in that. If the community, therefore, accepts the responsibility for a new member, then their own lives have been touched, for in the ways in which they put their lives together, from here on out their responsibility for this new member must be reckoned as a factor. They must offer the Jesus-event to *this* member. Baptism, therefore, takes hold of a community as well as a new member. Because it involves also a taking-hold of a community, it means a new presence of the Jesus-event within community as well as for the new member. And that is not an incidental to the workings of Baptism. Causal efficacy must result in shaping a community's becoming if it is to shape the life of the new member. Baptism may begin with the initiation rite and the pouring of the water, but it is an on-going event. It establishes reciprocal responsibilities. It initiates the process of becoming Christian. It initiates it in a special way for the new member, but it initiates it also for community members anew, for they too are taken-hold of. But for Baptism to work, that is, to make present the Jesus-event, a whole pattern of life must bring to fruition that which the moment of Baptism merely initiates. The symbol in a Sacrament effects what it symbolizes. But the initiation rite of Baptism—which is its symbol—needs a real community in which the symbol participates as well as the Jesus-event in which it participates in order to effect the New Being it promises.

CONFIRMATION

In discussing Baptism, I have stressed as essential to its working that an actual community takes up responsibility for a new member who seeks a new life in its folds. This places a stress in the relationship between new member and community upon the "receivingness" of the new member and the "giving-ness" of the already members. The community bears a great responsibility in the formation of its members. It would be inaccurate, of course, to make it that simple. There is indeed reciprocity in the give and take relationship. New members will often bring fresh and prophetic insights into the meaning and possibilities of adaptation of the society's defining patterns of life. But the dominant relationship of a new member is that of receiving into his life pattern that of his new community, of learning to adapt the pattern according to which he assembles the facts of his becoming so that it participates in the pattern of becoming which makes important sense to him in the lives of the community.

Baptism effects entrance into the new community. Confirmation effects full participation as an "adult" member. The Sacrament Confirms that the one who once came as a new member has now indeed taken up that structure of existence which he came to seek. And it Confirms his own choice to affirm that pattern of life as one which he wants to continue in the becoming of his experience. For Whitehead, an actual entity has a private life and a public life. Its private life is its own moment of becoming, and during this time it is not yet accessible to other actual entities as a datum for their becoming. Only after a drop of experience has reached its moment of satisfaction and has yielded to the succeeding moment of life experience can it in its turn be a datum for others. In a (very) analogous sense, Baptism and Confirmation mark similar distinctions. Baptism emphasizes the more private period of becoming Christian. Of course one must always be becoming-Christian in order to be Christian. Yet Confirmation acknowledges a certain successful satisfaction in the becoming-Christian period, and effects a change in official status whereby one is, as it were, certified as himself being a "there" of the Jesus-event for others; and the Confirmed one assumes an apostolic role (in the literal sense of apostolic, which is "being sent"). He is sent into the world with the "there" of the Jesus-event in himself and is asked to give to others since he experiences it as important to the meaning of life.

A few years ago there appeared in a publication by the Youth Department of the World Council of Churches an article describing the role of a "guarantor." While the article addressed itself to the ways in which an adult is sometimes a guarantor to a younger person, it said that the guarantor relationship takes places in many aspects of life. Confirmation changes a person's status in the community, and one aspect (and an important one) of that new status is the guarantor role, especially in regard to new and less experienced members. I want to cite some passages from the article, keeping in mind that in our context "Confirmed Christian" is to be understood for "adult" or "guarantor":

A guarantor is a significant other, who is farther along in life, who establishes us with a co-personal world. Knowing that he cannot live our life for us, but only affirm us as true and give us entree. "Entree" means both "the main course of the feast of life," and "the right and freedom to enter."

A guarantor is not a father-mother substitute, but an adult who has a respected place in some activity valued by us, who notices us personally, talks to us as equal, and by his dependable image of us enables us to feel "being the kind of person I am, I will make it." . . .

Whatever our age, we need a guarantor as we work into the inner circle of some new-for-us enterprise, having to become a new person in the process.

We need such a person as a *reference point of identity* within ourselves. Also as a source of courage. For we can stand up to change and tension, grow by leaps and risk, only if something remains throughout it all, i.e., relation with a guarantor. A person who trusts us and trust, *continues* us.

A guarantor firms in us expectation—as contrasted with wispy dreaming which we know is largely illusion. We begin, not only to vision the good life, to feel vaguely that we are desirable life, but to feel that it will come off. (Expectation is always both a *vision* of the desirable and a *belief that it will happen.*) Being what we are, we have a real chance in life. We can count on being something special.

Introduced by the guarantor, we become—often to our surprise—weavers of the social fabric. He does this partly by clueing others on the expectation they may have of us. Somewhat as when a person takes us to a social event and introduces us around, at first we are accepted not because of what we are (for no one knows that yet), but because someone has, in effect, said to both the introduced people, "You two are not enemies; neither of you is carrying concealed weapons, you can be trusted, something interesting may happen." . . .

The guarantor sees potential in us. And sanctions work in which we discover our "name," and our powers of creating. . . .

He senses us at the point of our life vocation.

We are also birthed by meeting the quality of his existence. By being exposed to "where he lives." We commune more with his consciousness than we do with his conclusions. Around him, we are "more than usual." And over a period of time, we are generated. . . . He is a fairly skilled interpreter of the events of our time and the meaning of life, can state fumblingly and in situation the faith out of which he lives. . . . The task is to find adults (guarantors) who are *living the becoming future* now. Who have some sense of what possibility God is offering in this moment of history. Who are living in New Time, rather than Old Time; are of the growing edge, rather than the rotting edge of civilization. . . . People who instead of talking about the past—and in pious language—are present incarnations of New Testament vitality. And know the truth of the Hasidic saying—

"Every day, man shall go forth out of Egypt, out of distress." [8]

I have cited the description of guarantor at length because it incorporates so many of the facets of relationship which a Confirmed Christian has with his Church. He is one to whom others ought to be able to look to see a workable "pattern of assemblage" according to which a Christian life has been put together. He is aware that he is able to guarantee the life, and is willing to do so—more than willing, even, for it is a responsibility. Someone(s) once became forever responsible for him; and now he in his turn is responsible for the Church. He is a lure to others to be "more than usual," that is, not to accept a life that does not promise transcendence. He is (to state it perhaps clinically) an expert at "conceptual reversion," for he has learned to interpret the events of our times in terms of the Faith out of which he lives. He is a lure for others to do that; but he does not impose his own way of bringing together Faith and contemporary events; each one must do that in his own way. The guarantor guarantees *that* it can be done.

The "concrescing stage" is a moment of great inward concern. "Objective immortality" looks out and beyond in its universal availability. Following the analogy that I have suggested along these lines, the Confirmed Christian faces outward to the world and to the whole Church in a way that the Baptized and not yet Confirmed Christian (the concrescing one) is not expected to do. (I cannot insist enough that the Confirmed Christian is of course a process of actually prehending the Jesus-event in an on-going way—I use the concrescing/ concrete analogy loosely.) A Confirmed Christian has a broader, more universal responsibility for the life of the Church (even though he normally lives out that responsibility through his insertion into a particular community). It is a fitting part of the Confirmation ritual, therefore, that a Bishop or someone delegated by him be the minister of Confirmation—for a Bishop, even though he presides over a particular Church, exercises his pastoral care for the entire Church. The fact that a Bishop presides symbolizes the much broader context of Church into which the Confirmed person is inserted.

Another analogy in which a traditional Confirmation symbol is rooted, an analogy indicating a whole-Church concern of a Confirmed Christian, is that of military service. The "slap on the cheek" is a symbol of a readiness "to do battle." At this moment of history that particular symbol (doing battle) may almost be an anti-symbol, a negative one. But the point of it remains. In tribal life as well as contemporary life, coming of age has meant the obligation to become a warrior when society is threatened. In modern life, coming of age frequently implies voting too, that is, participation in the life of the society (not just the inward life of one's family). We may well at this point need a new symbol and I am not suggesting one; but an essential of Confirmation, which needs an effective symbol, is the taking up of a very large responsibility for and participation in the life of the society.

I think that it should also be clear that Confirmation, which is a Sacrament of Maturity, should be the experience of those who are old enough to make the kind of mature decision which is implied. It means there has been enough experience of Christian life that deliberate choice is made of it, that it is believed in deeply enough that one wants to make it available to others, and that in some way the community accepts this person's appropriation of Christian life and approves it. The questioning session which is normally a prelude to Confirmation is a symbol of one trying to demonstrate his grasp of Christian life, his ability to articulate his life (the guarantor can state fumblingly—at least ·that—the Faith out of which he lives). In the recent revision of the Ordination right, the community is asked to manifest in some way its approval of the candidate for the priesthood. That makes sense, of course, only if those assembled know the candidate. Perhaps that sort of ritual would now be a better symbol in Confirmation than the questioning—that those who have actually formed Christian community for this candidate for Confirmation would express their acceptance of him.

The Pentecost experience of the New Testament is frequently a model for Confirmation. The Spirit comes upon those assembled, after which they face outward to the people and preach the Gospel of Jesus-Christ. There should be some counter-part in the Confirmation experience, some actualizing symbols, so that a newly Confirmed person does indeed include in the pattern of his life's events some new points of insertedness into his functioning in the Christian community.

I am trying to insist throughout this description that the Sacramental symbols must *in fact* participate in both the Jesus-event and contemporary possibilities for the Sacrament to do its work. For a symbol actualizes what it symbolizes in the Sacrament, and the symbol must have a real basis. If a person is not old enough to make a mature decision, the symbol is ineffective. If a person has not learned yet how to put together a Christian way of life, the symbol is ineffective. If a person is not willing to take up an active responsibility for the Church, the symbol is ineffective. If a community will not accept the service of someone, the symbol is ineffective. I emphasize here the nature of symbolism which Sacramental symbols must also respect if they are to work. Whitehead gave the analogy of a musical string and a tuning fork: the string may not sound until a tuning fork is struck; but not any tuning fork or any string will do. They must be tuned to each other. So also here for Confirmation; mere use of the symbols may have no effect whatsoever. If there is no effect, there is no presence. The availability or *disponibilité* of the Jesus-event is not enough for there to be presence: it must be tapped by a tuning fork that touches the same frequencies in it and in the contemporary situation.

EUCHARIST

The celebration of the Eucharist has been a central event of Christian life since the first days of Christian community. It is here that those who call themselves Christian have so often looked for the meaning and the expression of their common faith. It has been a constant in the faith of the celebrating community that the Risen Lord is present in the Eucharist. Theology has over and over again grappled with elaborations of the Lord's presence.

The theology of the Eucharist which has had the longest hold in the Church has been that of transubstantiation, a theological elaboration in Aristotelian-Scholastic categories. More recently we have become familiar with "transignification" or "transfinalization" as theological elaborations. If there is any point in suggesting a parallel word in a process theology of the Eucharist (and I mostly suppose there isn't too much point), it would perhaps be "transeventualization," since event replaces the notion of substance.

The fact that we are in the process of formulating new world views and new articulations of our world views is reason enough for attempting a new formulation of the Eucharist. But a second reason for taking up the topic again is the large amount of recent exegetical examination of the Lord's Supper. This research suggests that bread and wine have been understood much too narrowly as the Sacramental signs that bear the Lord's presence. In earlier theologies of the Eucharist there has been an almost physical emphasis upon "body" and "blood," which a narrow concentration upon the elements of bread and wine would certainly suggest. I cannot here deal more than briefly with the exegetical question—for that is not within the scope of either this work or my competency. I will mostly be depending upon the work of Eduard Schwiezer [9] and Willi Marxsen,[10] especially the latter.

There are four accounts of the institution of the Eucharist in the New Testament: those in each of the three synoptic Gospels, and that in Paul's first letter to the Corinthians. The Pauline account of the institution was written some fifteen years or so before the synoptic accounts, and is almost certainly closer to the very early practice and understandings of the community:

> For this is what I received from the Lord, and in turn passed on to you: that on the same night that he was betrayed, the Lord Jesus took some bread, and thanked God for it and broke it, and he said, "This is my body, which is for you; do this as a memorial of me." In the same way he took the cup after supper, and said, "This cup is the new covenant in my blood. Whenever you drink it, do this as a memorial of me."
>
> I Cor. 11:23-26

I want to note first of all the separation of the two symbols. The cup is taken only after the meal; and this is reflected also in the Lucan account, although there are two cups there, one

at the end of the meal and another earlier. The breaking of the
bread is earlier in the meal. The two actions involving the
bread and the cup are separated from each other. The particular symbolism of each of the actions should be inquired
after, to see how *each action in its own way* is a communication of the Lord's presence. It is later (though not by much)
that the celebration of the Eucharist is removed from an
actual meal. As soon as that happens, the two symbols are
juxtaposed. Then, through parallelism, the formula develops
into the one with which we have become liturgically familiar:
"This is my body. This is my blood." Jesus certainly made use
of the symbolism of the two actions that would have been
familiar to the apostles. And while they are inter-related
symbols (both have a place in the Paschal meal), they do not
exhibit the parallelism that later theologies attributed to them.
In Paul (and also in Luke), the words accompanying the
second action are, "This is the cup of the new covenant . . ."
and not, "This is my blood." The symbol here is not the wine
alone, i.e., not the contents of the cup, but the cup with its contents as a symbol of covenanting action. How repulsive it
would have been to a Jew to consider, even symbolically,
drinking blood! The blood reference seems surely to be to that
of covenant. Recall in Ex. 24:8 that "Moses took the blood
and cast it towards the people. 'This,' he said, 'is the blood of
the covenant that Yahweh has made with you . . .' " Paul also
says in I Cor. 11:28-29 that "everyone is to recollect himself
before eating this bread and drinking this *cup;* because a person who eats and drinks without recognizing the Body is
eating and drinking to his own condemnation." The symbol is primarily the cup of the Lord. Again in I Cor. 10:21, he
says that "you cannot drink the cup of the Lord and the cup
of demons." Then he goes on to say, which suggests a wide
understanding of the bread symbol also, that "you cannot take
your share at the table of the Lord and at the table of demons."
For not just bread, but blessing it, breaking it, and sharing

it are included in the symbolic action—and perhaps even the still larger action of a shared meal, which "breaking bread" also means. In the Emmaus account, Jesus is recognized "in the breaking of the bread." Also in Acts 2:46-47a: "They went as a body to the Temple every day but met in their houses for the breaking of the bread; they shared their food gladly and generously; they praised God and were looked up to by everyone." It is not certain whether "the breaking of the bread" is meant to indicate the Eucharist or just a meal; but in either event, the expression is used for the whole action of Eucharist or meal. Let me give a final text from Paul:

> The blessing cup that we bless is a communion with the blood of Christ, and the bread that we break is a communion with the body of Christ. The fact that there is but one loaf means that, though there are many of us, we form but a single body because we all have a share in this one loaf.
>
> I Cor. 10:16-17

It seems clear to me that the Sacramental symbols, as reported in Paul's letter (and for the most part, also in Luke's account), are *not things* of bread and wine, though they are part, but the *action* of breaking bread and partaking, and of blessing the cup of a new covenant in Jesus' blood, and partaking in it. It is worth noting that in the liturgical formula for the Eucharist given in the *Didache*, the symbolism is even more loosely construed than in any of the Gospel's accounts; there is not a parallelism between the things of bread and wine, and body and blood.

It is events and not things which are symbols through which the Lord is present in the Eucharist. The Eucharist is above all in *action* of the Lord and the Christian community. The actions of the Eucharist are already invested with symbolic meaning from their Old Testament context. Jesus re-invests them, but he makes use of the weight which they already carry, for that is how those who shared the meal with him would have understood the symbols. The entire Paschal meal re-presents the action (deliverance from Egypt) in which Yahweh became their God and they became his people. Yahweh became present to the Hebrews in their history, in their deliverance. The shared table (the "breaking of the bread") symbolizes the unity of the Hebrews, or perhaps the "people-ness" aspect of "the people of God." Only Hebrews came together at table for the first passover meal; they assembled so that Yahweh could act among them, and they were in readiness for him. And at the yearly Passover Feast, only Hebrews came to table and broke bread together. The meal celebrated the oneness and togetherness of a people, who were both one and together through the hold of Yahweh on their history and on their lives. In the New Testament, the new people of God are those who are one in and through Jesus. The unity of men is pre-eminently clear as a theme in Jesus' Eucharistic discourse in John's Gospel. The unity between Jesus and the Father is offered as a model of the unity among men. The taking-hold action of Jesus results, above all, in that men become one in him out of love for one another. Jesus is "for us" (this is my body, which is for you) and in the Eucharist we let him be for us, we let him take hold of us, and in so doing he is made present. In a sense, this is a personal happening for each one, for it is life by life that men become a society. But in a primordial way, the Eucharist is a social action through which a people is formed more deeply as a people, and the presence of the Lord is through his hold on a people: "The fact that there is only one loaf means that, though there are many of us, we form a single body because we all have a share in this one loaf" (I Cor. 10:17). The "breaking of the bread" symbol participates in the Jesus-event, therefore, in exhibiting through its sharing a single people that is a people because Jesus is "for us" and we have accepted his being for us. And very much like the father who told his children at the Passover Feast that "this is what Yahweh did for *me*," even though he was not *there* those hundreds of years before, so the Christian explains, this is what Jesus has done for *me*, for *us*. It is not necessary for us to have been *there*, for the *there* is now *here* in our new celebration. It is *here* because there is *now* an experience of the Jesus-event taking hold of our lives. For that is the deepest and most real meaning of presence.

The "cup of the new covenant" in the blood of Jesus carries a symbolic meaning that is related, of course, to the breaking of the bread. But it carries its own weight. The pouring out of blood is often associated with sacrifice in the Old Testament. And some of that meaning is perhaps present in the New Testament use. For the Eucharist recalls the death of the Lord until he comes. And later Eucharistic texts relate the shedding of blood to the forgiveness of sins, especially after parallelism has succeeded in juxtaposing bread/wine and body/blood both in action and in conceptualization. Scholastic theology has sometimes interpreted the essence of the *sacrifice* of the Mass in the separation of the body and blood. While some elements of a sacrificial notion of blood may not be lacking, the emphasis certainly seems to be upon that of covenant. Even after parallelism causes a shift from "This cup is the new covenant in my blood" to "This is my blood, the blood of the new covenant" (Mt. 26:28), the notion of covenant remains.

In the Exodus event itself blood identifies the Hebrew households; it is sprinkled on the door posts. It is also essential to Yahweh's agreement with the people, for he will protect them if they are identified with the blood. That is his covenant:

The blood shall serve to mark the houses that you live

in. When I see the blood I will pass over you and you
shall escape the destroying plague.

Ex. 11:13

Moses uses blood again to ratify the covenant. There is, in this
Mosaic covenant, a strong emphasis upon the contents of the
law and upon obedience:

> And taking the Book of the Covenant he read it to the
> listening people, and they said, "We will observe all that
> Jahweh has decreed; we will obey." Then Moses took
> the blood and cast it towards the people. "This," he said,
> "is the blood of the Covenant that Yahweh has made
> with you, containing all these rules."
>
> Ex. 24:7-8

In the New Covenant which Yahweh made with his people
and which Jeremiah proclaimed, the emphasis is now upon
the interior spirit. The people of Yahweh will know in their
hearts the meaning of being his people. There is no need for
a Book of Covenant since it is written in hearts:

> See, the days are coming—it is Yahweh who speaks—
> when I will make a new covenant with the House of
> Israel (and the House of Judah), but not a covenant like
> the one I made with their ancestors on the day I took
> them by the hand to bring them out of the land of Egypt.
> They broke that covenant of mine, so I had to show them
> who was master. It is Yahweh who speaks. No, this is the
> covenant I will make with the House of Israel when those
> days arrive—it is Yahweh who speaks. Deep within them
> I will plant my Law, writing it on their hearts. Then I will
> be their God and they shall be my people. There will be
> no further need for neighbor to try to teach neighbor,
> or brother to say to brother, "Learn to know Yahweh!"

No, they will know me, the least no less than the greatest
—it is Yahweh who speaks—since I will forgive their in-
iquity and never call to mind their sin.

Jer. 31:31-34

Jesus initiates still a New Covenant beyond that of Jeremiah. In a way, the content of Jesus' New Covenant is not
greatly different. The locus of it is in the spirit of love and not
in prescriptions of a written law. God does not call to mind
the sin of man, for he loves him regardless—he does not
want man's sin, but he does not stop wanting man. God wants
man more than he non-wants the sin of man. Jesus does,
however, un-nationalize the Covenant. It is meant for all
men. It is universalized. Hebrew history erupts into world
history in the Jesus-event.

The cup of the Covenant in Jesus' blood is a symbol above
all of an agreement, a commitment. It effects an acceptance
of the importance of the Jesus-event so that those who drink
of it agree to let their lives be taken hold of by it; they agree
that the Jesus-event will be a center of meaning in their lives,
that it will play a significant role in their becoming. And
because, as the bread signifies, all are one Body, the Covenant also means the responsibility which all of those take up
for each other who drink the cup. We are Covenanted to one
another in Jesus. The sharing of the cup of the New Covenant
in Jesus' blood is, therefore, a symbol of commitment. Its
effects (if the symbol works), therefore, are a Covenanting
action whereby we once again let the Jesus-event be important
to our corporate lives, and whereby we take up responsibility
for one another and affirm the responsibility which others have
for us. The Eucharist continually actualizes what Baptism
and Confirmation have begun: ties are established, we are
forever responsible for what we have tamed; new life is over
and over again proffered (it will be as if the sun came to shine
in my life). Each sharing of the cup recontracts the people of

God and their God with each other, in the blood of Jesus. A contract is a responsibility, and each contract (each covenanting action) radicalizes the responsibility of God for the community and of the community for building the Kingdom of God through the incorporation of community into the Jesus-event and the Jesus-event into community. It makes the Jesus-event into Real Presence.

The Sacrament of the Eucharist is the central Sacrament in that it sums up the entire Jesus-event: mankind becoming one Body in Christ through its emBodiment of him in their lives together; the acceptance of a Covenant among men and between man and God, made and lived out through Jesus, so that love can make men one, and man and God one. St. Thomas insisted upon the centrality of the Eucharist; it sums up the sense of the Jesus-event so fully in its symbols and in its presence of Jesus that all of the other Sacraments look to it. It is also in a pre-eminent way the *signum commemorativum, exhibitivum et prognosticum.* Jesus designated it as a *commemoration* of the meaning of himself in relation to his community of followers, and in the large content of its Sacramental symbol, the Eucharist more than any other Sacrament *exhibits* the full scope of the Jesus-event. And the Eucharist in its on-going appropriation of the Jesus-event for the Christian community is the pre-eminent sign of the Church's *future,* a sign that *effects* the Church's future through its ever new re-creation of the New Covenant of Jesus, its Christ and its Lord.

I have said enough about the interplay of survival dynamics and intensity dynamics that I do not want to dwell upon them here, other than to suggest that the principal ingredient of ritual sameness is certainly the re-presentation of the Lord's Supper through one of the New Testament accounts of the institution, and that includes the maintenance of the breaking of the bread and the sharing of the cup of covenant, for these are invested with meanings from their own past, meanings that are essential to the "forms of definiteness" of the Jesus-event through which the Eucharist makes Jesus present. The ritual sameness of each Eucharistic event puts every celebration in touch with the action initiated in Jesus' last celebration with his friends in the upper room, at which his own self-gift reached the culminating point soon to be consummated. The ritual sameness also keeps each Eucharist in touch with the large historical movement in which action—in a very large sense—moves toward fulfillment of the Jesus-event. The ritual sameness also confers an identity that should make each Eucharist, whenever and wherever, recognizable as being in touch with both the initial Eucharistic action and with every other fellow-celebration of it. But there must also be great particularity in each celebration, for there are particularities in the configuration of each Christian community's unity and there are special requirements that mark the nature of each community's covenant with God and with each other. That is where intensity of Christian life is generated. Each new celebration of the Eucharist must ally itself and assimilate itself to the continuing movement within man to become "more" by transcending each now into the becoming of New Man. Each new celebration of the Eucharist is a new front edge to the self-same action that is carving a constantly deeper unity out of the amazing multiplicity that Christianity learns to embrace without destroying.

6

SOME PASTORAL
IMPLICATIONS

As soon as one accepts that "the process is the reality," for both homiletics and catechetics it becomes more fruitful to ask "When is a Christian?" rather than "What is a Christian?" A man is a Christian when some aspect of the Jesus-event plays an *important* role in the pattern according to which he assembles the facts and events of his existence. I want to recall the Whiteheadian sense of the word "important": it means some aspect of experience that receives considerable attention because it provides a clue to the large part of experience; what is important serves as a clue to the interpretation of the whole. A woman becomes a mother in giving birth to a child, at least in a legal and a biological sense. But she is a mother as constitutive of her personhood *when* "mother" becomes an important factor in how she puts her life together in an overall way.

When I speak of "an overall way" of putting a life together, I mean that there is a pattern. In this case, "mother" dictates much of the configuration of that pattern. Many elements of the pattern situate themselves in relation to "mother" which is a key symbol in the woman's self-understanding. And that is

255

the sort of thing we mean when we speak of ego-content. (I am very much indebted to Cobb's *The Structure of Christian Existence* for many of these elements of a Whiteheadian psychology.) The woman who is not merely biological "mother" but "mother" in her personhood does not necessarily put her life together with constant conscious awareness of herself as mother. In fact, there may well be several other key symbols which tell her who she is, and which participate in an important way in her pattern of self-hood. But in an integrated personality, such key symbols, even if they are several, have been organically inter-related so that they do not negate or inhibit each other. (A personality conflict might arise if "mother" and "wife" and "writer" are not organized symbols, but are merely juxtaposed.)

A man may be a juridical Christian when he is Baptized, but he is only Christian to the extent that, and when, some Christian "form of definiteness" is an important constituent of his personhood, not in an incidental way but in a patterned way. He is a Christian when his personhood is importantly constituted by his own appropriations of the Jesus-event. Here I stress "his own" appropriations, but a little later I want to stress the deeply societal nature of each one's own-most appropriations of the Jesus-event.

The point that needs to be stressed is that one is never a Christian for all time on the basis of any single commitment. Only when that commitment is a central one (even if one central one among others) is my personal process a Christian process, and my personal reality a Christian reality. There are times in life when one is more Christian or less Christian; it's not just a matter of Christian or not Christian. And even when speaking of being more Christian or less Christian, there is more at stake than being good or bad. Someone may be doing some wrong and un-Christian actions, and all the while know deep within himself that things are not right; and it could be the presence of a Christian form of definiteness in his committed pattern of personhood, which he moves against, that makes him know his own dis-ease. There is a real way in which that person is a Christian in a more real sense than someone doing good things who has never heard of Christ. When I say that, I am not of course placing a higher valuation on the unfaithful Christian over the virtuous non-Christian. I am just saying that even in a moment of infidelity I may well have a Christian personhood, albeit that my Christianity at that point is at low tide. (Much as an unfaithful spouse may not at all want to back out of the "spousehood" which he affirms, and which largely constitutes his personal identity.) The pastoral point is the need to reckon with the fact that my life will never be without failure, and that I must, without condoning failure, learn to relate to it in such a way that even in its presence I do not unconstitute myself, in my self-understanding, as Christian.

Equally important is to pay less attention to individual actions and more to the overall configuration of life—or at least to be attentive to actions for what they are able to tell us about the patterns of our lives. For I am insisting that the name Christian belongs to an identity which is larger than individual actions, which is as large as a pattern of life, a pattern which inundates our process, communicating its identity to the whole assemblage of life's events.

There is a tension which frequently arises when someone tries to put together a life in which the Jesus-event is constitutively important. It is the tension between a very high intensity and a very reasonable and balanced appropriation of the Jesus-event. As we saw earlier in Whitehead, intensity in an organism results from a highly specified and very particular kind of interaction with its world. Men, too, who live very intense existences are captivated most often by something quite special; they are caught up in an intuition. They are relating to very particular elements in their world, and are relating and interacting in a very particular way, in a sense, an unbalanced way; unbalanced because the high particularity leaves much unsaid and untouched. Society is justified in desiring that what defines it be present and active in a balanced, proportional way. Lack of proportion in an organism is precisely what we denominate as monstrosity. But there are certainly two ways of achieving that necessary balance of composition within a society. One is to expect to find a good balance of all or most of its defining characteristics within each member. A second, and more difficult way, is to achieve a high degree of relatedness between the various members, each of whom works out of a highly particularized and partial version of the defining characteristics. The wholeness comes from the organic inter-relatedness of members. That wholeness is available on a large basis to the society, but conditions the various members too, for when they prehend each other in relationship, they set up a positive relationship to other parts of the defining characteristic. These considerations hold for the Christian world and would apply also within the historical Catholic Church. The latter society, throughout much of its history, has achieved, or sought to achieve its balanced hold on the Jesus-event through the balanced hold that each member has (a dynamic which also serves the survival quest). That has produced a high degree of standardization. The great diversity which arises in the Church today is threatening, both because there are surely more numerous partial holds upon the Christian intuition even at points of great Christian intensity, and also because there are not many historical paradigms out of our past to assist the Church in a new role as facilitator, that is, one whose authority function is less to regulate and more to occasion inter-relation in the most organic way possible.

To recapitulate thus far: in as much as being a Christian is a result of a personal identity resulting from a patterned importance of the Jesus-event in a man's life, "When is a Christian?" is undoubtedly a better focus for catechetics and

homiletics than "What is a Christian?" For the umpteenth
time, the process is the reality. Secondly, intensity in Christian
life often means a highly particularized hold on the Jesus-
event as part of a very specialized response to one's personal
relationship to the world. The more particularized one's version of Christianity is, the more does one need *to belong*
broadly to community. I intend *belong* to be taken in a very
strong psychological and experiential way: I know that I belong to you, and you belong to me. I think these dynamics are
also called for by the Whiteheadian aesthetic which pervades
his metaphysical schema. Intensity is a quality of major forms
of beauty, beauty being the aim of existence. Intensity is
achieved in a society when variety of detail enters into harmony, an achievement of effective contrast. Only a powerful
mode of inter-relatedness can effect such contrast, when items
that would ordinarily be dismissed as incompatible are made
whole together.

These approaches to "When is a Christian?" reflect a number of Whiteheadian themes. *The act of experiencing* the
Jesus-event creates "Christian." Baptism initiates and celebrates that act. One is more or less Christian when that act
effectively shapes the experiencing. One is more or less Christian according to the intensity with which the Jesus-event
shapes the experiencing, for intensity in a life always involves
a keen focus of both energy and vision. There is a risk in this
because a sharp focus is a limited one; it is particular and
highly defined. But there is small openness to the summons of
the future to be more without risk. "The worship of God is
not a rule of safety—it is an adventure of the spirit, a flight
after the unattainable. The death of religion comes with the
repression of the high hope of adventure." [1] Psychologically,
a carefully balanced statement or vision is not an effective
symbol around which to assemble the events of a life with
intensity, for that spreads rather than focuses energy. Yet
carefully balanced vision is essential for the life of a society

—in this case the Church. If the Church wants to manifest a balanced response to the Jesus-event that is *also* an intense response, the balance must come from an integration of accumulated and highly specialized appropriations of the Christian intuitions which individual Christians have achieved. The safety of Christian risk is in the cushioning that comes from community where "my people" round me out with a wholeness that values and needs my intensity. The call for openness to risk must be accompanied by the call to deep insertedness into Church, but a Church which is not identified as a rule of safety but as a summons to transcendence.

I would like to take a closer look at Whitehead's description of a society. He says that the common element of form, necessary in each member for there to be a society, "arises in each member of the nexus by reason of the conditions imposed upon it by its prehension of some other members of the nexus."[2] To state the issue as a question: If I am a Christian because there is some Christian form operative in the pattern according to which I put my life together, where did the Christianness come from? How did I get it?

I will let someone into my life who has made good sense to me. That "good sense" might come from a thousand different quarters. Human relations develop when people make good sense to each other. When I make a *full* decision to let someone into my life, I give that person leave to unpack his life here in mine. When that life has been unpacked, I give particular attention to that part of the baggage that helps account for the good sense which he made to me in the first place. Or, to put it another way, the central symbols in that person's pattern of significantly organized experience get unpacked in my life. They are the symbols which I have experienced as valuable though I may not have sorted them out yet; but because they are what makes sense out of my friend's life, I have already decided that I like them. When I let someone into the becoming of my own life, in that self-same decision I let into my life the dynamics of his becoming. When I prehend someone because he makes sense to me, the "what makes sense" of him imposes itself upon me. As I increase the number of people I let into my life who have similar and related symbols central to their various patterns of life, I begin to accumulate in amount in my own life the key elements that have gone into making sense out of their lives. The more those lives become central to my own, the more I develop patterns of significantly organized experiences which reflect theirs, or supplement theirs, or complement theirs—but in any event, relate organically to theirs. Of critical importance, therefore, to becoming a Christian is the need for a milieu of Christians who make sense out of life, in some way or other because they are Christians; and the dynamics by which Christians unpack their own lives in each other's lives in important ways. A reminder again: my concern is primarily with the dynamics of becoming Christian so I have not tried to delineate any kind of "essence" of the Christian common element of form that makes "Church." A least common denominator statement of it might be that the Jesus-event is (Whiteheadianly) "important," and is a clue therefore to the interpretation of the whole of life.

As one goes through life becoming a Christian, the New Testament of course has a primacy in a man's life. And from another point of view, the Sacramental system has a primacy in the becoming dynamics of Christianity. Those primacies have to be asserted and lived—each is a locus of the Jesus-event. But the nearest set of "hows," existentially and psychologically, have to do with lives which have appropriated the Jesus-event effectively and impressively, and when we appropriate those lives into our own, we appropriate their appropriation of the Jesus-event, and Christianity accumulates within us. What I am asserting here is the existential and psychological primacy of those dynamics which foster that individual Christians unpack their respective lives in the lives of each other, not merely as good human relations (as if that were "mere"), but as how Christianness gets let into a man's life. In the restoration of Sacramental ritual the societal character of those experiences is being stressed more again. For a long time historically the private and personal character overshadowed and sometimes hid the social nature of Sacramental experience. There is a lot of room in Sacramental experiences for fostering, in a ritual way, the unpacking of lives so as to turn loose "out there" the operative holds of the Jesus-event in contemporary life, making the Jesus-event not just neutrally available, but waiting to leap into life. Two ritual occasions that commend themselves to these dynamics, just for examples, are General Confession and the Prayer of the Faithful during celebration of the Eucharist. The Prayer of the Faithful is an occasion when members of a community expose their lives (they can, that is; one doesn't hear it often) by praying for intentions that reflect their real needs and their real insertedness into life, and the way that insertedness is conditioned and compelled by something from the Jesus-event.

Another formational value in stressing this aspect of how one becomes Christian is that when some Christian intuition is at work in a person's life, it is there not only as intuition, but as intuition that has already felt the world around, and learned how to engage itself. When we let someone in our lives like that, we not only get a feel for the Christian intuition which is at work, but also for how it has gone to work. Doing it that way often makes it possible to skip a step formationally, in that the intuition is not first appropriated with the subsequent task of working out active embodiments of it; when the intuition is first appropriated, it is already appropriated with its own *savoir faire*. I need to say, of course, that in stressing these dynamics of unpacking lives, I am not saying that they are (or even could be) exhaustive of how one becomes Christian. But I am saying that they are living ways that have not been sufficiently developed, and that they are ways which the process world view heartily commends to the structure of Christian experience.

I might indicate also that I have stressed here the "unpacking dynamics" with regard to individual Christians in relation to their more immediate communities. It is a more complex issue, but equally important are the similar dynamics by which individual churches unpack their experiences in the larger Church. I find it heartening to see that Vatican II was in many respects such an activity, and that the Church-wide synod of Bishops functions frequently in this way too. Nor would it be too farfetched to indicate the new importance of media in unpacking Christian experience all over the place—in fact, we've only just begun to experience the impact of media upon Christian life. The impact of "popular opinion" on Vatican II was immense because so much of its operation was exposed, and interacted with and reacted to with immediacy in the press and on television. But "popular opinion" can legitimately be translated into the interaction of different experiences, cultural and religious, with the experiences of the men who were themselves interacting in Council. And what once were theological discussions of a rather esoteric nature among the "experts"—these are now the common property of the religion section of *Time* and *Newsweek* and of many journals and newspapers. Presuming that various theologies are expressions of various religious experiences, it would certainly not be out of place if homilies and sermons sometimes dwelt upon these items, not for fadiness of newsiness, but for the sake of unpacking the Christian experience of other communities.

If rite and symbol are to help Christians unfold their experiences of the Jesus-event for each other, it is reasonable for lives that touch each other most closely to worship and celebrate Eucharist together, to ask forgiveness together, for the natural community of a child to be present at Baptism, etc. To some extent—not exclusively, but largely—the natural units of society and community recommend themselves as natural units of Christian society, that is, of Church. That was certainly the sense of parish structure as it arose in the Church. Until the kind of movement and interchange that transportation and communication have made possible, people who lived geographically close tended to be the natural units of society. Parish structure respected that naturalness. While that natural societal structure may still function in some rural areas and small towns, city life—which accounts for most of this country's population—does not tend to form societal units in terms of geography. There is enough mobility that societal units draw from all over a metropolitan area. I do not have practical suggestions to make, for at this juncture we must look to the sociologists for expertise in assessing the most operative bases for the formation of natural units of community in our country. Frequently there are several groupings in which the same family may participate with a sense of belonging. We need also to consult systems experts to look for ways to restructure the units and cross-units of societal belonging. The present system is obsolescent and in some places obsolete. The "underground" Church and the floating parishes are random essays at regrouping. Unfortunately these groupings have seldom had affirmation and official encouragement. But a process theology judges those dynamics which I have suggested to be existentially and psychologically fundamental and they are severely hindered when basic units of Christian community do not respect the natural groupings of human society.

Process theology has a lot of suggestions to make about man sharing life with God. I touched upon that in passing earlier and would like to come back to it. It was Whitehead's desire to arrive at metaphysical statements so adequately general and coherent that it would be possible to describe and interpret *all* of our experience without failing against those first principles. Yet he, probably more poignantly than all the Whiteheadians to follow, was in touch with the relativity and partialness of every vision. It is somewhat of a moot question among Whiteheadians whether or not he succeeds in that coherence when he speaks of God. I want to avoid the technicalities of many questions related to coherence in Whitehead's understanding of God. My own position is that Whitehead's philosophy helps me more than any other system to make sense out of my world and my experience—in a basic way, my own experience validates his vision. And the question areas have not seemed serious enough to me, even at those points where I feel there may well not be coherence, to invalidate his system. Whitehead points out that quibbling about a system means that as a living school of thought it's on its way out. I find that the critiques of Whitehead are not quibbling ones at this point, but good pressures on the process work going on. I feel inclined to make a distinction between the loose constructionists and the strict constructionists about Whitehead, and I feel comfortable being a loose constructionist. I have made these reflections because I want to work on the presumption that reality is such in its unity that only one set of rubrics is necessary throughout our interpretation of our experience. That amounts to saying that there are non-analogical statements that can be made about God, and that theology has an option for a *via positiva*. I want to say therefore that there are aspects of my experience of shared life with people in my life that are not just "sort of like" what constitutes shared life with God, but *quite* like. And I believe that is loaded with implications pastorally and catechetically, for we are talking about the heart of religious experience: union with God.

I want to make two reminders before entering into that discussion. The first is that I will be understanding God as "person" in the discussion that ensues, a position which Whitehead never states unequivocally, even though he uses personal

language about God; but it is a position that some Whiteheadians feel is not only a possible interpretation but a
necessary one for maximum coherence in Whitehead. The
second reminder points to something importantly different in
what I know about God and what I know about other persons
with whom I share life in union. I recur to Hartshorne's
distinction between rational knowledge and empirical knowledge. Rational knowledge yields information about the
abstract character of reality or some aspects of it; the empirical
method has concrete reality for its object. Both methods however have a valid yield about reality; and both, therefore, are
genuine experiences of what is real. What I know about the
people around me with whom I share life is effectively empirical knowledge, and forms the basis of my relationship.
What I know about God, which is the basis of a relationship,
begins with things I know rationally and therefore abstractly.
But I want to call insistent attention to the fact that this is
real knowledge and real experience. It is the Faith of Christians that the Jesus-event has a privileged yield about God,
and that through it we get a basis of knowing God which
is more than merely rational. It is Christian Faith that in
and through Jesus we learn what matters to God and what
matters to us in relationship with him.

When I share life with someone, process modes of thought
want to make me say that that person is not only present to
me, but he is present in me. In shared life a new reality comes
into being, for there is a new unity of what was multiplicity
before. The deepest meaning of presence is what (who)
shapes my becoming and is therefore *there* in my real, internal constitution. The kind of shaping that goes on that
makes someone be *there* in me can be of so many kinds and
can effect itself in so many ways. One dynamic of shared
life is that my friend and I like some of the same things.
While we once enjoyed the same things quite separately, we
learned to enjoy them together, that is, an additional reason

for my enjoyment is that it is the selfsame experience which shapes me and my friend, which jointly has a hold on our becoming. My enjoyment of my friend's enjoyment can not only increase the intensity of my own enjoyment, but can add dimensions to it that were not there before. The important point is that what is fundamentally the same external act of experience for my friend and for me before we met has been transformed by the addition of a new element of consciousness: we now know that this experience is important to the other. And though we may be doing the same simple thing we did before, the new element of consciousness transforms the experience into shared life. All the time and effort which I spend developing that new element of consciousness, whether I am with my friend or apart, are necessary for transforming events of my life into events of our life. That I understand to be the primary function of contemplation in a human relationship: developing the new element of consciousness that supports and sustains shared life. It needs to go on when two friends are apart, and that action apart is already a mode of presence for it is a means whereby the one increases his hold on the becoming of the other. It is likewise that contemplative act which accompanies an experience and raises it from a personal experience to a shared life experience; it is transformatively necessary even in the midst of shared life, contributing that element of awareness which conducts a life of union between two people who share in each other's lives. The contemplative act is for the sake of the process in which two people urge each other's active, creative presence upon and into one another, whereby a two becomes a one.

A growth in personal relationship is a growth in how deeply I am finally able to make another's life so *important* that his destiny becomes linked to my destiny, my satisfaction with his satisfaction. All that matters to him matters to me. I have made his "it matters" be my "it matters." What matters becomes an increasingly common possession. I know his loss as my loss, and in binding his wounds I bind what I too have suffered in his suffering. The contemplative act constantly underrides and facilitates the process by which we share in the creation of each other.

The act by which I link my destiny to that of my friend is not at all a surrender of my own destiny. It is almost as if the new unity that we generate has its own subjective aim, which includes taking the separate feelings of our two destinies and accommodating them to each other until they are embraced in a single feeling and appropriated by positive prehensions. I keep my destiny, though it may be reshaped in order to become appropriatable to another, and in order to be able to assimilate another. That is the basic pattern according to which two lives start becoming one at a single juncture, then at several junctures, finally at very many junctures. The other person's reality is present to my becoming in a deep interpersonal relationship so as to affect in a radical way the pattern of assemblage, according to which I put together the stuff of my own existence. And I become the same to him. Union is a process in which my care is tendered toward all (or approaching all) that matters to the one whom I love. My care embraces his "it matters," and because I care it is my matter too. To know what matters is necessary. To care is necessary. The contemplative act is necessary, for it opens up to me what matters, how it matters, and opens my caring to all that mattering.

The dynamics of union with God are those. Not like those, but those precisely. God desires for the world its openness to becoming more than it is, and its responsiveness to the call to be more. He invites increase upon everything. He invites transcendence. It matters to him that the world be more, that every person I know be more, that I be more. I may will this "more" for myself and my world without my desire being an act of personal union. It becomes shared life—union with

God—when my energies are pledged to caring for "more" because I have it as an element of my consciousness that it matters to him as well as to me, in fact that the "more" matters to him more than anything else, a fact which increases the power of my caring. That necessarily extends my caring beyond my own possibilities for more, to every possibility for more that I can get in touch with. We must understand that this extension of our caring to all that we know matters to God is precisely the stuff of union with God, of shared life. In our personal relationships we need to discover as best we can in the life of another his own-most possibility of becoming more —we cannot do that with infallible knowledge about what is best. We divine what is best as best we can. We are no different with God. We look at our world and divine as best we can what are its possibilities for increase, and we try to evoke the increase. We are limited with God as with other persons with selfishness and self-interest which keep us from a true assessment of what matters and where. But the primary locus for sharing in God's life is in creation, which matters to him. We and God do not have two different sets of "it matters," although his is larger than ours for his care extends to all that is, and we cannot take measure of that. Every possibility I have for becoming more is a possibility offered by God (an initial aim) who cares, therefore, that I do become more. My "it matters" and his "it matters" are already the same. What is needed is that new element of consciousness which makes me care also because God cares.

Whitehead and Teilhard both speak of God's concern over the hurt of the world. Teilhard understands God to be brooding over the world to heal its wounds and bind its hurts. Whitehead speaks of the tenderness of God that saves everything that can be saved. That tells us another locus of the "it matters" of God—wherever there is need. Whenever we bring caring to the pain of the world we have once again the stuff of union with God—we only need the compelling desire to do it also because God is already brooding over that suffering.

A Christian understands the Jesus-event to be the best clue there is to God's "it matters," so that to plumb the mind of the New Testament is to have access to the mind and heart of God. The contemplation of the New Testament with one eye and the new world with the other is, in a sense, what the life of the Church is about. It is a contemplation that intends action, that action which is a process of man and God experiencing each other in an act of co-creation.

I think that in our asceticism and in our prayer we have not yet begun to take with enough seriousness that what we do in the arena, which is our actual world, is the real stuff of union with God. In the Whiteheadian understanding of God (consequent nature) we understand that God takes into himself the life we create, and the richer that our decisions make our lives, the greater the gift we proffer. Creation, in a real sense, feeds the becoming of God's life. Our existence depends on what God offers us in a much more primordial way than what we can offer him. Yet we really do offer God his life in how we shape historical events which he takes into himself. Such is the intimacy of God and the world! I would like to cite again two passages which I have already indicated, but with the suggestion that both are to be understood quite literally (even though they are good poetry!):

To begin with, in action I adhere to the creative power of God; I coincide with it; I become not only its instrument but its living extension. And as there is nothing more personal in a being than his will, I merge myself, in a sense, through my heart, with the very heart of God. This commerce is continuous because I am always acting; and at the same time I can never set a boundary to the perfection of my fidelity nor to the fervor of my intention, this commerce enables me to liken myself, ever more strictly and indefinitely, to God.[3]

God is *in* the world, or nowhere, creating continually in us and around us. This creative principle is everywhere, in animate and so-called inanimate matter, in the ether, water, earth, human hearts. But this creation is a continuing process, "and the process itself is the actuality," since no sooner do you arrive than you start on a fresh journey. In so far as man partakes of this creative process does he partake of the divine. . . . His true destiny as co-creator in the universe is his dignity and his grandeur.[4]

These reflections suggest further ones about prayer and contemplation. What gives glory to God is a human life that is responsibly and tenderly co-creative with him. Prayer gives God glory, not so much because we have taken time to honor him, but because it shapes our lives to honor him. Prayer unites us to God when it informs our actions with his heart and mind. Prayer opens me to what matters in creation; it opens me to conformity with the intentionality of God, and it shunts the energy of my life into the creation of personal and communal history that is safe: salvation history.

The first prayers which children learn might already reflect a concern for shared life with God—though not necessarily in those words. "God bless Mommy, and Daddy, and Grandma, and my brothers and sisters," might be replaced with, "Thank you God for the good things that have happened to us (such as . . .) and help me to make more good things happen since that is what you want and it is what I want. I am sorry for bad things that happened which made someone hurt, or sad (such as . . .). I want to help them not hurt. I want to smile for them and laugh with them for you." Prayer postures us so that we can act in such a way as to achieve personal union with God in the selfsame act that we become ourselves.

It is not unimportant, certainly, to be thankful for all that is good. But a grace before a meal can posture us much more fully than thankfulness, though that is included. It can affect the intentionality which shapes a meal. "We are grateful for food which is necessary for life. We are grateful for food that is good. We want our zest for this meal to nourish our zest for the rest of this day. We ask that this meal be an occasion of great mutual presence to each other." Admittedly, such child- and meal-prayer might seem trivial examples. The point, I hope, is not trivial: that God is in the world, or nowhere—or better, that God is in my world, or nowhere for me; and prayer gives me access to God through the real particularities of my world where it matters, and where I actively care that it matters. The mind and heart of God, the matterful particularities of the real world, my intention and action: these are brought to bear upon each other in prayerfulness.

Presence, we have understood, means having an effect on my becoming. I am shaped by all that is present to and in me. Union between two people involves the mutual shaping of each other, that is, mutual presence. The Church is a locus of shaping where God, through the Jesus-event, participates in our becoming. The Church is likewise a locus where we return event and life to God, where salvation history is created and taken back into God:

> What is done in the world is transformed into a reality in heaven, and the reality in heaven passes back into the world. By reason of this reciprocal relation, the love in the world passes into the love of heaven, and floods back again into the world. In this sense, God is the great companion—the fellow-sufferer who understands.[5]

I want to come back now to symbol. Symbol points to something on the basis that it participates in that to which it points.

A symbol stands for something because of a natural con-
nectedness to it. Symbol invites us to interpret what it stands
for, and the act of interpretation lets what the symbol stands
for work on me. In getting to know someone, his "it matters"
becomes a symbol that mediates his presence to me. That is
not the only kind of symbol which mediates a relationship,
but it remains a key one, for what matters to someone comes
very close to the heart of his reality.

A humanist is one who knows what really matters to human life and to history and who responds vigorously with his
own life. He cares. He cares very much. A theistic humanist
also knows that everything that matters really, matters really
to God. Anything at all that matters, therefore, has the power
to become a symbol to mediate the presence of God. "What
matters" is what matters on the basis of how the real world is
put together at any given moment. It is the same "it matters"
for a humanist as well as for a theistic humanist. But with
the latter case, "what matters" becomes the stuff of union with
God. The stuff is no different. But that it can become an act
of relationship with God gives it new being. The Christian
adds to his humanism and his theism that the Jesus-event is
the important revelation of God concerning what matters
most, and that includes man's potential for union with God.
Jesus becomes central to our interpretation of human life for
he is the primordial symbol of God. Because of Jesus' participation in God, the Christian has access to God in his participation in the Jesus-event. The good Christian and the good
humanist do not have to do different things. What matters,
matters—as simply as that. What makes all the difference
about the world, life, reality, what matters, or whatever you
want to name it, is that for the Christian all of it can be
symbol of God and can mediate shared life between God and
man. Anything that matters *can* be what takes God's reality
into mine and gives mine to him.

Pastorally, it cannot be emphasized too strongly that the
Church and the Christian must have one foot in the Jesus-

event and one foot in the particularities of history. Prayers must have their feet in both places. Sermons and homilies must have their feet in both places. Sacraments must point man and the Jesus-event at each other through the concrete particularity of this life and this community within which the life is pitched.

Without ever unplanting the foot that holds to the Jesus-event, the Church needs to have the other foot planted squarely wherever life and history are in the making, so that it knows what matters and feels care for what matters. It is out of her own knowing and caring that the Church can make life with God available.

In the newly reformed Ordination rite, it is clear that a priest is called forth from and for the people to preside over their religious self-expression. Ministry in the Church (I do not intend a technical statement, but simply a descriptive—but real—one) must know where there is pain and hurt, and must care for it; must know where there is a need for reconciliation and must issue a call to it and facilitate it; ministry must know what is good and holy in life, must sense where the instances of God's experienced presence are, and gather them together and celebrate them; ministry must have a keen sense of what matters in the lives of people in order to transform their caring into an act of relationship with God; ministry must not only know that its people are called to be more, but must sense some of the real quarters from which the summons is issued, and must lure life into those quarters. It is clear to me that the life of ministers, whether ordained priests or any form of ministry, needs to be very close to the life of the people whom it serves. Its one foot must be really in the life of the people of God so that it knows. It needs to understand all pain that asks attention, all the alienation that needs reconciliation, all that is celebratable. Ministry in the Church has too often lived in shelter away from the daily life of the people it serves, apart and sometimes aloof. I believe that celibacy is an authentic personal charism, but that it is a separate call from that of ministry, although certainly the two can and do coincide. But celibacy, as a requirement for priestly ministry in the Catholic Church, has often served to set ministers outside the daily circles of life. Sometimes only a toe and not a foot has been planted in the life of the people who are asking for help in being one with each other and God; but sometimes even the gesture of a foot pointed in that direction is not in evidence. I think there is something telling in the reprimand of Pope Celestine in 428 of two bishops, because word had reached him in Rome that priests in their two dioceses were following the pagan custom of dressing in a way that set them apart from the rest of the people. Celibacy is inauthentic when it institutionalizes distance between the whole ministry and the people to whom ministry is tendered. Other contemporary ecclesiologies in addition to a process ecclesiology seem to be asking also for optional celibacy. To be sure, there is nothing in the "nature" of the Church which demands it.

Union with God—or with anyone—is a process. There is union when two persons are letting each other into their lives. The process of mutual presence is the reality of union. I have been stressing, therefore, our engagement in the creation of history as the locus of our presence to God and his to us. But in stressing the active side I want to stress equally the reflection which must undergird it, which must undergird any personal relationship. Reflection is not only requisite for the fact of mutual presence, but for the quality of presence.

As had been said many times already, presence is a matter of having effects. Things that are present are those that shape becoming. In the sense of physical thereness, the whole universe is mutually present to itself. So what we are speaking of is not physical proximity, nor temporal proximity, but how much of a hold one thing has on another. Presence has density. Awareness is important to the density of presence. Reflection generates awareness. Contemplation is a form of that reflection; its intention is to increase the density of presence between man and God; its purpose is to support that process which is union. For that matter, contemplation is already an act of union. But it must move beyond itself in support of man's vocation to be co-creators of history with God. Contemplative life, it seems to me, justifies itself in finding ways to make its experience available to life at large—and here I mean "contemplation" as a way of life as it has been found in the history of the Church. There is something of a paradox in our experience, that sometimes we distance ourselves ("to make a retreat") for the sake of the reflection that ultimately increases our closeness, that is, increases the density of presence. The time given to pulling away for reflection is an example of surrendering one mode of presence for another. One of the large considerations that makes sense out of celibacy is that it is basically a contemplative experience, even in the midst of things, or perhaps most of all in the midst of things.

There is a strong empirical strain in process thought that makes it hard-nosed. Pragmatism (à la Peirce, James and Dewey) is the best known expression of its hard-nosedness. The influence of the process world view upon theology also has a kind of a hard-nosed side, which I want to affirm. The deepest meaning of presence is exercising a hold on someone's or something's becoming: having effects. An effect is *only particular*. A "general effect" can only be a widespread and frequent occurrence of similar and inter-related particular effects. The presence of God is only as strong an experience as the accumulation of shapings that we have invited from him into our lives. We are never, in a sense, without the presence of God, for his function is essential in giving an initial aim to each concrescent event that makes up our reality. But consciousness is an essential element in an inter-personal relationship. We are conscious of the effects we have on each other; we welcome that hold of another on ourselves. Both the consciousness and the welcome express themselves in an increase in the number and importance of the effects whereby shared life is effected. Christians need hard-nosed effects in their lives of the Jesus-event! Because I have dealt with Sacramental life, I would like to point to a pastoral implication for ministers of Sacramental life. The Jesus-event is accessible through all of the Sacraments. Its presence is not a physical-thereness presence, but a Sacramental presence. The important issue is not whether the Jesus-event is present or not, but how much: quality of presence; density of presence; intensity of presence. Every person who participates in a Sacramental experience has something to do with the density of presence which accrues. The one who presides over the liturgical act has a particularly important role, however, in facilitating the accumulation of a large presence of the Jesus-event in the experience. Because effects are important, his role in seeing the particularities of the moment and their affinity for certain particularities of the Jesus-event is very important. He can aid and abet the presence of the Jesus-event, when through the shaping which a particular Sacramental symbol mediates, he is able to commend the lives of those doing liturgy and the Jesus-event to each other in terms of particular effects. It remains for each person to appropriate the Jesus-event with all the adaptations that his personal history demands, but he is helped greatly when life and the Good News meant for life are commended to him already standing in relationship to each other. For this reason, good homiletics and relevant prayer are not merely good practice, they are experiences which greatly condition the intensity of presence of the Jesus-event, for they facilitate greatly the *effect*iveness of the Sacramental experience. The priest is not a perfunctory instrument; rather, his personality and experience, his feel for the Jesus-event and for the actual world of himself and his people— these contribute greatly to the density of the real presence achieved in each Sacramental experience.

Whitehead holds that every prehension has a subjective form. Every feeling *of* something has its own way of feeling, its own "how." Subjective form is how something is noticed, how the prehension feels what is there and introduces it into the here. In eliciting the Jesus-event into the here and now, each Sacrament involves positive prehensions of the Jesus-event, each with its own subjective form—its own affective tone. If a Sacramental experience does indeed render the Jesus-event present in a new occasion, it always does so with an affective tone, that is, with some emotional accompaniment. I want to point out that the emotional elements in Sacramental experiences are not just possible concomitants, but necessary concomitants. The right affective tone greatly facilitates the prehension. In other words, emotion conditions the quality of presence. That to which we are emotionally attuned gets into us and touches us much more easily.

Emotions break a neutral stance toward something, and give us a Yes or No position. We walk into an unfamiliar room. There are uncountable pieces of possible data for our attention. Very quickly items come to our attention—what we like and don't like. What we come to know about the room is not the uncountable pieces of data that we have counted with our glances, but a selection of items, based on what pieces of data we have broken neutrality with. "Breaking neutrality" is an element of every prehension. Even a negative prehension breaks neutrality when it dismisses an item from feeling.

Every prehension has an affective tone. It is not as though we first take note of something and then respond with feeling toward it. The act of taking note is a "feeling" of what is there which already has an affective tone. Our subjectivity shapes the taking note. Whitehead insists in talking of the phases of a concrescence, that "phases" is but a way of speaking for the sake of analysis. The concrescence is a unit, albeit with temporal thickness—but an "atomic" unit: it can not be really broken down into consecutiveness. Actual occa-

sions have consecutiveness when they follow each other, but
there are no temporal divisions below that level.

The emotive response is closely tied in with value. An
actual entity's subjective aim gives it a certain stance toward
its actual world; because of that stance an actual entity has a
sense of what matters for itself. The aim, the sense of what
matters, the stance, the affective tone—these are organically
inter-related. They make an appearance, as it were, together
or not at all.

The pastoral plea involved in all of this is for keen attention to emotional tone, and that at many levels. Perhaps the
most significant inheritance we have from the Greeks is the
centrality of the rational element, which has tended to denigrate emotion as that which interferes with the rational. Oddly
enough in our ethics we have understood only intellect and
will to be necessary constituents of a genuine human act
—witness the three elements traditionally considered necessary for a human act to be a mortal sin. Emotion was understood as able to increase or decrease guilt in real situations,
yet it was basically something in addition to or alongside of
mind and will. I do not want to deal with ethics at this juncture, other than to say we need an ethical approach in which
the emotive element is rehabilitated as essential in its function in every human act. (Max Scheler, the German philosophical anthropologist from the turn of the century, has
worked out a system of emotive ethics. I think it would be
very fruitful to bring his work to bear upon our redeveloping
approach to Christian morality.)

I would like to generalize Whitehead's understanding of the
role of emotion in all process beyond the technical description of it in each concrescing entity—as I think Whitehead
himself did. All that data out there in reality which is not
likely to have an effect on the real internal constitution of an
occasion of experience is, for all practical purposes, inert. My
experiencing is my life; and corporately, as Church, our ex-

periencing is our lives. Whatever is not the stuff of our experience, either really or potentially, is inert. It is simply boring! I feel nothing! "A merely well-informed man is the most useless bore on God's earth," [6] and so is a merely well-informed catechism or catechist or homilist or theologian. Whitehead's remarks on education are, I believe, equally applicable to the areas I have just mentioned:

> In training a child to activity or thought, above all things we must beware of what I will call "inert ideas"—that is to say, ideas that are merely received into the mind without being utilised, or tested, or thrown into fresh combinations. . . . You cannot put life into any schedule of general education unless you succeed in exhibiting its relation to some essential characteristic of all intelligent or emotional perception. It is a hard saying, but it is true; and I do not see how to make it any easier.[7]

This does not mean that there is no room for the theoretical and speculative, but that even those need to stand in relation to real human quests; they must be useful for the interpretation and elucidation of experience, and the usefulness must make an appearance.

The ontological principle states that all reasons for everything come down ultimately to actual entities. The vitality of Christian experience comes down ultimately to the vitality of individual Christians and the influence of individual Christians in the experience of others. What is important in Christian knowledge is what relates to those to whose immediate experience it addresses itself. It is at those points, and only at those points, that what Christianity has to say becomes operative, that is to say, present. Christian understandings need to be indicated at points of importance, and in ways that illuminate importance of implementation. "That knowledge which adds greatness to character is knowledge so handled as to transform every phase of immediate experience." [8]

The emotional thrust that facilitates our experience relates intimately to values and goals: what I like enough to put myself in motion toward; what repels me and makes me avoid it. The quest for what is better or more, the active pursuit, is what Whitehead calls adventure. His books about the effects and influences of various ideas he calls *The Adventures of Ideas*. Inert ideas have no adventures. In a popular as well as a technical way, the affective response to adventure we have called romance. Sometimes "he's a romantic" has a very pejorative ring. But most of us own up to having romantic streaks, and without the central valuation that our Greek heritage has placed on the rational, we might more proudly and more regularly own up to Don Quixote who is at least a little bit in all men. The truth of the matter is that whether we name them romanticism and adventure, there is throughout experience a thrust to be more, and the excitement that nudges the thrust into the open arena of personal process and sometimes of corporate process. Religion dies when it no longer holds out the high hope of adventure. At that point it is a bore, one of the severest indictments that could be levied.

I am making a strong pastoral plea for keen attention to the emotive factor in religious experience. It is a concomitant of all experience, but it has not had the full citizenship that it deserves. As a full citizen it takes up its duties much more responsibly in creating desirable presences. And that applies equally to experiences that continue the presence of the Jesus-event in our lives. I have not attempted to make a balanced statement, relating the affective and the cognitive, nor the immediately practical with the speculative. I have rather tried to balance the picture by dwelling on the aspects which seem to me too long to have been on the light side of the scale. What is at stake is not balance for the sake of balance, but the activating of all possible resources that will help our lives and help history by disposing the Jesus-event to captivate our world, and disposing us to capture the Jesus-event in our experience.

When we are told that religious instruction is boring, or that episcopal letters are boring, or that Mass is boring, it behooves us to listen. That does not mean that the object of all of those is supposed to be entertainment. But if what is being said or done does not make us entertain it seriously, the chances of it having an effect upon our lives is about nil, and what suffers is the active presence of the Jesus-event to our becoming. It should be a power-full experience to entertain the Jesus-event!

The final reflections I wish to offer concern the "nature" of the Church. I am taking cues from two sources: process thought and some of the more recent New Testament scholarship (Bultmann, Käsemann, etc.). The process sources are not just Whitehead, but James and Dewey. The New Testament scholarship is out of my competency and my field as far as my personal endeavor is concerned; I depend upon such men as I have named, and others. I want to affirm at the ending what I affirmed at the beginning: that process theology is a relatively new endeavor in Catholic theology. I offer this work as a probe of its possibilities, and with the tentativeness that must attend all human endeavors because of the relativity of every perspective and every world view, and also because of the fluid and dynamic state of New Testament scholarship in the case of the Church (as also earlier in connection with my discussion of the Eucharist and the Institution texts).

Let us look briefly at the meaning of "nature" in a process framework. Scientists frame natural laws, such as the law of universal gravitation. At the popular level it is often supposed that things behave the way they do because of a law of universal gravitation which they obey. A more accurate scientific rendering is that the law of universal gravitation is the best description we can make of certain patterns of behavior in the world. The law of gravitation is framed because nature behaves the way it does, and the law is an attempt to generalize a description of that behavior. Similar reflections can be made about "human nature." Nowhere is there a revelation of the exact content of human nature. Rather, our formulations of "human nature" have been our best efforts to generalize our description of how man behaves, what aspects of behavior foster life and growth, and what aspects are detrimental. In both cases, our expressions of a "nature" are as good as our powers of observation, as good as our facility for accurate generalization, and as good as the stability of behavior which we observed and generalized.

That last observation ties in with another fundamental process conviction, that reality is open-ended, that history is on the move, that real newness happens to reality as it evolves. Man too is on the move. He came from someplace; he is where he is; he is going someplace. The description of human experience two thousand years ago or ten thousand years ago would not look like the description of present civilization. I highly recommend the process development of this topic in John B. Cobb, Jr.'s book, *The Structure of Christian Existence*, wherein he first develops a discussion of the various structures of existence. He uses "structure of existence" as a replacement for "nature." The structures of human existence vary even now, and they have been and are in the process of development. Teilhard is another process thinker who has tackled the "nature" question. That is apparent, for example, in some of his discussions of sexuality and sexual morality. (Cf. his treatment of sexuality in the recently published—in English, that is—essays titled *Human Energy,* and his attempt there to define "pure" and "impure" in terms of where he thinks man is today with sexuality.) I think there would have to be the same inclination in process theology, that is, to understand the nature of the Church as rather open-ended. That seems called for by understanding human nature and human society to be open-ended and plastic. The Church is for man, for human history. Its "nature" is not a packaged sort of givens. Its nature has emerged from authentic social responses to the Jesus-event; needless to say, the Jesus-event has its own reality and it shapes experience of it, the way every piece of data shapes future prehensions of itself.

There does not seem to be very compelling evidence that Jesus had the direct, conscious intention or the desire to be the founder of a Church or a new religion. Throughout his life he was faithful to the Jewish religion, although in word and practice he repudiated the legalism that had emerged within. He preached regularly in the synagogues. He encouraged those who heard him to be faithful to their Jewish faith, though without getting caught up in the hypocrisy which he rejected. He kept the Jewish feasts. It was the Passover which had brought him to Jerusalem when he was arrested, tried and condemned. His last act with his followers was the celebration of the Passover meal. The early activity of the apostles and disciples, after the death of Jesus and after the Easter event, was in the synagogues. The early Christians, we are told in Acts, celebrated together, yet also went together to the temple each day to pray. A number of factors are involved in the emergence of the Christian Church with an identity of its own. Acts recounts the first time and place where the name "Christian" appears. Although it happens soon after the Easter event, the realization that the Jesus-event calls forth the kind of response that makes it become something with its own identity was not an instantaneous response. It was an identity that emerged in awareness as it emerged in fact. Another factor at work was that Christian preaching was banned finally in the synagogues and temples, and Christians were expelled and soon persecuted. The newness of the Jesus-event revealed itself to experience as of such import and with such power that a new response with an identity of its own was the only authentic response. It was a response called for by the configuration of the Jesus-event as that configuration was made increasingly perceptible through historical event.

There is fairly general agreement that the foundation text of Mt. 16:16 ("You are Peter, and upon this rock I will build my Church.") is a post-Easter text. Likewise, the Church texts at the end of John's Gospel ("Feed my lambs . . . my sheep.") are rather generally taken to be later additions. The twentieth chapter of John is so clearly an intentional conclusion that the succeeding chapter could only be an addition. That is true also of the last dozen verses of Mark's Gospel which manifest a sense of Church identity. The Church foundation text of Mt. 16:16 is generally held to be a very early text, although not part of the original pericope (compare the same scene in Mark and Luke). In fact a dominant theme in Matthew's Gospel is the continuity of Jesus with Jewish faith. Matthew alone is the four accounts of the institution of the Eucharist does not have Jesus speak of the cup in terms of a *new* covenant. Jesus says: "This is my blood, the blood of the covenant."

Probably the most quoted (and perhaps most resented) sentence from the work of Alfred Loisy, the modernist theologian, is that "Jesus promised the Kingdom of God, but it was the Church that came forth." There are two ways of understanding that statement. The pejorative way is that the Church is a sort of a dirty trick, because we didn't get what was promised. The other understanding is that Jesus did indeed spend his life preaching the Kingdom of God (and not preaching a new Church with himself as founder). A small group of followers formed first, then a community of followers which became quite large already in Jesus' lifetime, and which multiplied rapidly in the early years after the Easter-event. The community that arose *had to* arise—the exigencies of an adequate historical response to the Jesus-event demanded it. The Church is clearly founded in the teaching and preaching of Jesus. It was what it was, it is what it is, it will be what it will be, because of him to whom it responds.

There are in the Church *sine qua non* forms and shapes which derive from what the Jesus-event was and is. But an immense amount of the Church's shape comes also from the historical conditions out of which the historical responses were made. The practical functioning of the Church bears much of the historical configuration of the Roman administrative experience and Roman system of jurisprudence. Rome, a city-state, directs the entire western civilization. (Suppose Christianity had spread to the Orient instead!) The structure of belief and dogma bears the heavy imprint of Greek experience and the Greek world view. That all of this happened seems very, very right. The Church incarnated itself in man and addressed itself to man with words and experience that he could understand. The problematic situation is that those historically formed words and experiences got canonized as the nature of Christian life and Christian belief. That too is easily understandable. One could not have expected history to evaluate itself with a sense of historical relativity or a sense of evolutionary movement. Those are perspectives that emerge from the nineteenth and twentieth centuries, and could not have been operative before. Given the shaping which Roman and Greek experience contributed, one would probably have to expect the canonization of historically and culturally conditioned forms (e.g., that there are and can only be seven Sacraments, no less, no more, and that each of these was instituted individually and directly by Jesus in his life).

What our perceptions of reality, of the Church, ask of us today is a deeper sense of the plasticity of the Church. The "structure of ecclesial existence" ("nature") which the Church is, is patient of immense variation. The pluralism developing within the Church is but one expression of this century's keener sense of historical and cultural relativity. One aspect of what some writers call the end of the Modern World, the World Come of Age, the New World, etc., is their perception that many of the *forms* which western experience has identified with human civilization are disappearing or being replaced. Many of the *forms* also with which Christianity has been identified in the past are disappearing or being replaced. Dietrich Bonhoeffer, perhaps more than anyone else, has helped us articulate and confront questions about the plasticity of the structure of Christian existence. A process ecclesiology should assist us in understanding and interpreting the real newness which comes to the Church, for real newness is a necessary condition of transcendence, of the summons and response to be MORE, to be GREATER.

I tell you most solemnly,
whoever believes in me
will perform the same works as I do myself,
he will perform *even greater works*.

Jn. 14:12

FOOTNOTES

CHAPTER 1

¹ *Webster's New World Dictionary of the American Language,* concise edition (New York: New World Publishing Co., 1958), p. 339.

² *Gaudium et Spes,* n. 54.

³ Harvey Cox, *The Secular City* (New York: Macmillan, 1966), p. 2.

⁴ Arend Theodor van Leeuwen, *Christianity in World History* trans. by H. H. Hopkins (New York: Scribner's, 1964).

⁵ Friedrich Gogarten, *The Reality of Faith* trans. by Carl Michalson and others (Philadelphia: Westminster, 1959), especially chapter 20.

⁶ John Dewey, *Reconstruction in Philosophy* (Boston: Beacon, 1966), pp. 60-61, p. 54.

⁷ Alfred North Whitehead, *Science and the Modern World* (New York: Free Press, 1967), pp. 188-189.

⁸ *The Reality of Faith,* p. 171.

⁹ John Dewey, *The Quest for Certainty* (New York: Putnam's, 1960), pp. 99-100.

¹⁰ *The Reality of Faith,* p. 168.

¹¹ *Gaudium et Spes,* n. 55.

¹² Alfred North Whitehead, *Process and Reality* (New York: Harper, 1960), pp. 315-316.

¹³ *Reconstruction in Philosophy,* p. 68.

¹⁴ Leslie Dewart, *The Future of Belief* (New York: Herder, 1966), p. 196.

¹⁵ Alfred North Whitehead, *The Function of Reason* (Boston: Beacon, 1962), p. 22.

¹⁶ Albert Schweitzer, *The Quest of the Historical Jesus* trans. by W. Montgomery (New York: Macmillan, 1969), p. 15.

¹⁷ *The Reality of Faith,* p. 174.

¹⁸ Fyodor Dostoevsky, *The Brothers Karamazov* trans. by Constance Garnett (New York: Random House), p. 259.

¹⁹ Jean-Paul Sartre, *Existentialism* trans. by Bernard Frechtman (New York: Philosophical Library, 1947), p. 14.

²⁰ *Ibid.,* pp. 16-17.

²¹ Carl Jung, (ed. V. S. DeLaszlo), *The Basic Writings of C. G. Jung* (New York: Random House, 1959), pp. 306-307.

²² Richard Rubenstein, *After Auschwitz* (Indianapolis: Bobbs-Merrill, 1966), p. 69, p. 204.

[23] George Tyrell, *Christianity at the Crossroads* (London: Longmans Green, 1910), p. 5.

[24] W. Paul Jones, *The Recovery of Life's Meaning* (New York: Association Press, 1964), p. 14.

[25] Paul Sabatier, *Modernism* trans. by C. A. Miles (New York: Scribner's, 1908), pp. 306-308.

[26] *Gaudium et Spes,* n. 62.

[27] *The Quest of the Historical Jesus,* p. 81.

[28] Maude Petre, *Alfred Loisy* (Cambridge: Cambridge University Press, 1944), p. 42.

[29] *The Future of Belief,* p. 116.

[30] George Tyrrell, *Through Scylla and Charybdis* (London: Longmans Green, 1907), p. 85. The essay, "The Relation of Theology to Devotion," is reprinted in this book in the chapter entitled "Lex Orandi, Lex Credendi."

[31] *Ibid.,* p. 87.

[32] *Ibid.,* pp. 87-88.

[33] *Ibid.,* p. 95.

[34] *Ibid.,* p. 104.

[35] *Christianity at the Crossroads,* p. 176.

[36] *Ibid.,* p. 176.

[37] *Ibid.,* p. 174.

[38] *Ibid.,* pp. 173-174.

[39] *Ibid.,* p. 176.

[40] *Ibid.,* p. 213.

[41] *Ibid.,* p. 9.

[42] *Ibid.,* pp. xxi-xxii.

[43] Charles Hartshorne, *The Divine Relativity* (New Haven: Yale University Press, 1948).

[44] Alec Vidler, *A Variety of Catholic Modernists* (Cambridge: Cambridge University Press, 1970), p. 11.

[45] Robert Speaight, *The Life of Teilhard de Chardin* (New York: Harper, 1967), p. 135.

[46] *Ibid.,* p. 140.

CHAPTER 2

[1] Aristotle, *Metaphysics* 1069.

[2] Alfred North Whitehead, *Process and Reality* (New York: Harper, 1960), p. 290, emphasis added.

[3] *Ibid.,* p. 28.

[4] Marshall McLuhan, *Understanding Media: the Extensions of Man* (New York: Signet, 1964), p. 19.

[5] Alfred North Whitehead, *Science and the Modern World* (New York: Free Press, 1967), p. 152.

[6] George L. Kline, ed., *Alfred North Whitehead: Essays on His Philosophy* (Englewood Cliffs, N.J.: Prentice-Hall, 1963), p. 8.

[7] *Process and Reality,* p. 65.

[8] *Ibid.,* p. 335.
[9] *Ibid.,* pp. 34-35.
[10] *Ibid.,* p. 290.
[11] *Ibid.,* p. 83.
[12] *Ibid.,* p. 252.
[13] Alfred North Whitehead, *Modes of Thought* (New York: Capricorn, 1958), p. 188.
[14] *Science and the Modern World,* p. 25.
[15] *Process and Reality,* pp. 79-80.
[16] *Ibid.,* p. 305.
[17] Alfred North Whitehead, *Religion in the Making* (Cleveland: Meridian, 1960), p. 109.
[18] *Process and Reality,* p. ix.
[19] *Science and the Modern World,* p. 152.
[20] Alfred North Whitehead, *Science and Philosophy* (Paterson, New Jersey: Littlefield, Adams, 1964), p. 9.
[21] Alfred North Whitehead *Adventures of Ideas* (New York: Mentor, n.d.), especially chapters 17 and 18.
[22] *Ibid.,* p. 252.
[23] *Ibid.,* p. 252.
[34] *Ibid.,* p. 31.
[25] Kline, pp. 33-40.
[26] *Ibid.,* p. 34.
[27] *Science and Philosophy,* pp. 105-121.
[28] *Ibid.,* p. 114.
[29] *Modes of Thought,* p. 163.
[30] *Process and Reality,* p. 128.
[31] *Adventures of Ideas,* p. 199.
[32] *Process and Reality,* p. 321.
[33] *Ibid.,* p. 53.
[34] *Process and Reality,* p. 31.
[35] *Ibid.*
[36] *Science and the Modern World,* p. 3.
[37] *Process and Reality,* pp. 27-28.
[38] *Ibid.,* p. 373.
[39] *Ibid.,* p. 37.
[40] *Ibid.,* p. 70.
[41] *Ibid.,* p. 73. It is disputed among interpreters of Whitehead whether "eternal objects" and "possibility" can be simply equated.
[42] *Adventures of Ideas,* p. 199.
[43] *Process and Reality,* p. 252.
[44] *Ibid.,* p. 254.
[45] *Ibid.,* p. 29.
[46] *Ibid.,* p. 35.
[47] *Ibid.,* p. 35.
[48] *Ibid.,* p. 83.
[49] *Ibid.,* p. 353.
[50] *Ibid.,* p. 133.
[51] *Ibid.,* p. 35.

[52] Alfred North Whitehead, *The Function of Reason* (Boston: Beacon, 1962), p. 20.

[53] *Ibid.*, p. 22.

[54] *Process and Reality*, p. 246.

[55] *Ibid.*, p. 250.

[56] *Ibid.*

[57] *Ibid.*, pp. 29-30.

[58] *Ibid.*, p. 51.

[59] *Ibid.*, p. 153.

[60] *Ibid.*, p. 154.

[61] *Ibid.*, p. 43.

[62] *Ibid.*, p. 71.

[63] *Ibid.*, pp. 79-80.

[64] Gabriel Marcel, *The Philosophy of Existence* (New York: Citadel, 1962), p. 36.

[65] Lucien Price, recorder, *Dialogues of Alfred North Whitehead* (New York: Mentor, 1964), p. 125.

[66] *Science and the Modern World*, p. 92.

[67] *Religion in the Making*, pp. 76-77.

[68] *Process and Reality*, pp. 512-513.

[69] *Ibid.*, p. 315.

[70] *Ibid.*, p. 521.

[71] William A. Christian, *An Interpretation of Whitehead's Metaphysics* (New Haven: Yale, 1967), Part Three; John B. Cobb, Jr., *A Christian Natural Theology* (Philadelphia: Westminster, 1965); Ivor Leclerc, "Whitehead and the Problem of God," *The Southern Journal of Philosophy*, VII (Winter, 1969-70), 437-446; Donald W. Sherburne, "Whitehead without God," *The Christian Scholar* L (Fall, 1967), 251-272.

[72] E. G. Hartshorne takes God as a society of actual entities rather than an actual entity, which Cobb accepts so as to understand God as person. Charles Hartshorne, "Whitehead's Novel Intuition," in Kline, p. 23.

[73] *Process and Reality*, p. 73.

[74] *Ibid.*, p. 523.

[75] *Ibid.*, p. 521.

[76] *Ibid.*

[77] *Ibid.*

[78] Charles Hartshorne, *The Divine Relativity* (New Haven: Yale, 1948).

[79] *Religion in the Making*, p. 97.

[80] *Science and the Modern World*, p. 74.

[81] *Ibid.*, p. 78.

[82] *Process and Reality*, p. 522.

[83] *Religion in the Making*, p. 149.

[84] *Ibid.*, p. 115.

[85] *Ibid.*, p. 97.

[86] *Process and Reality*, p. 134.

[87] *Religion in the Making*, p. 151.

[88] *Science and the Modern World,* pp. 191-192, passim.

[89] *Religion in the Making,* p. 91.

[90] *Process and Reality,* p. 522.

[91] *Ibid.,* pp. 525-526, passim.

[92] *Ibid.,* p. 528.

[93] *Religion in the Making,* p. 109.

[94] *Process and Reality,* p. 256.

[95] Alfred North Whitehead, *Symbolism* (New York; Capricorn, 1959), p. 53.

[96] *Ibid.,* pp. 50-51.

[97] *Ibid.,* p. 7

[98] Susanne K. Langer, *Philosophy in a New Key* (New York: Mentor, 1951).

[99] *Symbolism,* p. 88.

[100] T. S. Eliot, "The Love Song of J. Alfred Prufrock," *Selected Poems* (London: Faber and Faber, 1961), p. 13.

[101] *Adventures of Ideas,* p. 169.

[102] *Ibid.,* p. 169.

[103] *Ibid.,* p. 170.

[104] *Religion in the Making,* pp. 56-57.

[105] *Adventures of Ideas,* p. 173.

[106] Lionel Spencer Thornton, *Christ and the Church* (London: Westminister, 1956).

[107] Norman Pittenger, *Christ and Christian Faith* (New York: Round Table Press, 1941).

[108] Norman Pittenger, *The Word Incarnate* (New York: Harper & Row, 1959).

[109] Norman Pittenger, *Christology Reconsidered* (London: SCM, 1970).

[110] Norman Pittenger, *God in Process* (London: SCM, 1967).

[111] John B. Cobb, Jr., "A Whiteheadian Christology," *Process Philosophy and Christian Thought,* ed. by Delwin Browne, Ralph E. James, Jr., Gene Reeves (Indianapolis: Bobbs-Merrill, 1971).

[112] John B. Cobb, Jr., *The Structure of Christian Existence* (Philadelphia: Westminster, 1967).

[113] James M. Robinson, *A New Quest of the Historical Jesus* (London: SCM, 1963).

[114] "A Whiteheadian Christology," pp. 382-383.

[115] *Ibid.,* pp. 390-393, passim, emphasis added.

CHAPTER 3

[1] Pierre Teilhard de Chardin, *How I Believe* (New York: Harper & Row, 1969), pp. 10-11, passim.

[2] Claude Cuénot, *Pierre Teilhard de Chardin* (Paris: Libraire Plon, 1958), p. 292.

[3] *Process and Reality,* p. 8.

[4] *The Function of Reason,* p. 8.

[5] Pierre Teilhard de Chardin, *Science and Christ* (New York: Harper & Row, 1968), pp. 212-213.

[6] *Process and Reality*, p. 8.

[7] Pierre Teilhard de Chardin, *The Phenomenon of Man* (New York: Harper & Row, 1965), p. 40.

[8] *Ibid.*

[9] *Process and Reality*, p. 53.

[10] *The Phenomenon of Man*, p. 40.

[11] From *Comment je vois*, cited in Christopher F. Mooney, *Teilhard de Chardin and the Mystery of Christ* (Garden City, New York: Doubleday, 1968), p. 184.

[12] *Process and Reality*, p. 66.

[13] *The Phenomenon of Man*, p. 41.

[14] *Ibid.*, p. 107.

[15] *Science and Christ*, p. 13.

[16] *The Phenomenon of Man*, p. 69.

[17] *Ibid.*, p. 62.

[18] *How I Believe*, pp. 34-35.

[19] *The Phenomenon of Man*, p. 63.

[20] *Ibid.*, pp. 64-65.

[21] *Ibid.*, pp. 264-265.

[22] *Ibid.*, p. 49.

[23] *How I Believe*, p. 35.

[24] *The Phenomenon of Man*, p. 65.

[25] *Ibid.*, p. 301.

[26] *How I Believe*, p. 28.

[27] Letter from 1951, cited in *Teilhard de Chardin and the Mystery of Christ*, p. 69, emphasis mine.

[28] John B. Cobb, Jr., *A Christian Natural Theology* (Philadelphia: Westminster, 1965), p. 56.

[29] Pierre Teilhard de Chardin, *The Divine Milieu* (New York: Harper & Row, 1968), pp. 60-61.

[30] Pierre Teilhard de Chardin, *Science and Christ*, pp. 12-13; *The Future of Man* (New York: Harper & Row, 1969), pp. 261-262.

[31] *The Phenomenon of Man*, p. 71.

[32] *Teilhard de Chardin and the Mystery of Christ*, p. 46.

[33] *The Phenomenon of Man*, p. 271.

[34] *The Divine Milieu*, p. 78.

[35] *Ibid.*, p. 84.

[36] From *Comment je vois*, cited in Piet Schoonenberg, *Man and Sin* (Chicago: Henry Regnery, 1968), p. 44.

[37] *The Divine Milieu*, pp. 62-63.

[38] *Dialogues of Alfred North Whitehead*, p. 297.

[39] *Teilhard de Chardin and the Mystery of Christ*, p. 83.

[40] *How I Believe*, p. 64.

[41] *Ibid.*, p. 78 n.

[42] *Ibid.*, p. 78.

[43] *Teilhard de Chardin and the Mystery of Christ*, p. 35.

[44] *Ibid.*, p. 29.

[45] *How I Believe*, p. 88.

[46] Robert Speaight, *The Life of Teilhard de Chardin* (New York: Harper & Row, 1967), p. 140.

[47] From *Letters from a Traveller*, cited in *The Life of Teilhard de Chardin*, p. 260.

[48] *Religion in the Making*, p. 77.

[49] *Ibid.*, p. 76.

[50] *Process and Reality*, p. 513.

[51] *How I Believe*, p. 79.

[52] *Ibid.*, p. 63.

[53] *The Phenomenon of Man*, pp. 262-263.

[54] *Ibid.*, p. 258.

[55] *Ibid.*, p. 259.

[56] Scripture translations are from *The Jerusalem Bible*.

[57] From *Le Christique* and *Super-humanité, super-Christ, super charité*, cited in *Teilhard de Chardin and the Mystery of Christ*, p. 64.

[58] *The Future of Man*, p. 79.

[59] *How I Believe*, p. 80.

[60] *The Phenomenon of Man*, p. 233.

[61] *Ibid.*, p. 293, emphasis mine.

[62] *Ibid.*, p. 265.

[63] *Ibid.*, p. 293.

[64] *Ibid.*, p. 294.

[65] *How I Believe*, p. 80.

[66] From a letter to Père Valensin, cited in *Teilhard de Chardin and the Mystery of Christ*, p. 83.

[67] From *Super-humanité, super-Christ, super-charité*, cited in *Teilhard de Chardin and the Mystery of Christ*, p. 172.

[68] *The Phenomenon of Man*, p. 298.

[69] *How I Believe*, p. 64.

[70] *Science and Christ*, p. 13.

[71] *Teilhard de Chardin and the Mystery of Christ*, p. 110.

CHAPTER 4

[1] Chapters 8 and 9, passim.

[2] *Religion in the Making*, pp. 151-152; *Process and Reality*, p. 522; *Religion in the Making*, p. 151.

[3] *Science and the Modern World*, p. 191.

[4] *Ibid.*, p. 192.

[5] Lk. 21:12, 16-19.

[6] *Process and Reality*, p. 128.

[7] *Religion in the Making*, p. 16.

[8] *Ibid.*, p. 19.

[9] *Ibid.*, p. 16.

[10] *Ibid.*, p. 47.

[11] *The Phenomenon of Man*, p. 59.

[12] Ernst Bloch, *A Philosophy of the Future* (New York: Herder and Herder, 1970), p. 86.

[13] *Religion in the Making*, p. 104.

[14] *Process and Reality*, pp. 50-51.

[15] *The Structure of Christian Existence*, p. 125.

[16] *Dialogues of Alfred North Whitehead*, p. 79.

[17] Mt. 5:43-48.

[18] Charles Sanders Peirce, "Evolutionary Love," *The Monist* (1893), reprinted in *Philosophical Writings of Peirce*, ed. by Justus Buchler (New York: Dover, 1955), p. 363.

[19] *Ibid.*, p. 362.

[20] *The Phenomenon of Man*, p. 253.

[21] *Gaudium et Spes*, n. 5.

[22] Arthur Utz, *Ethique Sociale* (Fribourg, Suisse: Editions Universitaire, 1960), Vol. I, pp. 150, sqq.

[23] *Gaudium et Spes*, n. 26.

[24] *Ibid.*, n. 25.

[25] *Ibid.*, n. 74.

[26] *The Divine Relativity*, p. 50.

[27] *Religion in the Making*, p. 123.

[28] *Process and Reality*, p. 151.

[29] *Ibid.*, p. 153.

[30] *Ibid.*, p. 154.

[31] *Ibid.*

[32] *Ibid.*

[33] *Ibid.*

[34] *Ibid.*, p. 155.

[35] Norman Pittenger, *God in Process* (London: SCM, 1967) pp. 21-22.

CHAPTER 5

[1] *Process and Reality*, p. 133.

[2] *Religion in the Making*, p. 128.

[3] Mircea Eliade, *Myth and Reality* (New York: Harper & Row, 1963), cf. especially Chapter I, "The Structure of Myths."

[4] *Religion in the Making*, p. 127.

[5] *Process and Reality*, p. 83.

[6] *Symbolism*, p. 74.

[7] Antoine de Saint Exupéry, *The Little Prince* tr. by Katherine Woods (New York: Harcourt, Brace & World, 1943), Chapter XXI, passim.

[8] Ross Snyder, *The Ministry of Meaning* (Geneva: Youth Department of the World Council of Churches and World Council of Christian Education, 1965), Vol. 1, nos. 3 and 4, pp. 137-143, passim.

[9] Eduard Schweizer, *The Lord's Supper According to the New Testament*, tr. by James M. Davies (Philadelphia: Fortress Press, 1967).

¹⁰ Willi Marxsen, *The Lord's Supper as a Christological Problem*, tr. by Lorenz Nieting (Philadelphia: Fortress Press, 1970).

CHAPTER 6

¹ *Science and the Modern World*, p. 192.
² *Process and Reality*, p. 51.
³ *The Divine Milieu*, pp. 62-63.
⁴ *Dialogues of Alfred North Whitehead*, p. 297.
⁵ *Process and Reality*, p. 532.
⁶ Alfred North Whitehead, *The Aims of Education* (New York: Mentor, 1963), p. 14.
⁷ *Ibid.*, pp. 14, 19.
⁸ *Ibid.*, p. 41.

BIBLIOGRAPHY

Altizer, Thomas J. J. *The Gospel of Christian Atheism*. Philadelphia: Westminster, 1966.

Baltazar, Eulalio R. *God within Process*. New York: Newman, 1970.

————. *Teilhard and the Supernatural*. Baltimore: Helicon, 1966.

Barrett, William. *Irrational Man*. Garden City, New York: Doubleday, 1962.

Benz, Ernst. *Evolution and Christian Hope*. Translated by Hein G. Frank. New York: Doubleday, 1968.

Bloch, Ernst. *Man on His Own*. Translated by E. B. Ashton. New York: Herder and Herder, 1970.

————. *A Philosophy of the Future*. Translated by John Cumming. New York: Herder and Herder, 1970.

Bochenski, I. M. *Contemporary European Philosophy*. Translated by Donald Nicholl and Karl Aschenbrenner. Berkeley: University of California Press, 1965.

Bonhoeffer, Dietrich. *Letters and Papers from Prison*. Translated by Reginald Fuller. New York: Macmillan, 1962.

Bornkamm, Günther, *Jesus of Nazareth*. Translated by Irene and Fraser McLuskey, with James M. Robinson. New York: Harper & Row, 1960.

Brown, Delwin; James, Ralph E., Jr.; Reeves, Gene, editors. *Process Philosophy and Christian Thought*. Indianapolis: Bobbs-Merrill, 1971.

Browning, Douglas, ed. *Philosophers of Process*. New York: Random House, 1965.

van Buren, Paul. *The Secular Meaning of the Gospel*. New York: Macmillan, 1963.

Cauthen, Kenneth. *Science, Secularization, and God*. Nashville: Abingdon, 1969.

Christian, William A. *An Interpretation of Whitehead's Meta-*

299

physics. New Haven: Yale University Press, 1959.

Cobb, John B., Jr. *A Christian Natural Theology.* Philadelphia: Westminster, 1965.

————. *The Structure of Christian Existence.* Philadelphia: Westminster, 1967.

Congar, Yves M-J. *A History of Theology.* Translated by Hunter Guthrie. Garden City, New York: Doubleday, 1968.

Cousins, Ewert H., ed. *Process Theology.* New York: Newman, 1971.

Cox, Harvey. *The Feast of Fools.* Cambridge University Press, 1969.

————. *The Secular City.* 2nd ed. New York: Macmillan, 1966.

Cullman, Oscar; Leenhardt, F. J. *Essays on the Lord's Supper.* Translated by J. G. Davies. Richmond: John Knox, 1966.

Delfgaauw, Bernard. *Evolution: The Theory of Teilhard de Chardin.* Translated by Hubert Hoskins. New York: Harper, 1969.

Dewart, Leslie. *The Future of Belief.* New York: Herder and Herder, 1966.

Dewey, John. *The Quest for Certainty.* New York: G. P. Putnam's Sons, 1960.

————. *Reconstruction in Philosophy.* Boston: Beacon, 1966.

Eliade, Mircea. *Cosmos and History.* Translated by Willard B. Trask. New York: Harper & Row, 1959.

————. *Myth and Reality.* Translated by Willard B. Trask. New York: Harper & Row, 1968.

Fontinell, Eugene. *Towards a Reconstruction of Religion.* Garden City, New York: Doubleday, 1970.

Gilkey, Langdon. *Naming the Whirlwind.* Indianapolis: Bobbs-Merrill, 1969.

Gogarten, Friedrich. *The Reality of Faith.* Translated by Carl Michalson, et al. Philadelphia: Westminster, 1959.

Hartshorne, Charles. *The Divine Relativity.* New Haven: Yale University Press, 1948.

————. *A Natural Theology for Our Time.* La Salle, Ill.: Open Court, 1967.

Heinemann, F. H. *Existentialism and the Modern Predicament.* 2nd ed. New York: Harper & Row, 1958.

James, Ralph E. *The Concrete God.* Indianapolis: Bobbs-Merrill, 1967.

Jolivet, Régis. *Sartre, The Theology of the Absurd.* Translated by

Wesley C. Piersol. Westminster: Newman, 1967.

Kilmartin, Edward J. *The Eucharist in the Primitive Church*. Englewood Cliffs, New Jersey: Prentice-Hall, 1965.

Kline, George L. ed. *Alfred North Whitehead: Essays in His Philosophy*. Englewood Cliffs, New Jersey: Prentice-Hall, 1963.

Küng, Hans. *The Church*. Translated by Ray and Rosaleen Ockenden. New York: Herder and Herder, 1967.

Lafarge, René. *Jean-Paul Sartre: His Philosophy*. Translated by Marina Smyth-Kok. Notre Dame: University of Notre Dame Press, 1970.

Langer, Susanne K. *Philosophical Sketches*. Baltimore, Johns Hopkins, 1962.

————. *Philosophy in a New Key*. New York: Mentor, 1951.

van Leeuwen, Arend Theodor. *Christianity in World History*. Translated by H. H. Hoskins. New York: Charles Scribner's Sons, 1964.

Loisy, Alfred Firmin. *L'Evangile et L'Eglise*. Paris: Emile Nourry, 1930.

————. *My Duel with the Vatican*. Translated by Richard Wilson Boynton. New York: E. D. Dutton, 1924.

Lowe, Victor. *Understanding Whitehead*. Baltimore: Johns Hopkins, 1966.

deLubac, Henri. *The Religion of Teilhard de Chardin*. Translated by René Hague. New York: Desclee, 1967.

————. *Teilhard de Chardin: The Man and His Meaning*. Translated by René Hague. New York: Mentor, 1967.

Macquarrie, John. *God and Secularity*. New Directions in Theology Today, Volume III. Philadelphia: Westminster, 1967.

Marxsen, Willi. *The Beginnings of Christology: A Study in Its Problems*. Translated by Paul J. Achtemeier. Philadelphia: Fortress Press, 1969.

————. *The Lord's Supper as a Christological Problem*. Translated by Lorenz Nieting. Philadelphia: Fortress Press, 1970.

Mooney, Christopher F. *Teilhard de Chardin and the Mystery of Christ*. London: Collins, 1966.

Newbegin, Leslie. *Honest Religion for Secular Man*. London: SCM, 1966.

Overman, Richard H. *Evolution and the Christian Doctrine of Creation*. Philadelphia: Westminster, 1967.

Peters, Eugene H. *The Creative Advance*. St. Louis: Bethany, 1966.

————. *Hartshorne and Neoclassical Metaphysics*. Lincoln: University of Nebraska Press, 1970.

Petre, Maude. *Alfred Loisy*. Cambridge: Cambridge University Press, 1944.

Pittenger, Norman. *Alfred North Whitehead*. Richmond: John Knox, 1968.

————. *Christology Reconsidered*. London: SCM, 1970.

————, ed. *Conference of Modern Churchmen*. London: SCM, 1968.

————. *God in Process*. London: SCM Press, 1967.

————. *Process Thought and Christian Faith*. New York: Macmillan, 1968.

————. *The Word Incarnate*. New York: Harper & Row, 1959.

Powers, Joseph M. *Eucharistic Theology*. New York: Herder and Herder, 1967.

Price, Lucien. *Dialogues of Alfred North Whitehead*. New York: Mentor, 1965.

Reese, William, and Freeman, Eugene, editors. *Process and Divinity*. La Salle, Ill.: Open Court, 1964.

Rideau, Emile. *Teilhard de Chardin: A Guide to His Thought*. Translated by René Hague. London: Collins, 1967.

Roberts, David E. *Existentialism and Religious Belief*. New York: Oxford University Press, 1957.

Robinson, James M. *A New Quest of the Historical Jesus*. London: SCM, 1963.

Roth, Robert J. *American Religious Philosophy*. New York: Harcourt, Brace, 1967.

Rust, Eric. *Evolutionary Philosophies and Contemporary Theology*. Philadelphia: Westminster, 1969.

————. *Positive Religion in a Revolutionary Time*. Philadelphia: Westminster, 1970.

Sabatier, Paul. *Modernism*. Translated by C. A. Miles, New York: Charles Scribner's Sons, 1908.

de Saint Exupéry, Antoine. *The Little Prince*. Translated by Katherine Woods. New York: Harcourt, Brace, 1943.

Sartre, Jean-Paul. *Being and Nothingness*. Translated by Hazel Barnes. New York: Citadel, 1965.

————. *Existentialism*. Translated by Bernard Frechtman. New York: Philosophical Library, 1947.

Schillebeeckx, Edward. *Christ the Sacrament of Our Encounter with God.* Translated by Paul Barrett, Mark Schoof, and Laurence Bright. New York: Sheed and Ward, 1963.

―――. *The Eucharist.* Translated by N. D. Smith. New York: Sheed and Ward, 1968.

Schoonenberg, Piet. *The Christ.* Translated by Della Couling. New York: Herder and Herder, 1971.

―――. *Man and Sin.* Translated by Joseph Donceel. Chicago: Henry Regnery, 1965.

Schweitzer, Albert. *The Quest of the Historical Jesus.* Translated by W. Montgomery. New York: Macmillan, 1961.

Schweizer, Eduard. *The Lord's Supper According to the New Testament.* Translated by James M. Davies. Philadelphia: Fortress Press, 1967.

Sherburne, Donald W. *A Key to Whitehead's Process and Reality.* New York: Macmillan, 1966.

Snyder, Ross. *The Ministry of Meaning.* Geneva: Youth Departments of the World Council of Churches and World Council of Christian Education. Vol. I. Nos. 3 and 4, Third and Fourth Quarters, 1965.

Speaight, Robert. *The Life of Teilhard de Chardin.* New York: Harper & Row, 1967.

Teilhard de Chardin, Pierre. *Building the Earth.* Translated by Nöel Lindsay. Wilkes-Barre, Pa.: Dimension, 1965.

―――. *The Divine Milieu.* Translated by Bernard Wall. New York: Harper & Row, 1968.

―――. The Future of Man. Translated by Norman Denny. New York: Harper & Row, 1964.

―――. *How I Believe.* Translated by René Hague. New York: Harper & Row, 1969.

―――. *Hymn of the Universe.* Translated by Simon Bartholomew. New York: Harper & Row, 1965.

―――. *The Phenomenon of Man.* 2nd ed. Translated by Bernard Wall. New York: Harper & Row, 1965.

―――. *Science and Christ.* Translated by René Hague. New York: Harper & Row, 1968.

de Terra, Helmut, *Memories of Teilhard de Chardin.* Translated by J. Maxwell Brownjohn. New York: Harper & Row, 1964.

Thornton, Lionel Spencer. *Christ and the Church.* London: Westminster, 1956.

―――. *The Incarnate Lord.* London: Longmans, Green, 1928.

Tyrrell, George. *Autobiography and Life of George Tyrrell*. London: Longmans, Green, 1912.

------. *Christianity at the Crossroads*. London: Longmans, Green, 1910.

------. *The Programme of Modernism*. New York: G. P. Putnams, 1908.

------. *Through Scylla and Charybdis*. London: Longmans, Green, 1907.

Utz, Arthur. *Ethique Sociale*. Translated from German into French by Etienne Dousse. Fribourg, Suisse: Editions Universitaires, 1960.

Vidler, Alec. *The Modernist Movement in the Roman Church*. Cambridge: Cambridge University Press, 1934.

------. *A Variety of Catholic Modernists*. Cambridge: Cambridge University Press, 1970.

Whitehead, Alfred North. *Adventures of Ideas*. New York: Mentor, n.d.

------. *Concept of Nature*. Cambridge: Cambridge University Press, 1964.

------. *The Function of Reason*. Boston: Beacon, 1962.

------. *Interpretations of Science*. Indianapolis: Bobbs-Merrill, 1961.

------. *Modes of Thought*. New York: Capricorn, 1958.

------. *Process and Reality*. New York: Harper & Row, 1960.

------. *Religion in the Making*. Cleveland: Meridian, 1960.

------. *Science and the Modern World*. New York: Free Press, 1967.

------. *Science and Philosophy*. Paterson, New Jersey: Littlefield Adams, 1964.

------. *Symbolism*. New York: Capricorn, 1959.

Wieman, Henry N. *The Source of Human Good*. Carbondale: Southern Illinois University, 1964.

Wildiers, N. M. *An Introduction to Teilhard de Chardin*. Translated by Hubert Hoskins. New York: Harper & Row, 1968.

Williams, Daniel Day. *The Spirit and Forms of Love*. New York: Harper & Row, 1968.